KANHA *to* KRISHNA

THE JOURNEY *to* DIVINITY

PRANAB MULLICK

Readomania

Readomania Publishing
A division of Kurious Kind Media Private Limited
466, DDA SFS Apartments, Pocket 1, Sector 22, Dwarka,
New Delhi – 110077
books.readomania.com
email: support@readomania.com
Facebook: facebook.com/iamreadomania
Twitter: twitter.com/iamreadomania

First Published in 2018 by Readomania

ISBN: 978-93-858547-2-9

Typeset in Palatino Linotype by Shine Graphics

Printed and bound at Thomson Press India Ltd.

Readomania

India has traditionally been the land of storytellers and a lot of us have an inherent skill of creating good plots, good stories and good narrations. With a little encouragement and support, many more authors will be widely read and attain a place in the sun. This is the essence of *Readomania*—an initiative that nurtures emerging stars of the literary world.

It would not be an exaggeration to say that *Readomania* is the talent hunt in fiction. It goes a step beyond by not just identifying the talent but also nurturing it and showcasing it to the world. In the process, we have created a powerhouse of content.

Readomania has four principle interest areas – traditional print publishing, online library of short stories and poetry, literary events and products.

The print publishing works towards delivering good quality content to the readers. We publish good authors in meaningful anthologies, novels and works of narrative non-fiction. Our books stand out for their perspectives, the plots, the language and most importantly their ability to enrich lives.

Take a break, read something nice, write something beautiful. Read our books or visit us at www.readomania.com and enjoy a whole new world of literature.

Dedicated to

Lord Krishna

Who became a part of my existence
as I wrote the book

Maharishi Ved Vyas

Who wrote the greatest epic
ever written

Dr Raghunath Mullick

My grandfather, an authority on Kalidasa
whose books Kalidas Pratibha, Stories from
Kalidas and Kalidaser Golpo instilled in
me love for our culture

K.S. Mullick

My father who taught me the art of writing,
the love of language and the love of mythology

Author's Note

Mookam karoti vachalam, pangum langhayate girim
Yatkripa tamaham vande, paramananda madhavam.

I salute thee, O Madhava, by whose grace even a mute becomes loquacious and a lame conquers the mountains.

Sri Krishna is different from other gods in the Hindu pantheon in that he is not confined to the pedestal but is regarded as family. Mothers see His image in their children while comely maidens seek Him in their lovers. A major part of India's religion, literature, music, dance, art, culture revolves around the theme of Krishna.

Maybe that is one reason why books have been written trying to explain his supernatural powers and treating him rather as an extraordinarily talented, multifaceted but adorable human being—someone whom we can readily identify with. Bankim Chandra Chattopadhyay did it in his *Krishna Charitra* and has been followed by innumerable other authors. I have merely attempted to follow their footprints.

I should however, hasten to clarify at the outset that Krishna is as much a part of my existence as anyone else's and I worship Him as everyone else. The book is only a mythological fiction, intended to be read as a mere story and there is no intent whatsoever to cause any disrespect to anybody's religious belief.

The theme of the book is that when God takes avatar on Earth, He follows *all* the laws of nature. Otherwise there would be no necessity for Him to take birth as He could have killed the enemies with a flash of lightning from the sky, so to say. In my humble opinion, God takes avatar to set an example of what we humans can achieve through hard work, intelligence, focus and dedication. We, the lesser beings, being unable to emulate such feats either due to laziness or lack of dedication, take the easy way out and ascribe the feats to supernatural powers.

Applying this theme to the popular story of Krishna's life, which we have heard since childhood, I tried to build a fiction that gives a realistic and rational explanation of his birth, his *leelas* and how he achieved his goals. It is a journey of a cowherd boy Kanha to that of Vishnu's avatar Krishna in which he is forced to toil, encounter caste and colour prejudices, cross obstacles and face betrayals from those he trusted. The transition to *avtarhood* was aided in no small measure by the politics of the time and the *inter se* rivalry amongst Kansa's own advisers. The novel explores what Krishna gained and what he lost in the process of his transition.

In writing this book, I must acknowledge the contribution of my family comprising of my mother Mrs Dolly Mullick, my wife Soma, my daughter Ananya and my son Arnab who not only encouraged my writing but also patiently suffered my absence through the hours I wrote. They are all integral to my very existence and of this book.

The book would not have been the same but for the suggestions given by my great friend Mr C. Mohan Rao, Advocate.

I must thank Google and Wikipedia for facilitating instant research. What would we do without them?

I thank my publisher *Readomania* and Mr Dipankar Mukherjee for putting their faith in my book and publishing it. My editor Ms Indrani Ganguly did a yeoman's job in editing it. My special thanks also go to my Literary Agent M/s Book Bakers and Mr Suhail Mathur.

And finally, the question that may dog all readers: Did it actually happen this way as described in this book?

Maybe....

Hare Krishna

Part I

I

The Birth

Your birth proclaims the victory of life
May the mysteries of the infinite unravel themselves through you
... Tagore

It was midnight on the eighth day of the dark phase of moon in the post-monsoon month of *Bhadra*. Nandrai, the headman of the Gops, paced nervously in front of the delivery room in his cottage. Outside, the wind howled across like a raging wolf, threatening to blow away the roof itself. Trees swayed in the storm and smashed against one another. It seemed as if a war had broken out between the gods and demons. Uprooted trees and branches were hurled like spears across the horizon. Lord Indra lit up the firmament in succession as he hurled thunderbolts towards an invisible foe. Torrential rains in swirling motion, lashed at the doors. From afar, the river Yamuna roared as a caged lion pounding against its barriers, the sound carrying through the howling wind and lashing rain. All over the colony, herds of cows mooed in fright, tugging at their tethers. It was as if the Earth was preparing for another Great Deluge.

Inside the delivery room, the midwife and two other ladies attended to Nandrai's wife, Yashoda, who was in labour. Nandrai could only helplessly look on as now and again the door opened a bit and one of the ladies hurried out to the kitchen to heat water or get dressings.

A loud clap of thunder shook the whole cottage, followed by the sound of something crashing outside. Was it the cowshed? Nandrai cautiously unbolted the door and immediately the gale prised open the door and forced him back. For a moment, Nandrai was left dazed and by the time he regained his wits, a shower of rain had waltzed inside the room, drenching the floor.

'What are you doing, *Mukhiyaji*? Have you lost your senses? For heaven's sake, a delivery is going on.' The *dai* had come out of the delivery room and her professional fury was directed at Nandrai. He might be the *mukhiya* of the Gops, but here and now she was the one in charge.

Nandrai pushed the door with all his force and barely managed to lock it back. 'Sorry, *Daiji*,' he mumbled. From inside the delivery room, Yashoda shrieked and the *dai* rushed back into the room.

Each moment seemed like an eternity. The clapping of the sky alternated with Yashoda's shrieks and the terrified mooing of cattle. *It was not a night, but a nightmare.*

'O Lord Indra, please control your fury, please spare us,' Nandrai prayed fervently in his mind. He could visualise the condition of the village. God knows how many cottages and cowsheds would collapse, how many trees would be uprooted. The cottages and cowsheds could be rebuilt, but God, please protect the people and the animals. A storm of this magnitude would not depart without claiming its sacrifices.

As if in answer to Nandrai's prayers, little by little, the storm started subsiding. An hour later, as the torrent of rain receded considerably, there was an urgent knock at the door. '*Mukhiyaji, Mukhiyaji,* please open.'

Nandrai hesitantly looked at the delivery room before opening the door. Two villagers stood there.

'*Mukhiyaji*, please come. A tree fell on Budhiya's cottage and he and his wife are injured. We have pulled them out. Please come and see.' The same instant another villager came rushing in. '*Mukhiyaji*, Bantu and Nandan's cottages have collapsed. In seven other cottages the roofs have blown off. All their belongings are in a mess.'

So, the ordeal had begun. Nandrai shook off his stupor. 'I'm coming in a moment. You go and call *Vaidji* immediately.' Just then Yashoda shrieked and immediately thereafter one of the attendants came out of the delivery room and proceeded to the kitchen. Nandrai stopped her. 'Is everything alright?'

'As of now it is alright, *Mukhiyaji*. But it is taking time and Yashoda*ji* is getting exhausted.'

For a moment, Nandrai wavered. He was needed as much at home as outside. But he steeled his mind. There was nothing he could presently do at home but to wait. The *dai* and her attendants were there to take care of Yashoda. But out there in the village, he was the headman and nobody would be able to organise a rescue or give directions in his absence.

'Alright. Tell *Daiji* that I am in the immediate neighbourhood. I will keep making rounds of the house from time to time. In case there is any emergency, just send someone to call me.' Nandrai took a *diya,* covered it with a plate and went out in the rain.

It was a scene from the Apocalypse. Uprooted trees and branches blocked the road every few yards. Nandrai carefully made his way in the dim light of the *diya* through the sputtering rain and the sprawling mess. A huge peepul tree had uprooted and smashed Budhiya's cottage. It was a miracle that Budhiya and his wife had survived, albeit with injuries. The *Vaid* had arrived and was attending to them. A large group of villagers had gathered, discussing the storm with the same intensity with which it had occurred.

Nandrai immediately took charge of the situation. He called the villagers and made several teams. The first task was to help those whose cottages had collapsed.

Two teams were deputed to shift the belongings from the collapsed huts to their neighbours'. With Nandrai at the helm, the village stood as one family. What if a cottage had collapsed—the village community would rebuild it. The persons whose huts had collapsed, would live as family in their neighbours' huts.

Another team was deputed to pacify the terrified animals. It was only a few hours to the morning and the cows would have to be milked. It was necessary that they be calmed as soon as possible and rested before the milking time.

Most of the remaining teams were given charge of clearing the roads of debris. In a few hours, it would be time to go to Mathura to supply milk to the palace and the city. And, having regard to the tyrant King of Mathura, it was a task that could not be avoided, even if the sky itself came crashing down or Yamaraj himself knocked at the door. It was not only the road to Mathura that had to be cleared, the roads to the other Gop villages too needed clearance.

The main work done, Nandrai sent errands to the other Gop villages to ascertain their condition and convey his instructions regarding the organising of relief and rescue. He was explaining the errands when someone tugged at his *gamchha*. He turned around to find a ten-year-old village kid. 'They are calling you at your house immediately.'

Nandrai's heart leapt to his mouth. While organising the relief operations in the village, he had totally forgotten about Yashoda's delivery.

'Did they tell you anything? Why are they calling me?' Nandrai in his anxiety almost held the child by the neck.

The child's blank face made him realise the futility of the query. He left the child and made a sudden dash towards home.

'What happened, *Mukhiyaji*...O *Mukhiyaji*...?' The villagers' shouts fell on deaf ears. Nandrai leapt over fallen trees and sprinted through thorny hedges. The rain had reduced the road to slush and mud. Twice he stumbled, the thorns bruised his skin, the mud spattered his clothes, but he ran as if his life depended on it. Finally, as he turned the corner, his cottage stood in front of him. And suddenly, he stopped. He felt as if his feet had turned to lead. Butterflies sputtered in his stomach. He felt his lungs would burst. For an instant, his brain was clouded with doubt. What if....

One step at a time, Nandrai fumbled towards his cottage door. His hands shaking, he pushed the door and stepped inside. It was dark, one small *diya* waging a losing battle against the agents of darkness. His throat choked. With a supreme effort he blurted out one word: '*Daijiiii*...'

After what seemed an eternity, the sharp cry of a newborn answered his call. Immediately thereafter, the midwife emerged. Holding out her dupatta, she said with a smile, '*Mukhiyaji*, congratulations, it's a boy!'

'And, Yashoda? How is she?' Nandrai's voice quivered in anxiety.

'Both the mother and child are fine, my lord.'

A smile finally spread across Nandrai's face. He took out the heavy gold ring from his finger and threw it in the outstretched dupatta of the midwife.

'God bless you, *Mukhiyaji*. May your son live a thousand years and bring fame and fortune to your family.' The midwife withdrew into the room.

A little while later, Nandrai washed and changed and thereafter was allowed inside the delivery room. Yashoda lay on the bed still recovering from her exertions and suckling a tiny bundle of joy who clung to her with his tiny arms. For several moments Nandrai stood transfixed by the sight. It was his first child and he took time to come to terms with it. Then he took off his heavy gold chain, touched it to the newborn and proceeded to see its face. 'O my God!' he laughed aloud, 'this can't be a human being, it's a doll!'

Yashoda smiled weakly at his astonishment. The baby, which had fallen asleep, awoke with a cry and immediately resumed suckling.

A bolt of lightning lit up the night sky followed moments later by a deafening roar of thunder. Nandrai sat beside Yashoda and held her hand. 'Thank you, my love.' Yashoda merely pressed his hand in reply. Nandrai continued, 'We will now have to think about a name for our son.'

'I have already thought of that,' Yashoda said softly, 'We will name our son "Kanha".'

There was a rustle at the main door of the cottage. Some of the villagers had come over to enquire.

'What's the news, *Mukhiyaji*?'

'What, a son? Congratulations! So, we will wait for the treat.'

'See *Mukhiyaji*, even the skies lit up and the gods clapped their hands to herald your son's arrival. Take my word, one day he will make you proud.'

'*Mukhiyaji*, there must be a big celebration on the *chhathi*. You must send a word to the singing and dancing *tolis* immediately.'

'Yes, yes, and arrange for adequate laddoos and *pedhas* also. Satyaa himself will finish one mound of sweets.'

Nobody slept in the village that night. The men cleared the roads, while the women swept the courtyards and cowsheds of the debris. As the jet black of night turned to grey, they roused the cattle and brought out the milking pots. They also brought out the pots of butter and curd which had been left to settle the night before. The men completed their assigned tasks and returned to their homes.

They finished their ablutions, brought out the hay and started milking the cows.

One by one, carts from the nearby villages congregated near Nandrai's house. It was the headman's duty to maintain details of the milk and milk products being supplied to the city. Today, however, was an exception. The Gops themselves made a quick compilation. Then all the pitchers were loaded on a few carts. Nandrai and several other Gops stayed back. Apart from attending to his duties at home consequent to the birth of his son, Nandrai intended to attend to the reconstruction work in his own and the neighbouring villages. The remaining Gops perched themselves on the other carts and soon, the caravan of milk carts snaked their way towards the city of Mathura, through the muddy trail of what had once been a road.

Understandably, the storm during the night dominated the conversation during the journey. An elder claimed that there had been fiercer gales in his childhood, while the others laughingly ascribed the claims to his fading memory. A fierce debate ensued on the question. After sometime the conversation veered round to how *mukhiyaji's* son's birth should be celebrated. In particular, the sweets that should be ordered and the dancing *tolis* that should be brought in to add spice to the occasion. The gloom of the night before was soon submerged in collective laughter and gaiety even as the darkness diffused and gave way to dawn.

'O Haridas*ji*, please egg on your bullocks. If we are late, King Kansa will flay us alive.' Bhavya interjected.

The mention of King Kansa's name brought a hush on the conversation. A while later, there were muted whispers on the carts.

'Just think, after yesterday's storm, we should have been attending to our homes rather than going like this. But for our King...'

'Remember, his gardener had absented one day due to his wife's death and the King had him flogged for not delivering flowers! So, it does not matter whether we die or our homes are devastated or the roads are blocked, but milk must be delivered at the hour!'

'Really, such a cruel king has not been seen in the entire history of Aryavarta.'

'Cruel? Rather, wantonly cruel. Every other month he feeds one of his convicts to his dogs and watches the spectacle. He is not a human, he is a demon…' the voice tailed off.

'Yes, and he is also an expert in devising new ways of torture. None of his forefathers were like that!'

'*Arre,* what can you expect from a person who imprisons his own father and puts him in the dungeon, in order to become the King?'

'This is *yugdharma,* my friend. In the last *Treta yug,* you had Prince Rama who went to exile to keep his father's word. And, now in this *Dwapara yug,* you have a person who confines his parents in prison. God knows what shall follow hereafter.'

'Arre, he has not stopped at imprisoning his parents. He has gone ahead and put our kingdom itself under a foreign army. After imprisoning his parents he disbanded the Yadava army and stationed a division of the Magadhi army to protect Mathura.'

'Well, his father-in-law is the King of Magadha. What else do you expect?'

'Truly said, *Bhaiya.* This King of ours is no more than a vassal of Jarasandha, the King of Magadha. As soon as Jarasandha finishes his military campaigns in the East, he will come and take over reins of our kingdom.'

'In fact, this King has destroyed all our institutions. Not only has he disbanded our *Parishad,* which used to elect the king, but has inducted tribals as his chief advisers and ministers. Leave alone Brahmins, Yadavas are themselves excluded in their own kingdom. Strange are the ways of politics.'

'Nothing strange about it, brother. This King does not trust anybody. He thinks the Yadavas may have a soft corner for his father, so he has inducted tribals both as ministers and soldiers.'

'Rightly said, *Bhai*. But the Yadavas themselves are also to blame for their fate. Their chief landholders are divided on clan lines. They are recognised not as Yadavas but as Andhakas, Vrishnis and Bhojas. Kansa has only utilised this division to further his ends and perpetuate his reign.'

'And on account of this division the common man has to bear the day-to-day cruelty, not to forget the burden of taxes. The King and his dastardly ministers and advisers are squeezing the residents of Mathura to the last dime. And if someone cannot or does not pay, they just flay him alive.'

'God knows when we would be delivered from this tyrant.'

'What deliverance to us common folks? Haven't you seen what he did to his cousin Devaki and brother-in-law Vasudeva*ji*? If the royals could be treated in this manner, how do you expect the common man to fare any better?'

'My heart really goes out to them. Even before Devaki could go to her matrimonial home, Kansa threw her and her husband in the dungeon! Just think, a prince and princess, newly married, chained like animals and passing their days in the dungeon! And, each of their offspring killed before their very eyes! All this just because a sadhu predicted that Devaki's eighth progeny would kill him!'

'Forget your sadhus and their predictions, it is all the politics of power,' Bhairav said. 'Sadhu or no sadhu, Kansa would have got rid of Vasudeva in his own interest. Vasudeva's father and grandfather had been kings. Obviously he posed a challenge to the throne and therefore Kansa wanted him out of the way. This is how politics works.'

'But, politics sans even basic humanity? This cruel King has killed one after another of Devaki's newborns… flinging them to the walls! He has already decimated six of them. How can one be so ghastly in one's acts? He is indeed a demon.'

There was a clamour amongst the audience. 'Yes, yes, only a demon could do such a thing.'

'And, even if we go by that sadhu's words, it is the eighth child who would kill Kansa. Why kill the others?'

'*Arre* my innocent friend, that is what I was talking about. It is again the politics. He wants to end Vasudeva's legacy altogether. So when Kansa has a son, he will not face any threat from Vasudeva's line.'

'God knows how long our travails will continue. I for one have given up hope of deliverance during my lifetime.'

'No *Kaka,* this demonic act just cannot continue. I really believe what that sadhu said. God will certainly intervene and send his avatar to deliver us from this evil. The entire kingdom is waiting for the eighth child of Devaki. Six children have already perished and at present Devaki is pregnant with the seventh. Just some more time till the eighth child is born. Till then just persevere, keep low and pray that we remain safe and sound.'

'Well, the *kaalchakra* is already turning for Kansa. Have any of you noticed, he has not produced a son yet? He has already been married for more than nine years!'

'But, does Kansa really need a son? After what he has done to his father, he would always be afraid that his son would do the same to him. For all you know, if he begets a son, he would put him in the dungeon too.'

'Arre, whether it is Kansa or anyone else, the lot of us Gops will remain the same. The Yadavas, irrespective of which clan they belong to, all look down on us cowherds.

If they have a demon or tyrant as their king, it is just desserts for their own actions.'

About one *kos* before the city gates, the caravan was forced to stop. The Yamuna was in spate owing to the heavy rainfall during the night and a sheet of water, about knee deep, spread in front. It was as if the Yamuna itself was flowing in front of the city gates. A few Gops jumped down from their carts and went to the front of the caravan, tapping the ground with their sticks. The carts followed their progress, finally reaching the city gates.

At the city gates, there appeared to be unprecedented security that day. Each and every person entering the gate was thoroughly frisked and their goods were checked. Within the city, groups of people were spotted whispering amongst each other. They dissolved as soon as any soldier came into sight. The shops were shut and a strange silence prevailed. The Gops tried to enquire the reason from some bystanders, but they hurried away with a fearful look.

The milk carts proceeded to the palace but were stopped at the palace gate. Entry to the palace was barred. The King's troops took charge of the milk pots and other goods at the palace gate itself. The Gops were in a quandary. Should they give delivery to the troops guarding the palace? What about the accounts? And, what about supply to the shops? The shops remained closed and milk was perishable... Today, Nandrai was also not there to handle such a situation.

Finally, Satyabal managed to spot an old acquaintance and asked him what had happened. What he heard, sent shivers down all the Gops.

'Yesterday midnight, Devaki gave birth to her seventh child—a girl—and today morning King Kansa went and slaughtered her.'

II

The Pain

The wound is the place where Light enters you

...Rumi

Vasudeva's eyes roamed about the ceiling and walls of the dungeon. The spot on the ceiling where that morning Kansa had flung his seventh child, still bore a big red mark. There were six other marks on the wall, reminders of the fate of the other six of his children. There had also been one miscarriage, after the sixth and before the seventh child. Those six marks had been obliterated by dirt and grime, but Vasudeva could still remember the spots where his children had met their end. There was nothing else to do in the dungeon, day after day, year after year, except to ruminate the memories... The left side of the wall, about one and half cubits above the ground, the spot where there was a slight bulge, was where the first child was flung. The second was on the right side about two cubits from the ground, a little away from where the hook was embedded in the wall. That spot where a peculiar human face seemed to form, that spot...that spot... was that the spot for the third child or the fourth? If that belonged to the fourth, then that rack on the wall would be the spot where the third child was flung. Vasudeva tried to remember. These days, his memory seemed to be failing him. How he hoped that his memory would fail him altogether. Being sane was maddening! Every moment the visions floated before his eyes—Kansa grabbing his babies and flinging them against the wall. For years together, every night, either he or Devaki would have a nightmare and then, scream and wake up. Then both would remain awake for the rest of the night.

'Death to Kansa, death to Kansa, death to Kansa, death to Kansa, death to Kansa...' he continued to mutter under his breath.

Devaki was still in faint. In fact, her health had been a concern ever since her miscarriage and she had not fully recovered from the ordeal. Giving birth to a baby every year, that too in these conditions, did not make her condition any better. Killing of the seventh child today in front of her very eyes had triggered a collapse. Vasudeva seemed to have lost count of the number of times Devaki had fallen unconscious this morning.

Vasudeva moved towards the pitcher and drew a little water. He proceeded to sprinkle the water on Devaki's face but stopped midway. *Why revive her just now?* He pondered. Being conscious was a torture. But...but...no...the eighth child had to be conceived...as early as possible...Devaki must get up right now... He threw the water on Devaki's face. 'Devaki, get up quickly, you have to conceive our eighth child...time is running... Don't be late Devaki... get up...get up.' He shook her again and again. 'Devaki, you know, this is the last child that the *rakshas* Kansa has killed. He won't be able to kill any more. The next child will be our eighth...our eighth child, Devaki! The avatar of Vishnu himself! Remember what the sage had forecast? Devaki, come on now, get up,' Vasudeva's voice became impatient.

'Death to Kansa, death to Kansa, death to Kansa, death to Kansa, death to Kansa....'

How many years had passed by? Eight, ten, twelve? In the dungeon there was no difference between night and day. There was nothing by which one could keep track of date or time except a small skylight at the end of the corridor which could not even be seen from the cell. The years could be counted only by the number of summers or number of winters undergone. Vasudeva in the initial stages of confinement had tried to keep such a count by making a mark on the dungeon wall. But then the red marks on the wall had numbed his senses. There was now only one count...how many gone and how many yet to go before the eighth. Today, with the death of the seventh, that wait had ended. Now the final count...how many days for the eighth child to come. 'Devaki, Devaki, are you still asleep? The eighth child is knocking on the door...Let him in Devaki... get up, this is the time to prepare, not to sleep....'

When he was a child, while exploring the palace, Vasudeva had once come to these dungeons with his younger sister Pritha. Their father, King Surasena was then the ruler of Mathura. Every afternoon, with nothing to do, he and Pritha used to roam about and explore the palace. One day, the duo chanced upon an unlocked secret door leading to a staircase which led to another door. On opening the second door, they found themselves in this dungeon. They tiptoed along the corridor peeping from one cell to the other. Most of the cells were empty, while in a few others the inmates were asleep. One guard was on patrol but he did not see them as they hid behind a stone column. As they passed by one cell, an inmate called out to them. They went near the cell. He asked who they were. Vasudeva replied that they were the King's children and were exploring the palace. The man asked them if they would like to hear a story. They nodded in anticipation and went near the iron bars. The man commenced his story about a beautiful princess who was kidnapped by a demon. Suddenly Pritha shrieked. The man had put his hand out of the iron bars and grabbed her throat. Even after so many years, Vasudeva still remembered how in an instant the man's expression changed to demonic and the pure unadulterated fear in Pritha's eyes. The guards came running and were petrified at the sight.

'Release me immediately or I shall kill the princess,' the prisoner shouted. And, as if to prove his point, he slowly turned his hands which had grabbed Pritha's delicate neck. Another shriek filled the corridor. Meanwhile, King Surasena, on receiving the news from the guards, came running. Vasudeva did not remember what exactly happened thereafter. What he did remember was that the guards eventually rescued Pritha from the man's clutches. The next day, the man was brought to the King's court and sentenced to death. Both Vasudeva and Pritha watched the proceedings from behind the latticed curtains. And throughout the proceedings, Pritha kept tugging at his robe that their father should ask the man to complete the story!

Pritha was then only about five years of age. And Vasudeva, about eight. Merely a year later, the brother and sister had to separate, Pritha having been given in adoption to King Kuntibhoja. It was a decision which was resisted tooth and nail by both Vasudeva and Pritha. They howled, cried, refused food, did all that children of that age could do. But King Surasena's decision was intractable. Pritha was sent away to the kingdom of Kunti. Neither Vasudeva nor his family members were allowed to meet Pritha, nor was she allowed to visit Mathura. It was said that meeting her would hinder Pritha's assimilation in her new family. Vasudeva never forgave his father for the decision. Till his present incarceration, the separation from Pritha was the most traumatic event of his life and his heart was permanently scarred. Pritha's condition was no different. Her angst at being torn away from her parents and brother and left to live with strangers, shaped her future personality. Years later, Vasudeva had overheard his father telling his mother that Pritha had become very vain and wayward in her ways, always ready to rebel against the established tenets. In fact, during King Surasena's entire lifetime, Pritha did not visit Mathura. Like Vasudeva, she too never forgave her father. She refused to come to Mathura even at the time of King Surasena's death. It was only long after her father's death that Pritha came to Mathura, the occasion being Vasudeva's marriage to his first wife Rohini. The brother and sister met, but almost as strangers. Both had changed. Time had passed on... Later, Pritha had been invited at the time of Vasudeva's marriage to Devaki but could not make it as she was away from Hastinapur with her husband Pandu.

Throughout his childhood, Vasudeva had wondered why his father had given away his only daughter in adoption. Repeated questions to his father had elicited no response. It was only now that he could understand the exigencies of politics for which his father took the step.

Rapid political changes were taking place in the nearby kingdom of Hastinapur. The pleasure-loving King Shantanu had died. His eldest son Devavrata had during his father's lifetime, taken oath not only to renounce the throne but also not to marry so that his father could re-marry and his step-brothers from that marriage and their heirs could rule Hastinapur unchallenged. For this momentous oath, he was popularly known as 'Bhishma'. But, although he did not sit on the throne, it was Bhishma who, on death of his father, actually controlled the kingdom as Regent for his step-brother Chitrangad.

Chitrangad detested Bhishma. He wanted full powers of King without the looming shadow of the Regent. He set out to prove himself a greater warrior than Bhishma. But the field of war does not brook teenage adventures. Chitrangad died in battle in a stupid misadventure against the Gandharvas. He was succeeded to the throne by his brother Vichitravirya but it was Bhishma who continued to remain in control of the kingdom.

Bhishma was a disciple of the legendary Guru Parashuram and even surpassed his guru in the art of war. He did not believe in his father's policy of peaceful co-existence. He subdued the neighbouring kingdoms and extended his boundaries. Not content with that, he started ostensible demonstration of his power. The King of Kashi had organised a *swayamvar* for his three daughters—Amba,

Ambika and Ambalika. Hastinapur had not been invited as the King of Kashi was allied to the kingdom of Magadha which was trying to develop as a counter power to Hastinapur. That did not deter Bhishma. He went to Kashi and abducted all the three daughters from the *swayamvar sabha* itself on behalf of Vichitravirya. The timing of the assault was such that the King of Kashi did not have any defences in place. Jarasandha, the King of Magadha was away fighting King Bhagadatta in Kamrup and in no position to intervene. King Salva of the Mlechchhas rallied his soldiers and tried to stop Bhishma, but he was not only defeated but also humiliated in battle. That was not all. On finding that the eldest Kashi princess Amba had a crush on King Salva, Bhishma refused to get her married to Vichitravirya and sent her off to Salva as a loaded gift. Salva deemed it as an insult and did not accept her. Rejected by both Hastinapur and Salva, Amba was driven to suicide. The remaining two princesses Ambika and Ambalika were married off to Vichitravirya.

But Amba did continue to haunt Hastinapur. The family line seemed to be cursed by her. Vichitravirya soon died due to some mysterious illness, without leaving behind an heir. Bhishma declined to ascend the throne saying that he was bound by his oath. Dark rumours, however, abounded that the sudden demise of both Chitrangad and Vichitravirya were not above board. Could Bhishma not have restrained Chitrangad from the misadventure? Was Vichitravirya's ailment natural or induced by some slow poison? Some said that Bhishma did not ascend the throne because he feared the public would have revolted. Yet, the throne could not remain unoccupied. Finally, Ambika and Ambalika were compelled to bear children by *niyoga* method. Rishi Ved Vyas was chosen for the purpose. But the results proved disastrous. Ambika bore a blind son, Dhritarashtra, while Ambalika gave birth to a frail and perpetually ailing Pandu. The infant Pandu notionally ascended the throne and Bhishma as the all powerful regent again concentrated on empire building.

The manner in which Hastinapur was flexing its muscles, made Mathura nervous. It sought an alliance with King Kuntibhoja of Kunti, who was a famed warrior in his own right. King Surasena did not have any daughter of marriageable age, so he devised a novel plan to give his daughter Pritha in adoption to King Kuntibhoja in order to cement the alliance. The daughter was sacrificed in the altar of diplomacy.

It was, however, not the only occasion when Pritha made sacrifices for diplomacy. A little over a decade later, following the death of King Kuntibhoja, his son did not have the guts to stand up to Hastinapur. To placate Hastinapur, Pritha was married off to the ailing younger prince Pandu. It was not marriage, it was politics.

But Pritha's ordeal did not end there. While Bhishma controlled the kingdom, King Shantanu's widow Satyawati controlled the royal household with an iron hand. Pritha's very name was obliterated. She was renamed 'Kunti' as a reminder that she was a conquest from that kingdom. This had earlier been done for Dhritarashtra's wife too. Her homeland Gandhar having been defeated in battle, she was renamed 'Gandhari'. In fact, Gandhari suffered a worse fate. Satyawati convinced her that an ideal Aryan wife must feel and share the sorrows of her husband. Since Dhritarashtra was blind, dharma ordained that Gandhari should also cover her eyes. Gandhari tied her eyes with a cloth...forever....

At Satyawati's insistence, even before Pritha's marriage could be consummated, Pandu was sent off with a large army to Madra, from where he came back with a new wife, Madri. And then it transpired that apart from his physical frailties, Pandu was impotent....

They say that fate is like a wheel where good and bad luck constantly change their ends. Yet, there are people in whose lives the night is unending and even the first speck of dawn is obliterated by dark clouds. Pritha was one such being. At long last her husband Pandu was crowned the King of Hastinapur since his elder brother Dhritarashtra was blind and Pritha became a queen. But, the happiness was too good to last. Before the year had passed, Pandu abdicated his throne and went to the forests with his wives. It was said that he had accidentally killed a sage during a hunt and wanted to perform penance. Yet rumours flew thick and fast that disagreements with Bhishma had led to the abdication. It was said that with the blind Dhritarashtra now crowned as King, there would be no impediment to Bhishma in exercising full control over the administration. What the truth was, no one knew.

Vasudeva and Pritha... One incarcerated in prison, the other exiled in forest with an impotent husband. And yet the cup of their sorrows were not yet full and each remained unaware of the other's plight. In the forest, Pritha and Madri gave birth to three and two sons respectively through the *niyoga* method. But soon after, Pandu died, Madri immolated herself in her husband's pyre and Pritha was left a widow, in charge of five small children.

Is Pritha aware of my incarceration? Vasudeva wondered, unaware of Pritha's own condition. *If only she could use her influence to get Hastinapur to attack Mathura and secure my release....*

Devaki had still not recovered from her unconsciousness. Vasudeva drew some more water from the pitcher. While doing so, he saw his image in the water. What he saw, shocked his senses. Vasudeva had been the most handsome of the young men in Mathura. Fair complexioned with sharp Aryan features, tall, muscular build, large, intelligent eyes, he was known not only for his looks but also for his knowledge and empathy. While the man who peered out from the water vessel was nothing but a lowly beggar. Long, unkempt hair and beard, teeming with lice, dark burnt face and body, nails that looked like claws, tattered clothes that even a beggar would consign to garbage and everything from head to toe covered with layers and years of dirt and grime. Was it really him? For the first time in years he looked at Devaki. Was this the princess he had married? The princess of Mathura had transformed into an old, haggard beggarwoman. Her tattered dress hardly covered her. It was rather a stiff layer of grime and dirt that acted as a shroud and protected her shame. Vasudeva hit his palm on his forehead. *Oh God, are you testing me like you tested King Harishchandra? Does one have to go through so much to bear a divine child?*

Vasudeva walked about the prison cell, his footchain clanking about him. It was a long chain, one end attached to his left foot and the other secured to the cell wall. The chain was long enough to allow him freedom of movement within the cell. Another similar chain secured Devaki to the cell wall. In fact, in the initial months they were brought here, they were not shackled. Then one night their first son was born and early next morning, Kansa came to the cell. Vasudeva and Devaki cried and pleaded with him to spare the newborn, saying it was not the eighth child. Kansa replied with a booming laugh, snatched the infant from Devaki's lap and proceeded to smash the tiny bundle against the wall. It was at that point that with a blood-curdling roar, Vasudeva fell upon Kansa. He punched Kansa on his nose, kicked him on the groin and felled him to the ground. He retrieved the child, gave it to Devaki and again fell on Kansa, repeatedly boxing him on the face with vehemence. The suddenness of the assault and ferocity of his blows was such that Kansa, a burly and ferocious warrior, could not even move a finger. Vasudeva caught his throat and banged his head against the floor. Suddenly there was a hard blow to the side of Vasudeva's head. Kansa's guards had come inside the cell and one of them hit Vasudeva's head with his baton. Vasudeva's head reeled and he fell to the ground.

The other guards fell upon him and pinned him to the ground. Someone brought chains from an adjoining cell and tied him up.

Kansa got up. His lips were split. Blood oozed out of his nose and stained his dress. His eyes were blackened. Without bothering to even clean the blood, he turned on Vasudeva and gave him a stinging slap across the face followed by a resonant kick that almost made him unconscious. Devaki tried to come in between but was kicked away. He then snatched the child from Devaki's arm, showed it to Vasudeva and then flung it against the wall. A big red mark stained the cell wall.

That day onwards, Vasudeva and Devaki had one foot each chained to the cell wall and on days when Kansa was to visit, their hands and feet were so secured that they would not be able to move a finger. One by one their children were flung against the wall before their very eyes. Vasudeva spat and cursed in frustration but was unable to lift a little finger. One by one, the number of stains on the cell walls increased....

Even today morning, when Kansa came, Vasudeva and Devaki were securely chained to the wall. Kansa came and took the newborn girl in his arms. Devaki shrieked.

'It is only a girl, Kansa,' Vasudeva shouted. 'Why, why should you kill a girl?'

'Babies of snakes need to be crushed, Vasudeva,' Kansa replied jovially. 'You do not check whether they are males or females. Babies of snakes will grow up to be snakes one day.'

'Don't Kansa, don't,' Vasudeva pleaded.

Kansa started playing catch, flinging the baby towards the ceiling and then catching it.

Devaki swooned. Vasudeva spat at Kansa. The spit did not carry, but Kansa turned towards him. 'You dirty beggar, see how great I am. Despite your provocations,

I am delivering your child from the hell of this prison, directly to heaven. Be thankful. Ha ha ha ha ha ha....'

He threw the baby to the ceiling with force. The ceiling was splattered with blood and gore. This time Vasudeva fell unconscious.

The palace at Mathura, built by King Andhaka, reflected the opulence and arrogance of its builder. King Andhaka on ascending the throne, set out to build a grand palace and capital that would reflect his power. He commissioned a stone palace in an era when palaces were built of burnt mud bricks. His successors added battlements and fortifications to the structure, to make it an object of awe and splendour.

It is said that when a new city is built, the gods should first be propitiated with an offering of human sacrifice. The city of Mathura extracted its cost in human sacrifice even before it was constructed. When King Andhaka came to inspect the site, he found miles of undulating grasslands bordered by dense forests, with the mighty Yamuna flowing by. Nearby was the Govardhan hill which could be used for security purposes. It was an ideal place for establishing his new capital, he felt. The grasslands were inhabited by the Gops, who were cattle grazers, while the forests were inhabited by various forest tribes. The solution was simple. The inhabitants—both the Gops and the tribals—were driven away. The few who dared to oppose were mercilessly cut down. The homes, hearths and forests were burnt down and from those ashes, the new city rose like a Phoenix. The stone palace stood at the centre of the city, surrounded by palaces of the nobility. Other houses ringed the palace complex in order of wealth. Commerce brought in wealth and prosperity while the lands outside the city limits were harnessed for agriculture and building country houses of the ministers and the overlords.

The Gops were later resettled miles away from the gates of the city, close to the Govardhan hill, on the edge of the kingdom. The only concession granted to them was that they were allowed to manage their own affairs without any interference from the King, subject only to payment of a token annual tribute. In return, they were obliged to meet the dairy requirements of the city.

The tribals fared worse. They were driven into the forests on the southern fringe of the kingdom where they set up small settlements deep inside the forests. Being non-Aryans, they were looked down upon and often referred to by derogatory terms like *'rakshasas'*.

Over a period of time, the absolute power hitherto held by the kings of Mathura diminished and the overlords gained power. At this time there were three main clans in the kingdom—Andhakas, Vrishnis and Bhojas. Instead of hereditary monarchy, the overlords of the three clans formed a committee or *parishad* and elected a head who would be King for his life. The King would choose his minister from the *parishad.* On the death of a King, the *parishad* would meet again and elect one amongst them as the new King, who would rule the kingdom till his death. That new King was sometimes an Andhaka, sometimes a Vrishni and sometimes a Bhoja, depending upon the power and prosperity of the clan leaders at the particular time and upon the inter- and intra-clan politics.

Vasudeva's father King Surasena was a celebrated king from the Vrishni clan. He and his minister tragically died in an accident during a royal hunt. The deaths were a great loss to Mathura, but for the Vrishnis, it was catastrophic. They were left completely leaderless. Surasena's son Vasudeva was only fifteen years of age. The minister's son Akrur was only fourteen. The vacuum at the top led to internecine quarrels amongst the Vrishni clan leaders. Each tried to outdo the other to grab leadership of the clan.

With the Vrishnis divided, Vasudeva did not stand a chance to succeed his father as the King. The Andhakas and Bhojas seized the opportunity and got into the fray. After protracted deals and counter deals, Bhoja leader Ugrasen finally managed a pact with the Vrishnis by promising to marry his niece Devaki with Vasudeva, as soon as Devaki would attain marriageable age. Of course the marriage proposal evoked opposition from some of the Bhoja clan leaders who had fancied their own chances with Devaki, but nevertheless the proposal went through.

The issue of succession resolved, Vasudeva vacated the palace while Ugrasen was crowned the King of Mathura.

The day Devaki's seventh child was killed, Kansa's tribal minister Chanur and his tribal advisers Bhoumya, Dhenuka, Agha and Pralamba sat in their meeting chamber in the palace, nursing their wine and discussing the developments.

The lot of the tribals had changed with the advent of Kansa. Since he was a mere boy, the game of hunting was Kansa's favourite pastime. For days together he would wander about alone in the forest, searching for animals to hunt. During this time, he came in contact with the various forest tribes. He would often accept their hospitality, their wine and women. He would share his trophies with them, learn from them the techniques of hunting, wonder at their keen sense of hearing and smell, speak their language... He made his friends amongst tribals—friends who would accompany him in the hunts and orgies and in the various adventures of rapine and plunder. They would eat, drink and share with each other their thoughts and dreams. Bhoumya, Agha, Dhenuka, Pralamba...all friends who would kill and die for him. His main adviser however was Chanur, who had been a disciple of the famed Guru Rudracharya. When Kansa finally came to power after deposing his father, he chose Chanur as his Minister while Bhoumya, Dhenuka, Agha and Pralamba were appointed his advisers.

As Kansa entered the room and took his seat, Bhoumya handed him his gold tumbler while Dhenuka raised a toast. 'Here's to the death of the seventh serpent,' he roared. The others joined him but strangely Kansa was silent.

'What happened to you, Raja?' Pralamba quizzed. 'Why are you sitting with that sullen expression? Don't you want to celebrate the death of one more thorn in your path?'

Kansa kept silent for a moment and then bellowed, 'Chanur!'

'Yes Raja?'

'Seven are gone but now is the turn of the eighth—the incarnation of Vishnu. The danger is now right at my doorstep. What will happen when the next child is born?'

'Raja, as I was telling my friends, that view may not be correct,' Pralamba interjected before Chanur could reply. 'In my opinion, Raja, the eighth child of Devaki has already been slain. If you remember, apart from the seven children whom Raja has killed, Devaki also had a miscarriage. So this child whom you killed today, was not the seventh, but the eighth. Rejoice, Raja, we are out of danger altogether!'

'No, Pralamba,' Chanur stopped him. 'A miscarried child or an unborn child for that matter, cannot be counted. We cannot rest till the eighth born child is destroyed. As for your question, Raja, the eighth child of Devaki will also go the same way as the other seven.'

'But, how do you know that an incarnation of Vishnu will also meet the same fate as the other seven siblings? What if that child survives? What if by some miracle that child cannot be killed? Have you ever thought of the possibility? Do you have any second plan whatsoever? Have you taken any steps in preparation of such an eventuality?'

'Raja, don't panic. Immediately after you killed the seventh child, I have doubled the security both inside and outside the prison. Devaki will be subjected to medical examinations every day. I will be getting daily reports and thrice a week I shall go on surprise visits to ensure that the security is foolproof and the guards are all on their toes. Just as you killed seven, the eighth will also be killed in a similar manner.'

'Chanur, don't you realise that all these steps are sufficient for mortals. But they would not be sufficient to contain an incarnation of Vishnu. This Vishnu is a very wily god and uses all tricks in the texts. Haven't you heard how he killed Hiranyakashipu, the King of demons, who had the boon that he could not be killed by a man or animal, on land or in air or by any weapon?'

'I have read the Puranas, Raja,' Chanur replied. 'It is said that Vishnu took the form of *Nrisingha,* a cross between a man and lion, took Hiranyakashipu on his lap, so that the victim was neither on land nor on air and tore apart his entrails with his claws, without the use of any weapon. But Raja, these are mere stories for promoting the cult of Vishnu. These things do not happen in real life. Have you heard any such thing in all these years or in your father's time or even your grandfather's or great-grandfather's time? There is no need for you to panic. Nothing is going to happen to you and we will not let anything happen to you.'

'Ah, it is very well Chanur to say such things when the danger is not to you but to someone else. Only the receiver of a threat knows how upsetting it is... You just don't understand my position.' Kansa was beginning to get agitated. He got up and in his rage kicked a huge vase, breaking it to pieces.

'Raja...' Chanur began to speak, but Bhoumya stopped him with his eyes. Chanur squirmed uncomfortably in his seat.

'Don't get excited, Raja,' Bhoumya spoke up. 'I am sorry to say, you do not appreciate the extent of your own powers. Don't you realise you are equal to Vishnu in terms of power?'

'What the hell are you talking about?' Kansa again flew into a rage. 'Make good your submission just now, Bhoumya, or you know the consequences.'

Bhoumya remained impassive. 'Raja, in the *shastras* they say that there is fight only amongst equals. A king will fight only with a king. The gods are bound by dharma. So if Vishnu chooses to fight you, it is obvious that he considers you to be equal to him. That is to say, if he is divine, so are you.'

Kansa looked up, interested. 'Well, this never occurred to any of us before. Well said, Bhoumya.'

Agha took up the cue. 'Raja, what Bhoumya says is correct. When it is predicted that Vishnu will take incarnation to fight you, it is certain that in the times to come, there will be none else in the world but you, who can match Vishnu in terms of power, wealth or wisdom. It is obvious that Vishnu is afraid that you would seize from him the control of *Vaikuntha lok* in the times to come. It is time, Sire, that you realised your true powers. You are the invincible, you are the Almighty, you are Supreme Divinity in human embodiment. You are fit to be worshipped in temples by all and sundry.'

Kansa's breast puffed up in pride. He took out his seven-stringed bejewelled necklace and threw it at Agha, who received it with both hands and touched it to his forehead. Chanur shook his head in disgust.

'And there are several instances in history also, Raja,' Agha continued. 'King Dasaratha of Ayodhya, father of

King Rama, had fought on the side of gods when they were in trouble. It is obvious that his powers were at least equal to those of gods. Even in your exalted Chandra dynasty, your ancestor King Pururuva helped Indra in defeating Keshi, the King of Danavas, who ruled Hiranyapur. In fact, Indra offered him the famed *apsara*, Urvashi, as a gift. Another of your ancestors, King Nahush was selected to be Indra, the King of Gods. King Nahush's son King Yayati also helped the gods in their war against the Asuras. Indra gave him his own chariot. King Yayati's son King Yadu, after whom your subjects are called Yadavas, is also mentioned in the Rig Veda as having travelled to meet Lord Indra.'

Bhoumya interjected, 'Not only that, Agha, our Raja is a direct descendant of the gods themselves. Our Raja's ancestor is Soma, the Moon God and his dynasty is that of the Moon God, Chandravansh. He is divinity personified. Let Vishnu come. It will be a fight amongst equals.'

Chanur now spoke up. 'Raja, I would like to answer your apprehensions regarding our preparedness. First, we shall decimate this so-called incarnation of Vishnu at birth itself. That will not happen until at least ten months from now since Devaki has to conceive and then give birth. Since Vishnu will take human form, he would be subject to the same failings as any other human body and can be killed. But if by any miracle that does not happen, even then Vishnu cannot challenge you till he grows up. We have adequate time to finish him off before that time arrives.'

'In fact, Raja, till that time we shall eradicate the name of Vishnu himself from the minds of people,' Bhoumya said. 'In all the temples we will replace the idols of Vishnu with those of the superior God, our Raja Kansa.'

'That is a good suggestion,' Dhenuka took up the cue. 'We will make it mandatory for all people to go to the temples and worship His Divine Grace Bhagwan Kansa Maharaja.'

Kansa was beside himself. All these years he had been living in fear of the prophesy, without realising what it really meant! Bhoumya and Agha had really opened his eyes. He felt the Supreme Power rising within himself. If Vishnu were to come, let him. He was himself a god and his fight with Vishnu would be one with an equal.

Chanur was sitting quiet, almost in deep meditation. Kansa's eyes fell on him. 'Chanur, why are you so quiet? What do you say to Bhoumya and Agha's proposal? Shouldn't we start the work of replacing the idols of Vishnu with my own?'

Chanur looked up. 'Raja, my Guru Rudracharya, a descendent of the famed Guru Shukracharya, used to say that any act, howsoever great, must be done at the proper time and in the proper circumstances, otherwise it would be doomed to fail.'

Kansa shrugged impatiently. 'I really do not want any of your lectures, Chanur. It does not matter to me what your guru might have told you. You well know that when I was sent to the *gurukul*, I sniped off the *shikha* of my guru with a blade and that was the end of my association with any guru whatsoever.'

Bhoumya laughed out loud but Chanur's cherubic face turned beetroot red at the insult to his guru's name. He took a moment to regain his composure and then continued, 'Raja, your divinity is unquestioned. The only question is when to declare it. I would suggest some preparatory steps before we do it. To proclaim himself as God personified, the King is required to rally his supporters around him and promote himself as a cult. Even gods would be insignificant if they do not have a dedicated band of worshippers.'

'What exactly do you want to do?' Kansa was impatient.

'Raja, to create your cult we need to rehaul our education system, especially in respect of the curriculum. All *gurukuls* in our kingdom should teach a common curriculum where you should be projected as the Supreme Divine incarnate and the Great Leader. Your temples should first be set up in the *gurukul* premises. From their very infancy, every child should know and worship you as God. It should be so ingrained in their minds that they would be prepared to die and kill for your cause at your command.'

Kansa's face expanded a beatific smile. 'Well, at last Chanur is saying something I like to hear.'

'That is not all, Raja,' Chanur continued, 'We need to devise texts which will spell out your previous avatars and the deeds done by them, as well as set out the purpose for which you have taken your present avatar. You are here in your present avatar to protect the Earth from Vishnu, the evil one, who is set to take birth with the aim of destroying the world. The texts will project you as the ultimate *Purushottam* and Vishnu the ultimate evil. You will be projected as one who loves children. Your childhood pranks will be highlighted as your *leela*. These will be in the nature of stories which the children will relate to and find easy and interesting to learn and remember. This will then remain etched in their memories throughout their lives.'

'A great thought,' Pralamba spoke up. 'In fact, Raja, even if that eighth son of Devaki per chance survives, he will grow up reading of your divinity and worshipping your idols. The question of fighting you will then never arise. The danger, if any, would be nipped in the bud.'

'Ha ha ha ha ha ha...' Kansa's laughter shook up the entire hall like an earthquake. 'Vishnu's incarnation growing up worshipping my idols...ha ha ha ha... Well said, Pralamba, ha ha ha ha,' Kansa found it difficult to stop his laughter. His ministers and courtiers joined him and the hall resounded with their collective laughter.

'Go ahead and implement your plans, Chanur,' Kansa said after the laughter subsided. 'Give grants to *gurukuls* to set up my temples and revise the texts…just do it and report back to me.'

'That will not be enough, Raja,' Bhoumya interjected. 'I have something further to say.'

'What is it? Come out with it fast.' Kansa could not hide his impatience.

'Raja, Chanur has prescribed that your cult needs to be promoted, but changing the education system and texts is a long-term measure and will impact only the next generation at the most. But what about your subjects today? You need allegiance from your subjects of today. Who knows what happens a generation later. So, I am going to suggest measures to promote your cult amongst the immediate masses.'

'You are right, Bhoumya,' Kansa agreed. 'Come out with your suggestion.'

Chanur twitched his brow as Bhoumya continued.

'Raja, to develop a cult, you require an immediate and complete image makeover. We, who regularly have access to you, know of your remarkable qualities. But, pardon me for saying this, the common man on the street who does not get to see or know you, often thinks of you as a tyrant who ousted his father to usurp the throne, someone who violated the tenets of the Republic, is wantonly cruel and whose only interest is in hunting, rapine, plunder and watching convicts eaten alive by dogs. This is inconsistent with the image of divinity that you wish to project. Unless your present image is changed in the minds of people, they will not accept your divinity. You require a complete image makeover.'

'Bhoumya, a King has to be harsh and cruel to his subjects to get their obedience.' There was a hint of harshness in Kansa's voice. 'As to my deposing my father and ascending the throne, you are well aware that my father was too soft. Under him the clan leaders had become too powerful and had developed big private armies. There was hardly any central authority. My father was constantly making compromises in order to survive. See, he fixed the marriage of Devaki with Vasudeva in order to placate the Vrishnis. And, how can you forget the riots that took place between the three communities? If I had not intervened, there would have been a civil war between the three clans and our kingdom would again have split into three parts. After deposing my father, I restored the central authority. It was I who curbed the private armies and developed a standing army instead of borrowing forces from the clan leaders everytime. All this would not have been possible if I was a nincompoop like my father. It is on account of my harshness that revenue collection has improved. My subjects know that if they evade taxes, they would be thrown to my dogs and I would willingly watch the spectacle.'

Bhoumya smiled inwardly. Kansa was merely repeating what Chanur and he had been telling Kansa all these years. Outwardly he maintained an impassive face. 'Of course, Raja. you have restored order to this kingdom. But now that central authority has been restored, we need to change how the subjects view you.'

'What changes do you want?'

'Raja, people worship God for two reasons. They expect that God will solve their problems and they fear that if they don't worship, God will punish them. So you have to be a benefactor to your worshippers and cruel to your detractors. For this, the first step has to be improving contact with people so that they can pay obeisance to you and inform you of their problems. People approach gods with their problems and so they will approach you. And like the gods bless them, so should you. If they get tangible results from the interaction, you shall be a living God to your people.'

'How do you want these interactions to take place?' Kansa enquired.

'Raja, I would suggest that you should hold one *sabha* a week for the common people where they can come up with their problems. We shall all be around and try to solve the problems.'

'But, if somebody comes up with ludicrous demands or it is not possible to solve their problems?'

'Raja, I have thought of that also. In the first few *sabhas*, we shall bring in only people whom we have selected in advance. The problems shall be only those which can be solved by us expeditiously. The word shall go out of the tremendous success of the *sabha*. The only thing you have to do is merely to keep your cool and show interest in solving the problems which will be raised.'

'That will be the beginning. But later people may come with problems which it may not be possible to solve. What happens to my divine image if I cannot solve such problems?'

'Raja, even God cannot solve all problems. If there is something for which the people must suffer, it is their fate. They must have done sins in their past life due to which they have to suffer in this life. But, if they pay obeisance to you, then they will be cleansed of sins they commit in this life and in their next life they will prosper,' Bhoumya smiled. 'In any case, we are there to vet each problem before it is presented to you.'

'Well said, Bhoumya, you are a real rogue,' Kansa laughed heartily.

'Raja, we shall rope in some of the Bhoja clan leaders and provide them with incentives. They will enlist their followers to support you and vouch for your divinity. We shall also ask our spies to conduct a whisper campaign about the miracles brought about by you.'

'All this is very good, Bhoumya, but as you said, as of today the common man has a very negative view of our Raja. Will they believe that he has changed overnight?

Will it not take a good amount of convincing?' It was Pralamba this time.

'I just thought of that also, Pralamba,' Bhoumya said. We shall invite some *rishi* to visit our kingdom and after meeting him and being blessed by him, our Raja shall undergo a total transformation.'

'That's what you call a true politician,' Pralamba laughed. 'There is a solution for everything.'

'Great, Bhoumya, you are a real thinker. Others here need to learn from you,' Kansa laughed out loud and the others joined in. In their laughter no one noticed the momentary glint of steel in Chanur's eyes even as his mouth contorted in laughter.

Agha was quietly hearing out the others. He interjected, 'In our laughter, we are forgetting the most important thing.'

'What is that?' Kansa enquired.

'What is to be done with Vasudeva and Devaki? I think our first task should be to ensure that the eighth child is not born at all.'

'The best way out is to go and kill Vasudeva,' Kansa said. 'I do not know why Chanur has kept me back from killing Vasudeva for all these years. If there is no Vasudeva, then there will be no eighth child. Then Devaki will also not have to go through the torture.'

'Raja is right, Chanur,' Bhoumya interjected. 'We do not need to live with the problem when we can uproot it in an instant.'

'Raja, from the time of King Surasena, father of Vasudeva, we have a friendship pact with the kingdom of Kunti to help us against any attack from Hastinapur. To seal that friendship pact, Vasudeva's sister Pritha was given in adoption to King Kuntibhoja of Kunti. She subsequently married King Pandu of Hastinapur. Till now the kingdoms of Kunti and Hastinapur have not reacted to

Vasudeva being kept a prisoner, but if we kill him, both will become our sworn enemies. It is possible that Pritha may induce these two powerful kingdoms to declare war on us. Why should we take that chance at all?' Chanur remained firm in his views.

Agha came out with a middle path solution. 'Keep Vasudeva and Devaki apart in prison, Raja. They will neither be able to conceive the eighth child, nor will your hand be soiled by killing your sister. You can also make a mockery of the prophesy.'

Kansa thumped Agha on his back. 'Right, that is the way to do it,' he shouted in glee. 'Chanur, put up a wall between Vasudeva and Devaki. There should only be a small hole in the wall by which they would be able to see and hear each other, but no more. I just would love to see Vasudeva's frustration in not being able to conceive a child. Ha ha ha ha…Vishnuuuu…let's see who wins in this game…ha ha ha ha ha.'

His laughter echoed for long through the high-domed hall.

Chanur smiled.

Unknown to Kansa, Chanur had his own reasons for keeping Vasudeva alive.

Somehow a sparrow had flown inside through the skylight at the end of the corridor. It flew inside Vasudeva's cell and circled round and round, unable to find its way out. Vasudeva sat still, so as not to frighten away the little being. Finally, the bird perched on a small ledge on the cell wall. Vasudeva found a few leftover crumbs of bread, pushed them towards the bird and sat away. The bird hesitated and after a few minutes, flew down and hopped towards the crumbs. It looked left and right and started eating. Vasudeva looked intently at the bird. It was almost two years that he had looked at a free being, the last being his wife Rohini (The guards were mere slaves of the King).

'What news do you bring me, my little bird?' Vasudeva softly enquired. 'Is Kansa anxious that my eighth son will soon be born? Are the people rising in revolt?'

The bird looked to the right and left and hopped on to another piece of crumb.

'Have you been to my house, little bird? No? Will you go and meet my beloved wife Rohini and get her news? She will feed you all you can, my little bird. Just find out if she has given birth to a baby... Will you do it for me, little bird?'

Two years back, after Devaki had miscarried, she had almost died. It seemed as if the life blood had withdrawn from her person and only a few breaths remained. Kansa had offered to shift her to the palace and place her under the care of his royal physician, but Devaki stoutly refused. She also refused the services of any maid or even of any relative connected to her parents' side to look after her. It seemed she had given up on the very will to survive.

Finally, after a lot of persuasion, she agreed to be taken care of by Rohini, Vasudeva's first wife. For three whole months, through day and night, Rohini nursed Devaki like a mother. Gradually, as a month passed, a dull pallor returned to Devaki's cheeks. Another month and she was able to sit up. Finally, after three months, she was up on her feet.

And then under Kansa's order, Rohini had to go back. It was after years that Rohini had tasted marital bliss and time had flown away too soon... With tears in her eyes, Rohini took leave of Vasudeva and Devaki, nursing a faint hope in her heart that she was carrying her husband's progeny in her womb. Since then, Vasudeva had been unable to get any news about her. Unknown to him, Rohini had given birth to a boy who she named Balarama.

There was a small stir at the back of the cell. Vasudeva turned back and saw Devaki had come out of her unconsciousness. She was sitting straight, looking at the bird with a vacant expression.

The bird looked left and right, then picked up a piece of crumb in its beak and flew outside into the corridor. Minutes later, it fell in front of Vasudeva's cell, an arrow piercing its tiny breast. Vasudeva heard Devaki shriek and saw her body collapse. He rushed to pick her up, when the prison guard came up to the cell.

'In this cell, even a bird is not allowed to flutter its wings.'

III

The Politics of Matrimony

Marriage is not simply a romantic union between two people; it's also a political and economic contract of the highest order

...Elizabeth Gilbert

Ensconced behind the prison bars, with nothing to see except the grimy bare walls of the prison cell stained with blood of his babies and nothing to do but wait till eternity, Vasudeva ruminated on the events that led to his present condition.

It had all started on a sunny spring morning when Mathura woke up to the beat of drums. Heralds went round the city announcing the marriage of Prince Kansa with Princesses Asti and Prapti, the daughters of King Jarasandha of Magadh, seven months later, on the full moon day in the month of *Ashwin*. The heralds further announced that exactly two months thereafter, on the full moon day in the month of *Agrahayan*, the much awaited marriage between Princess Devaki, the niece of King Ugrasen and Prince Vasudeva, would be celebrated. The heralds were followed by pages who showered coins, wheat puffs and flower petals along the road. Children ran onto the streets, jostling amongst themselves to collect the goodies. Men and women alike rushed out of their houses and started discussing the developments. A large congregation assembled at the palace, which was being decorated with mango leaves, marigold flowers and painted earthen pots.

The announcement of marriage between Vasudeva and Princess Devaki came as no surprise. It had been a term of agreement between the Bhojas and Vrishnis. But, what was surprising was the match between Prince Kansa and the two daughters of King Jarasandha of Mathura. Even Vasudeva had been surprised at the announcement.

Jarasandha's name was an amalgam of two words—'Jara' and 'Sandhi'. The name literally meant 'conjoined by Jara'. The official version was that King Brihadrath of Magadha had no son and therefore went to a Rishi for his blessings. The Rishi gave the King a fruit and asked him to give it to his queen. The King had two queens, both daughters of the King of Kashi. He divided the fruit into two and gave half a fruit to each of them. After nine months, the two queens each gave birth to one half of a lifeless baby. On the King's orders, the two half bodies were thrown away. Late that night, a *rakshasi* by the name of Jara, who lived outside the city and came in at night to scour for food, found the two body pieces. When she put the two pieces together, immediately they joined into one and the baby came to life and started crying. The *rakshashi* then took the baby to the King. The grateful King named the baby 'Jarasandha', or 'joined by Jara'. In fact, a brown birthmark ran from the baby's throat to below the navel and gave credence to the version that two half bodies had been joined in one. Later in his life, Jarasandha revelled in the story of his conjunction. He added fodder to the grist by claiming that he had two lives, was invincible to all weapons and could only be killed by tearing him apart along the brown birthmark.

Rumour however abounded that King Brihadrath, who was childless through his queens, had fathered a son through a tribal woman named Jara. Hence the name 'Jarasandha', which could also mean 'through conjunction with Jara'. But since a child of such a match would be regarded as a '*dasiputra*' and would not be able to claim the throne, the King made up a story that the child was actually born to his two queens in two halves and conjoined by Jara.

Whatever be the truth, the apparent conjunction was not only limited to the name or physical appearance. Jarasandha's personality was a conjunction of contradictory characteristics. He was capable of unspeakable cruelty and infinite charity. It was said that he had the strength of ten thousand elephants. A champion wrestler, he was infamous for crushing his opponents at *mallayudh* meets. However, despite his valour, he preferred to win battles through the sly rather than on the battleground. He was arrogance personified, had no friends, and yet maintained contacts with a large number of people in different areas and belonging to different spheres of life.

When he succeeded to the throne, Magadh was a small principality. It comprised only the capital city and some adjoining territories by the Ganga. On the east were hill ranges while on the south were deep forests and thereafter plateaus and ravines. Not many Aryans had settled in the area and even amongst them, not many belonged to the *Kshatriya* or warrior caste. The population was predominantly tribal who had their own clans, beliefs, rituals and practices and were wary of the Aryans. The limited number of *Kshatriya* Aryans meant that the army was small and most of their energies were devoted to keeping the resident tribals in check.

Jarasandha was a man of foresight. If Aryans were few, he reasoned, the army could be increased only by inducting tribals into the armed forces. The very idea was however abhorrent to his ministers, advisers and generals. The *shastras* prescribed a caste-based society. There were four castes in the Aryan society—the *Kshatriyas* who would fight, *Brahmins* who would devote their lives in pursuit of learning, *Vaishyas* who were traders and merchants and the *Shudras* who performed all other work, including the menial and lowly jobs. When the Aryans extended their settlements in Aryavarta, the conquered tribals and locals were consigned to the caste of *Shudras*. If King Jarasandha's plan was to be implemented, these *Shudra* tribals would be fighting alongside the *Kshatriya* Aryans!

But Jarasandha was not one to let go. Soon after he became King, he placated the tribal chiefs with expensive gifts and secured their allegiance. He got the tribals to fight under his flag and order as the Magadhi army in return for one half of the loot while he kept the territories won in the battles and the balance loot. With the induction of the tribal territories, Magadh's size and its army increased fourfold. The naysayers were soon rendered powerless and in course of time, replaced. At the same time, Jarasandha took care to ensure that the tribal chiefs did not unite against his authority. This he achieved by playing the tribal chiefs against each other through clever propaganda and trained agents.

Jarasandha's tryst with tribals did not end there. He was a connoisseur of men and appointed two very able and knowledgeable tribal brothers, Hansa and Dimvaka, as his ministers.

Elated with his success in inducting tribals in his army, Jarasandha went a step further and denounced the caste system itself in army recruitment. Now, any person, irrespective of his caste or parental occupation, could join the army, provided he passed the various tests devised to test the fitness, ability and skill of the incumbents. Consequently, a large number of able-bodied non-*Kshatriya* Aryans joined the army and swelled its ranks.

With his back secured and in command of a large army raring to go, Jarasandha next set out to realise his vision—to become a *Rajchakravarti*, an emperor! For that purpose he envisioned the need for a trained army, where each soldier would fight with skill and unity of purpose, rather than merely provide guard duty to one *Rathi* or *Maharathi*. He therefore employed trainers to train his soldiers in the art of fighting and in improving their physical fitness.

One battle after another, Jarasandha progressed towards his goal. One by one the kings of Aryavarta fell to his strategies and to his trained army. But, while he added territories to his kingdom, it was another story on the social and matrimonial front. The kings of Aryavarta were rigid adherents of the caste system. Aryavarta was a country where even a poor *Brahmin* was socially superior to the *Kshatriya* King and entitled to respect from the King. Rumours of Jarasandha's mixed parentage coupled with his open endorsement of tribals, resulted in his being looked down upon by his peers. The other kings could be jealous of his prowess, fearful of his army and be his vassals in true sense of the term, but they would not send proposals for marriage with Jarasandha's daughters.

It had been a very hectic year for Chanur, albeit with a sweet ending. It was just over a year back that he was sitting with Prince Kansa and his other companions along the bank of the Yamuna. The sun was setting and its rays had set the river on fire. It was a week since they had returned from their last marauding expedition from a Panchala village. And the entire week had been spent in drinking wine and devouring the women who were part of the loot. Today's discussion started from comparison of maidens from Panchala and Mathura, snaked round to the next theatre of operation and finally settled on how uncannily that day's colour of the river, resembled that of a week back when the river reflected the burning fires of the Panchala village. It was Kansa who made the remark about colour of the river and his companions caught onto it.

'See Bhoumya, our Kumar has become a poet. Only a poet could point out the similarity in the reflected colours of the setting sun with that of a burning village,' Agha laughed aloud.

'Well, just ensure that our Kumar does not become Maharishi Valmiki,' Pralamba joined in. 'You see, Maharishi Valmiki was a dacoit before he turned tail and composed the Ramayana.'

'But what *mahakavya* will our Kumar compose?'

'Well, you never know. It could be paeans on the beauty of one of the Panchala maidens. I have heard maidens from Panchala know secret mantras by which they can turn a man into a lamb. Otherwise who could have imagined our Kumar commenting on the beauty of nature! It must be that dusky Panchala girl, who was the daughter of the headman.'

Kansa joined in the merriment. 'What would you fellows do if I turned to writing?'

'I will bear your ink and quill,' Pralamba quipped.

'That job is not for me. I have an altogether different job in mind,' Bhoumya winked.

'And, pray what is that job?' Kansa enquired with a smile.

'I will maintain a steady supply of Panchala girls to you so that you are never short of inspiration!'

The river exploded with laughter.

It was Chanur who broke the spell. 'But for how long, Kumar, how long?'

Kansa choked on his laughter. 'What do you mean "how long"?'

'I mean Kumar, how long will you go on with these activities?'

'What activities?'

'This drinking, marauding, looting villages...you are a Prince, Kumar. Behave like one. Not a measly dacoit. The kingdom is yours, yet you settle for a village! Get up and realise your potential instead of wasting it away like this.'

'Bhoumya,' Kansa boomed, 'why have we brought this spoilsport? He has ruined my intoxication. I am sure if

I were to take to poetry, Chanur would surely take the job of a preacher and roam about the kingdom preaching his nonsense.'

There was another echo of laughter.

Chanur stood up. 'My Prince, I am going to tell you a very unpleasant truth. This is Mathura—the only place in Aryavarta, where the son does not inherit the throne on death of the King. If today, God forbid, your father King Ugrasen were to come to any harm or succumb to destiny, then not a single Yadava would want you to succeed to the throne.' Chanur's lips curled into a sarcastic smile. 'Then you actually won't have any job but to write poetry and there won't be any muses either.'

'Don't beat around the bush, Chanur,' Kansa thundered. 'Get to the point and tell me what you want to say.'

'Kumar, what I am saying is that you would not want to remain a mere prince all your life. This is the time for you to develop your alliances so that you can succeed to the throne of Mathura.'

'But, you just said that not a single Yadava would want to see me on the throne. Then how do I go about it?' There was desperation in Kansa's voice.

'Kumar, if you have alienated those of your own, then you need to reach out to others, those who will back you without questioning your past.'

'Who will back me in this manner?'

'Kumar, my Guru taught me that alliances can be built in various ways, and one of those ways is matrimonial alliance. Your in-laws will back you without questioning whether you are right or not.'

'But matrimonial alliance with whom? Who will have the power and authority to dictate to the people of Mathura to select me over others?'

'Slow, Kumar, slow. One step at a time. First step is developing matrimonial alliance with a very strong ruler.

If you are able to do that, then your in-laws will have an interest in ensuring that you succeed to the throne so that their daughter becomes queen.'

'Chanur,' Kansa struck an impatient note, 'I asked—matrimonial alliance with whom? Answer that question first. You are just beating around the bush. Do you have anyone particular in mind?'

'Kumar, have you heard of King Jarasandha?'

Kansa paused for a moment and then shouted, 'What? You mean that *Shudra* King? You want me to get married to a *Shudra* King's daughter?'

Chanur did not even bat an eyelid. He was prepared for the reaction. Calmly he said, 'Kumar, it seems you do not know the facts. Jarasandha is reviled by the Aryavarta kings because of his affinity to tribals. But if affinity to tribals would make a person a *Shudra,* then even you should be called so in view of your proximity to us. The real fact is that Jarasandha has organised the tribes in his kingdom to build a force which no other king can beat and hence their jealousy. He combines power with cunning and industriousness. His dream is to become a *Rajchakrabarti* and he will certainly achieve it. Kumar, this is the time to hitch on to his bandwagon and reap the benefits as he rises in power.'

'But can't it be any other option?' Kansa was still hesitant.

'No, Kumar, no. Just think, after your raids on the Panchala village a week back, will the Panchala King or any of his allies give their daughter in marriage with you? Similarly, you have ravaged villages of almost each one of our neighbouring kingdoms. News travels fast to the other kingdoms beyond. That is why I have been repeatedly advising you to stop these raiding parties and concentrate on performing your princely duties by helping your father in administration. But you have never paid any heed to anything I have said.'

'But why will Jarasandha accept me if others don't?' Kansa was curious.

'First, he does not have many alternatives. No king is coming forward to seek his daughters in marriage. Second, he will find much in common between him and you. Your physical prowess, your friendship with us tribal chiefs, your ruthless behaviour are very similar to him. But it is the third reason that will make him accept you.'

'And pray what is that?'

'This is a political reason. Since Jarasandha began his victorious march, Hastinapur has been wary of him. It does not want a parallel centre of power. If Jarasandha becomes *Rajchakrabarti,* he will become that parallel centre of power and conflict with Hastinapur will become inevitable. It is for this reason that Hastinapur provided arms and men to the kingdom of Anga, to the east of Magadh, to halt Jarasandha's advance. He did try but could not succeed in conquering Anga. Hastinapur has achieved three objectives by doing this. It has effectively prevented Jarasandha from going south, added Anga to its list of vassal states and also sort of surrounded Jarasandha on one side.'

'So?' Kansa was now getting interested.

'Now, Jarasandha could not expand westward since there was Kashi, which was his maternal uncle's kingdom. He could not go south due to the rocky plateaus and forests there. In the north, flows the mighty Ganga. So the only option left to him was to proceed east, bypassing Anga. This was a direction away from Hastinapur, so they initially did not mind. But then Jarasandha conquered huge territories in Banga. This was a rich, fertile and large revenue generating land. This again raised the heckles of Hastinapur. So they started instigating King Bhagadatta of Kamrup, who was another king of similar status to Jarasandha. Huge consignments of arms were sent to Kamrup. Eventually on account of Hastinapur's conspiracy, Jarasandha and Bhagadatta were locked in a mammoth battle. It was like the Puranic tale of the elephant and the crocodile. In battles fought in Banga, Jarasandha won while in battles fought in Kamrup, Bhagadatta was victorious.

For full five years, the battle waged on, bleeding both Bhagadatta and Jarasandha and weakening them considerably. Hastinapur's objective was achieved. To rub insult to injury, Bhishma then raided the *swayamvar* of the princesses of Kashi—Amba, Ambika and Ambalika—and took them away for marrying his stepbrother Vichitravirya. Magadha had long regarded Kashi as its protectorate. However, Jarasandha was busy in Kamrup and had no option but to digest the insult.

It was then that Jarasandha took his lesson. He initiated a peace pact with Bhagadatta, who too was weary of the war. After that, Jarasandha has been taking his time to rebuild his finances and his army. Three years through the peace, he started building a new capital at a place called Girivraja. I have heard that place is surrounded by hills and therefore very secure from external invasion. And after the new capital is built, we can expect that Jarasandha will start with the second round.'

'So is Magadh now going to attack Hastinapur?'

'Of course not, Kumar. Hastinapur is a *"hasti"* (elephant) of mammoth strength and proportions. Jarasandha is a very cunning person. He will not stake his all in attacking Hastinapur. Even otherwise, Hastinapur is very far from Magadh. Taking a huge army to such a distant place and winning the war there, is well nigh impossible.'

'So, you are saying that Jarasandha will not take revenge?'

'Kumar, I have not said that. Jarasandha is not a person who either forgives or forgets. But where the enemy is mighty, you do not fight open wars with him, you try to bleed him and wait for the suitable opportunity to strike. Therefore, he will be interested in a matrimonial alliance with Mathura.'

'But, why with Mathura?' Kansa was curious.

'Because Mathura is near Hastinapur. Just like Hastinapur surrounded Magadha with Anga and Kamrupa, similarly, Jarasandha will look to surround Hastinapur with his friendly states. Mathura can be one such friendly state. At an opportune moment, Jarasandha can strike Hastinapur through Mathura.'

'But just now you said that Hastinapur is like a mammoth elephant. So how can he even dream of attacking Hastinapur?'

'Kumar, just think, Hastinapur is today great because of Bhishma. If tomorrow Bhishma dies, then what happens? The throne would be occupied by mere children. That would be the appropriate time to strike Hastinapur.'

'I agree with you on all this, Chanur,' Kansa retorted. 'I also agree that with a person of such strength and cunning backing me, I would stand a good chance to succeed to the throne. But why should Mathura agree to such an alliance? How would you persuade my father, who is of the old school and would look down on Jarasandha, to agree to this alliance?'

'I have thought of that also,' said Chanur. 'Mathura has always been at a risk from Hastinapur. Earlier, we entered into alliance with the kingdom of Kunti since King Kuntibhoja was a very big warrior and a counterfoil to Bhishma. King Surasena even gave his daughter Pritha in adoption to King Kuntibhoja. This ensured that till the kingdom of Kunti was safe from Hastinapur, Mathura would also remain safe. But, this position does not hold any longer. With King Kuntibhoja's death, his son is no longer in a position to hold his own against Hastinapur. He had had to capitulate and give Pritha in marriage to the prince of Hastinapur. This has brought Hastinapur to our doorstep. If Vasudeva were to become king, the threat of Hastinapur would have considerably subsided since Vasudeva is Pritha's brother. But that is not the case. In fact, Hastinapur may think of deposing your father and installing Vasudeva as their vassal. So what Mathura requires today is to develop alliance with a counter-power so that Hastinapur would have to think twice before attacking Mathura. And, there is no power other than Jarasandha, who can check Hastinapur. Therein comes the mutual interest of both Mathura and Jarasandha in forming an alliance.'

Chanur was a man not only of words but also of action. But convincing King Ugrasen was easier said than done. Chanur's argument that Mathura would benefit by aligning with Magadh, did not cut ice with Ugrasen. According to Ugrasen, Magadh was not sufficiently powerful to take on Hastinapur. On the other hand, such a move may enrage Hastinapur and provoke them to attack Mathura. The end result would be another humiliation like Kashi had suffered.

Then there was the caste factor. Why should Mathura align with a person of reportedly mixed parentage, who hobnobbed with the *Shudras?* What if all other monarchs shunned the King of Mathura for aligning with Jarasandha?

When arguments failed, Chanur instigated Kansa to plead for the marriage. He said that he had seen the portrait of King Jarasandha's daughter and had fallen hopelessly in love with her. If he could not get her, then he would not marry another girl all his life. Contrary to Chanur's expectations, even this ploy failed. Ugrasen reminded Kansa of his looted girls and wayward ways and severely rebuked him. Finally, when all failed, Kansa, on Chanur's advice, unleashed the *brahmastra*—the ultimate weapon. He went on a fast. On the third day, Ugrasen capitulated. Soon, armed with a letter of accreditation from King Ugrasen, Chanur went to Girivraja to meet Jarasandha to discuss if a formal marriage proposal could follow.

Seated on a rock on top of Mount Swarnagiri, Chanur looked down at the city under. Girivraj was under construction.

At the centre of the city, atop a huge mound, was being constructed the biggest and grandest palace ever built by man—the *rajgriha*. The area was a beehive of activity. A haze of dust rose from the construction sites and mixed with plumes of smoke from the coal ovens outside the workers' tents. The potent mix refracted and split the rays of the setting Sun to form fleeting rainbows, giving a tinted view of the ugliness below. Jarasandha's words rang in Chanur's ears: 'Today this city is like an ugly pupa. Tomorrow it will develop into a butterfly. Today I am constructing the capital of Magadha. Tomorrow it will become the capital of Aryavarta....'

It was almost more than a month since Chanur had come to Girivraja to meet King Jarasandha. On the third day itself he had managed to secure a private audience with the King. The first impression that Chanur formed of Jarasandha was that of a lion raring to go. Jarasandha was not wearing a crown and his fuzzy locks spread over his shoulder like a lion's mane. Later, Chanur realised that the lion's appearance hid behind it the cunning mind of a fox.

Chanur received a very patient hearing from Jarasandha. He set out the qualities of Kansa, which he felt Jarasandha would find desirable. He skilfully brought out the advantages of a matrimonial alliance between Mathura and Magadha to both the kingdoms.

Jarasandha heard him out without interruption and finally asked him just one question: 'Mathura is a republic. What happens if after King Ugrasen, Kansa is not selected as the next king?'

It was a question which Chanur had long apprehended and was ready for it. 'Your Majesty, I am sure you will not allow your daughter to remain a mere princess.'

With an impassive face, Jarasandha asked Chanur to stay as a state guest and await his reply. So Chanur stayed on in Girivraja.

One afternoon Chanur sat on his favourite rock on a ledge on Mount Swarnagiri and contemplated. Jarasandha and

Kansa were the only two royals at present in Aryavarta who were dependent on tribals. The others were openly hostile. All over Aryavarta, day after day, tribals were being evicted from their homelands, subjected to rapine and plunder. The forests were being burnt down to construct new towns and cities. Whatever forests remained were being reserved for hunting expeditions by the King.Chanur's tribe was one of many that suffered through years before they were coerced to submit to the King of Mathura.

Chanur had in his childhood, heard these stories from his grandfather, who had heard from his grandfather... The stacks were clearly pitted against the tribals, at least for now. There was no unity amongst them. Their antiquated cane bows and arrows were not sufficient. The Aryans had much better weaponry and their rishis were constantly researching into new types of annihilating weapon systems. The tribals did not have a Bhishma or Jarasandha who could transcend any weaknesses of their armies with their personal valour. Simple minded and uneducated, they did not know the intricacies of governance and politics. What chance of survival did they have! Yet, Chanur could sense, the chance was coming. In Magadha, after Jarasandha, the tribal ministers could, if they wished, take over the reins of power. And in Mathura, if Kansa ever came to power, tribals would become ministers. They could then keep Kansa under influence of wine and women and control the kingdom and its treasury. It was Guru Rudracharya's dream to create a tribal homeland. If resources of Magadh and Mathura could be controlled, that dream could turn into a reality.

During the last one month, after the initial meeting, Chanur had met Jarasandha twice. During one of his meetings, Jarasandha had waxed eloquent on the palace. 'You'll see Chanur, this *rajgriha* that I am building, will be like no other. It will be a massive fort-palace, which would be visible from any part of the town. The fort will be surrounded by a moat which will have to be crossed by a drawbridge. The huge iron doors of the fort will be plated with silver and studded with spikes to prevent elephants from bringing it down. Inside, the iron doors will be further fortifications and battlements as a next line of defence. The palace will be constructed of white marble with rich inlay work of gold and semi-precious stones. Chanur, it will be a work that even a thousand years later, people will find it difficult to match.'

Chanur smiled to himself. His Guru had taught him that the vanities of emperors will all crumble to dust one day. Dug up ruins of old, dead civilisations yield not the magnificent palaces and tombs but the pottery of the common man and the playthings of children. But yes, if Jarasandha did build a *rajgriha* as described by him, then surely he would become a folk legend whose name would outlast his buildings.

Towards the end of the third month of Chanur's stay, Jarasandha agreed to the marriage proposal, but with a condition that both his daughters, Asti and Prapti, be married to Kansa. Chanur was elated. If both of Jarasandha's daughters were to get married to Kansa, Jarasandha would have a much higher stake in him and would promote him like no other.

The meeting communicating the acceptance was followed by a series of other meetings between Jarasandha and Chanur. They discussed the various modalities and strategies. Although marriage is usually held at the girl's place, in this case it was decided that the venue of marriage will be Mathura. The ostensible reason was the construction activity at Girivraja. It was decided that the marriage would be held on the full moon day in the month of *Ashwin.*

Almost four months after he had come to Girivraja, Chanur finally left for Mathura. His ears were ringing with the parting words of Jarasandha: 'Chanur, if you ever need a job, come to me. I need persons like you and I know how to honour them.'

Fixing Kansa's marriage with Jarasandha's daughters was just the first step. Chanur's work had in fact just begun....

IV

The Marriage and the Coup

The real act of marriage takes place in the heart, not in the ballroom or church or synagogue

...Barbara De Angelis

Two months before Kansa's wedding, Mathura presented a picture of utter chaos. By the King's decree, all homes in Mathura were being repainted. At every street corner, huge vats of limestone mixture were being burned. A thick pungent odour of lime hung in the air, numbing the senses. There was no respite from the odour even inside the privacy of one's home. The smoke from the vats caused irritation to the eyes. A cloud cover ensured that the pollutants could not escape into the atmosphere. A dull haze hung about the town, subjecting the inhabitants to coughing fits. The palace fared no better as a steady stream of bullock carts brought in stones and materials for construction of a new building for Kansa's brides.

King Ugrasen, who had finally shed his inhibitions about Kansa's marriage and personally went about the city with his minister to take stock of the situation, was aghast. 'Bindudev, it is not a city, it is a cesspool. You all will ruin my reputation!'

'No Maharaj,' Bindudev replied. 'Two months from now, Mathura will emerge like a lotus from this murky cesspool.'

On the outskirts of Mathura, the scene was no different. About five *kos* from the eastern gates of Mathura, a huge township of tents was coming up to house King Jarasandha and his retinue who would be coming for the wedding. That would also be the venue for the wedding. Dimvaka had personally come from Magadh with hundreds of Magadhi workers and elephant-loads of resources to ensure that the arrangements were fit for the future Emperor of Aryavarta. The venue of the marriage may be Mathura, but being the father of the brides, it was King Jarasandha who would be the host for the ceremony and therefore the marriage tents were being erected at Jarasandha's instance and cost.

The marriage tent conceived by Dimvaka was a scaled down replica of the *Rajgriha*. That such a tent could be even erected, was beyond the comprehension of even the best architects. Dimvaka's idea was to project to the outside world, the majesty of Magadh, its power and grandeur and it being the alternate power centre to Hastinapur. Huge arches and pillars of hardened clay mixed with a special grass were erected and then adorned with the finest fabrics, to recreate a palace, of which the only parallel was the palace of Lord Indra. The gateway to the palace was guarded by *Yaksha* and *Yakshini* figurines and inside the gateway, lifelike nymphs gave a welcoming guard of honour.

Even more spectacular than the marriage tent was the manner in which Dimvaka had planned the brides' entry into the marriage arena. He drew upon the mythological *Pushpaka vimana*, the swan-drawn chariot owned by King Ravana of Lanka, which could fly in the sky. It was the vehicle in which King Rama returned to Ayodhya with his wife Sita and brother Laxman after vanquishing Ravana in battle. A grand chariot was constructed with figurines of swans in front, instead of horses. An immense crane with wheels was commissioned to lift the swan chariot from the brides' tent and carry it to the marriage arena. The crane would be hidden by figures of white clouds and blue sky, which would give the impression that the chariot was emerging from the clouds. Dimvaka smiled to himself as he imagined the jaws of people hanging in wonder at the spectacle.

A different tented community had come up on the south of the city, along the banks of the Yamuna. Folk dancers from Matsya, bangle sellers from Panchala, *mahua* liquor sellers from Nishada, astrologers from Kashi, sweetmeat sellers from Kuru, textile sellers from Chedi, singers from Gandhara, acrobats from Kosala had all come down to Mathura to display their skills or wares and earn money. A *kos* away, in an open ground, they set up their wares and skills on display. It was a festive carnival atmosphere and day after day, almost the whole of Mathura turned out in their best attire, to be a part of the festivities.

The best singers and dancers were summoned from all over Aryavarta to come and perform for the ceremonies. *Halwais* and confectioners came from distant lands with their varied traditional cuisines and special offerings. New 'marriage special' sweets were designed for the occasion. Life-size statues of Kansa with his two brides sitting beside him were made out of *khoya.* Suppliers of exotic fruits came in from Gandhara and Vidharbha, seeking contracts for the ceremonies. Hunting was banned to preserve the game for hunting parties to be organised for the guests during the festivities. To ensure a seamless supply of meat, special enclosures for deer, peacock, goats and sheep were created. Fine textiles were brought in from Banga and Avanti. The ladies of the palace kept busy selecting from the varied wares while goldsmiths were kept busy working out the prescribed designs on the ornaments. King Ugrasen got a new diamond-studded crown prepared for the occasion, with a novel design that would ensure that it took the spotlight off Jarasandha. Dimvaka's men kept a close watch on the arrangements made by Mathura and in return, were as closely watched upon.

Exactly one month before the wedding, Kansa was anointed the Commander-in-chief of the Mathura army by King Ugrasen. Ever since the match was finalised, Chanur had tried to persuade Ugrasen of the need to appoint Kansa to a high office as it would be demeaning for Mathura itself if Jarasandha's daughters were to be married to a prince who did not have any power. Being Commander-in-chief would also mean that Kansa would have control over the Mathura armies, which was of pivotal importance in Chanur's scheme of things.

The first step that Kansa took as Commander-in-chief was to send troop battalions to guard the borders. According to Chanur, King Jarasandha would come to Mathura for the wedding and Mathura's neighbours were not particularly enamoured of either Jarasandha or Kansa. It was therefore necessary to guard against any possible incursions or misadventures by Mathura's neighbours during the wedding ceremonies. Simultaneously, intelligence and counter intelligence units were beefed up. Troops patrolled the streets day and night. Bars and dancing houses were kept under surveillance while history sheeters were kept under custody. Amidst all this, Chanur kept up a steady connection with Dimvaka and the two discussed and furthered their plans.

The festivities now began in Mathura in right earnest. Every day one or the other overlords would invite Kansa and his retinue over for bachelor parties. Liquor flowed freely, dancing girls displayed their dancing and other skills while chefs whipped up exotic cuisines. And behind the scene, Chanur secretly negotiated with the overlords....

King Jarasandha arrived with a huge contingent five days before the marriage date. Apart from the two brides-to-be, his retinue comprised of his family members, rulers of some of the vassal states, housekeeping and other staff, large bands of musicians, dancers and performers, elephants and horses laden with gifts and supplies and a large army to provide security. With their arrival, Mathura exploded in celebrations.

The day after Jarasandha's arrival in Mathura was kept for blessing of the brides. King Ugrasen with his family and the leading overlords of Mathura went over to Jarasandha's tent to bless Asti and Prapti for the wedding. Ugrasen blessed the duo with suits of ornaments of gold, diamonds and precious stones, carved to perfection by celebrated goldsmiths of Banga. A huge feast was organised for the occasion by Jarasandha. The next day, Jarasandha came into the Mathura Palace with his family and retinue and an elephant-load of gifts, to bless Kansa. As the celebrations continued, Vasudeva, who was invited as a guest by King Ugrasen, suddenly felt a tug on his upper garment. A distant aunt motioned him to follow her. He followed her through the halls and the maze of rooms in which he had spent his childhood and three years of his teens, to a room in the internal quarters.

'Please wait here. I will just be back.'

'But Aunt, tell me why have you brought me here?'

'All in good time, my son. Patience brings its own rewards.'

The aunt left. Vasudeva wandered across the high-ceilinged room, looking at the vases, statuettes and paintings. It was odd enough for him to be here and would cause a lot of embarrassment if someone was to enter and ask what he was doing here when all the other overlords were at the function. Never mind that he was born and brought up in these rooms and was to be the son-in-law of the King....

Vasudeva waited and waited and finally made up his mind to leave. He turned round to the door and suddenly froze. His aunt had just entered the room and held the hand of the most beautiful and sublime damsel that he had ever seen. Her face was the radiant golden of the moon on a full moon night. Her eyes were serene and evocative. She was wearing on her slim frame, an elaborately embroidered lehenga of sunflower yellow and maroon, embellished with small mirrors and coloured beads. A yellow embellished veil covered her hair, pinned with a gold ornament that encroached upon her forehead.

'Devaki, see who we have here. Do you recognise him?'

So this is my bride Devaki, Vasudeva thought. The bud he had seen years before had blossomed into a *swarna champa* flower.

Their eyes met and in a flash, Devaki covered her face with her hand. But in that instant, Vasudeva had seen the radiant golden of the full moon change to the crimson of the rising sun.

With a jerk, Devaki freed her hand from the aunt and ran away. 'Devaki...Devaki...come back,' the aunt shouted but to no avail. Apologetically she turned to Vasudeva. 'Well, my son, I tried my best, but she is too shy....'

Vasudeva found his own ears turning beetroot red. 'Thank you nevertheless, Aunt,' he said and beat a hasty retreat.

Throughout that feast and celebrations that day, Vasudeva's eyes searched in vain for that elusive yellow and maroon lehenga and the embellished yellow veil. The feast was grand. Fifty preparations of meat, fowl and fish of different varieties were arranged and a dozen different wines to wash them down, yet Vasudeva could hardly eat a morsel. The overlords around him gossiped and laughed, but their sounds passed him by.

After the feast, Vasudeva flitted from one hall to the other, lonely in the crowd, looking out for the doe-like eyes, the yellow and maroon lehenga, the embellished yellow veil....

'May I help you? Are you looking for anyone in particular?' A damsel with smiling eyes confronted him.

'No...no, I was just taking in the festivities,' Vasudeva stammered.

'Oh, by the way I am Vanshini, a cousin of Devaki. I thought you were looking for her. Anyway, if you are not looking for her, then it does not matter.' The girl proceeded to leave.

In an instant, Vasudeva grabbed her hand. 'Where is... ahem...where is Devaki?'

'*Jamai Raja,* please let go of my hand. Devaki is nearby and if she sees you holding my hand, she may construe otherwise.'

Thunderstruck, Vasudeva let go of her hand.

'But *Jamai Raja,* they say once a true man holds a woman's hands, he does not leave it for a lifetime. You seem to be too fickle. I may have to tell Devaki.'

'No...no...' Vasudeva stammered once again. 'I did not mean to... I did not want to hold your hand in the first place... I was just enquiring about Devaki... Please don't take it otherwise and please don't tell Devaki anything about my holding your hand... It was just accidental, you see... Please accept my apologies....'

The girl laughed out. 'Alright, if you are so sorry about it, I won't tell.'

'But where is she?'

'Whom do you mean by "she"?'

'*Oho,* please don't torment me any further. Please tell where she is,' Vasudeva could control no longer.

'Well well, it seems the fire is equally burning in both the hearts. Cross the courtyard and go to the first hall on the left and you will find your beloved. She is waiting for you.'

Devaki waiting for him! Vasudeva could hold himself no longer. With a throbbing heart and leaden feet, he crossed the sun-drenched courtyard and into the first hall to the left. The movement from light to darkness blinded him for an instant. At first glance, the hall seemed vacant. Then Vasudeva's eyes took in a splash of colour and a clamour of bangles. Along one of the pillars, standing with her back to him, was the now familiar figure in the yellow and maroon lehenga and the embellished yellow veil.

With a dry throat and trepid steps, Vasudeva stepped forward. His muse still stood with her back towards him, one arm resting on a pillar.

'I am sorry if I frightened or embarrassed you in the morning,' Vasudeva managed to mutter out.

The figure still did not move. Vasudeva wetted his parched lips and continued.

'But ever since I saw a glimpse of you, my heart has not ceased to ache for you. You have been constantly in my thoughts. The celebrations here have just passed me by. Will you not favour me by revealing your beautiful face, my beloved, to sustain me till our marriage?'

After a moment, which seemed an eternity, the figure turned around. Her head bowed, the veil covering her face. With nimble fingers Vasudeva took the veil, lifted it...and froze....

It was NOT Devaki!

Suddenly a large band of laughing damsels came out and surrounded the duo.

'Tsk...tsk...what were you upto *Jamai Raja*?' A cacophony of voices demanded of Vasudeva.

The figure in the lehenga joined in. 'He was expressing his love for me and asking me to marry him. He specifically said that he wanted to see my face to sustain him till our marriage.'

Vasudeva again felt his ears getting hot and red. 'I am sorry, but....'

Another cacophony of voices drowned his voice.

'Well, *Jamai Raja* now has to marry Srinjini instead of our princess. That seems the only way out. Let's take him to Kumar Kansa's *vivaha mandap*. The two marriages can take place together.' Twenty hands grabbed Vasudeva, jostled and pushed him and ten others lent vocal support to the effort.

The swordsman *par excellence* had no defences against a bevy of flirtatious young girls. His pleas fell upon deaf ears, he was shouted down by the laughing and quarrelling beauties.

'Revati, Sundari…stop all of you. Leave him alone.'

A soft, flute-like voice from behind Vasudeva's back intervened to his rescue.

'You have tormented him enough. Now let him go.'

'Well, who are we to hold him? He is your property. We were just taking care of him on your behalf. Now that you have come, you take charge of your property.' The girls left Vasudeva and ran away together, laughing.

Vasudeva turned towards his saviour. 'Uff…that was close…thanks for saving me….'

'Save from what? It seems you go about professing your love to any girl you see.' There was a hint of anger in Devaki's voice, though the eyes could not hide their smile. 'First it was Vanshini, now it is Srinjini. I think you would have loved marrying them also. I may have to speak to King Uncle about it.'

Vasudeva fell on his feet. 'My apologies, beautiful lady. Since forenoon, my eyes have been scouting for the moon and only now it is visible. I would willingly bear any punishment that you give me if my eyes get to feast on your lotus eyes. Deny me the privilege and you see me dead….'

Devaki clapped her hand on Vasudeva's lips. 'Don't say such inauspicious things.'

'Then promise that you will meet me every day during these festivities….'

The bevy of girls burst in. Vasudeva, unwilling to be again a prisoner in their hands, bolted through the opposite door. For long, the peals of Devaki's laughter rang in his ears. For the next four days of festivities, their eyes sought each other out. Their eyes spoke of love and togetherness as their hearts sought each other's out and claimed it as its own.

It was Kansa's wedding ceremony. The marriage tent designed after Jarasandha's new capital Girivraja, drew gasps of admiration from the visitors. There were artificial mountains, streams, lakes and forests and in the midst of nature was the replica of *Rajgriha* at Girivraja resplendent in the light of a million earthen lamps. And, when the two brides Asti and Prapti arrived in the *Pushpaka vimana,* it seemed as if they descended from the clouds in a celestial chariot. But all this did not register with Vasudeva and Devaki who saw this all with unseeing eyes, their very consciousness imprisoned with the other.

The next two nights were fixed for Kansa's nuptials with his two brides and the last day for the ceremonial lunch at Kansa's new palace where the new brides would cook a dish apiece for the guests. Asti cooked a mutton item and Prapti cooked a dessert. Of course, the items were cooked in huge vats by experienced chefs and the new brides merely stirred the ladle once under the watchful eyes of their mother-in-law Queen Padmavati.

Vasudeva went around the halls, his furtive glances looking for Devaki, when a damsel approached him with a small gold container.

'Devaki has sent this for you, Sir.'

Vasudeva opened the container and found a spoonful of *payasam*.

'Devaki has cooked this for you with her own hands, Sir.'

Vasudeva consumed the contents with relish. 'Tell your mistress, that even the nectar of paradise would fail in taste before this. But this only torments my senses as my heart, mind and tongue yearns for more. Please ask her when she would end my torment.'

The damsel smiled and moved away. Vasudeva sighed. Little did he know that it would be decades since he would again be able to eat a dish cooked by Devaki....

The ceremonial lunch ended and the guests started leaving after heaping effusive praise on the dishes supposedly cooked by the brides. Kansa invited his parents to take a round of his new palace. The new palace had been constructed in a grand style and decorated in a grander manner. The King and Queen strolled with Kansa through the new palace, admiring its design and décor and reached the easternmost wing. There was a maze of rooms in the wing and as they reached one such room, a posse of guards came in and surrounded the King and Queen.

'What is the meaning of this, Kansa?' King Ugrasen could not believe his eyes.

'I am sorry, *Pita Maharaj*, but there was no other option. My forces have arrested a man and recovered a letter written by you asking Hastinapur to conduct a sudden raid on Mathura and kidnap King Jarasandha.'

'What are you talking about? I have never written any such letter. Who gave you the authority to insult me in this manner? Let me go immediately or....'

'The truth is out Maharaj,' Chanur came into the room. 'To save the honour of Mathura, there is no other option but for Kumar Kansa to assume the mantle of monarchy. In any case, Maharaj, you are old enough to renounce the world, the burden of monarchy need not detain you any longer. Spend the rest of your life in prayer and all will be well.'

Ugrasen looked around. His bodyguards had been left behind at the entrance to the new palace. There was not a single weapon on his person. 'Kansa, you wretch...,' he shouted.

Chanur turned to the guards. 'What are you all waiting for? Take them away and guard them well. A single mistake and our new King Kansa will feed you to the dogs. Go!'

A fuming and resisting King Ugrasen was dragged out by the guards. Queen Padmavati shouted, 'Kansaaaa, my sonnnn...' but her voice was drowned by the guards. A group of maids surfaced and dragged her behind the hapless King.

The room resonated with Kansa and Chanur's loud laughter.

V

The Overture

Life is a matter of choices, and every choice you make makes you

...John C. Maxwell

All through his years in prison, Vasudeva was tormented by the thought whether he had failed Mathura at the crucial time by not standing up against Kansa's usurpation of the throne. And more importantly, whether it was on account of his love for Devaki that he did not stand up and fight. For years, Vasudeva fiercely debated in his mind, but could not reach a definite conclusion.

The palace coup remained a closely guarded secret for two days. Jarasandha left Mathura on the evening of the coup with his family members and a part of his army. Almost the whole of Mathura had turned up at the farewell. It was however a surprise that neither King Ugrasen nor his minister Bindudev were present to bid farewell and it was Kansa who did the honours. It was officially stated that King Ugrasen was indisposed and had met the departing guests at Kansa's new palace. The next day, an ambassador arrived from Avanti but instead of getting a royal audience, was ushered to meet Kansa in the new palace. Another curious fact was that the Magadhi army which had stayed back in Mathura, began to patrol the streets while the Mathura army remained stationed at the borders. But the people had not got over the whirlwind of excitement over the last one month and the absence of King Ugrasen was too minor a topic for discussion.

Finally, on the third day, Mathura woke up to the beat of drums. Heralds went about the town announcing that King Ugrasen had invited Hastinapur to attack Mathura and kidnap King Jarasandha. On account of his seditious activities, King Ugrasen had been deposed and Commander-in-chief Prince Kansa had 'temporarily' assumed powers of the King of Mathura. The heralds further announced that there was an imminent threat of invasion by Hastinapur and therefore a three-member council for national reconciliation had been constituted, comprising of Kumar Vasudeva, the leader of the Vrishnis, Kiritavarman, the leader of the Andhakas and Rudrasen, the leader of the Bhojas to advise on the affairs of the three clans. The people of Mathura were asked to maintain peace and forbidden from spreading rumours.

In the Mathura palace, Chanur paced about his room. Every few minutes a messenger would come bringing in news from the city. He had planned the coup in meticulous detail and it had been executed to perfection without spilling a single drop of blood. It was his idea to bring King Ugrasen to visit Kansa's new palace and confine him there. In fact Dimvaka had proposed that Ugrasen be confined when he went to attend a feast hosted by King Jarasandha. Chanur opposed the plan. The Yadavas were a very self-respecting lot. If Jarasandha was to arrest Ugrasen, it would be construed as foreign occupation and every Yadava would fight against it to the last drop of his blood. The city was presently peaceful but Chanur knew better. Mathura was on the crater of a volcano and there were rumblings deep down. To buy time he had inserted the term 'temporarily' in the announcement. Again, the inclusion of the three clan leaders was not to his liking, but he did it to quell dissent in the short term. Once Kansa got settled in his new position, then through money and power, the script would be rewritten. Dimvaka had opposed the plan. A coup was a coup, he argued. There was nothing unusual in one king giving way to another. Kansa was to be the King, the repository of all powers, period. There was no need for window dressing by constituting a council. The Magadhi army was there to quell all rebellion. Chanur differed with Dimvaka. Mathura was a republic while Magadh was a monarchy. There was a wide difference in circumstances and public perceptions in the two systems. The overlords of Mathura were fiercely protective of their powers and would not give up so easily. Even the Bhojas would not rally behind Kansa. A civil war would ensue if Kansa tried to foist himself as King at this juncture. It was necessary to play for time and in the meantime, subvert the system from within. After a lot of arguments, Jarasandha and his ministers ultimately fell in with Chanur's view.

Vasudeva was stunned when he heard the proclamation announcing Kansa as the new King and even more so on hearing about his appointment to the three-member advisory council. For some time he was undecided. Should he first meet Kansa to find out what was going on or should he call a meeting of the Vrishni overlords to decide his next course of action? His thought process and options were cut short by the announcement that Kansa had summoned him to the palace immediately and had sent his own gold chariot for the purpose.

Now when he looked back at the events that day, Vasudeva realised that his first folly was to go to the palace on Kansa's chariot rather than on his own. Actually it was still early morning and summoning his chariot and charioteer would have taken some time. Still, the move created an impression that Vasudeva had allied himself to Kansa's cause. The other folly was to rush to the palace in haste instead of first meeting the other overlords of the three communities and then deciding the course of action. Was his haste on account of his anxiety for Devaki in the aftermath of the coup? No, obviously not, Vasudeva told himself. On second thoughts, he wasn't so sure. In his heart of hearts, he knew that the first thought that struck him on hearing of the coup, was the question if Devaki was safe.

When he reached the palace, Vasudeva was ushered in, not to the King's court but to Kansa's private chambers. Kansa was getting dressed with the help of two maids.

'Vasudeva, my friend, come, come,' Kansa came up to the door and gave him a warm hug.

'Kansa, I heard...' Vasudeva remained unmoved.

'Yes, yes, we will discuss about all that. That is why I have troubled you early in the morning. Come in, my friend. In fact, in another few days, this is also going to be your second home....'

Kansa held Vasudeva's hand and took him to a seat. 'Be seated, my friend, while I finish getting dressed.'

The maids strung a seven-stringed pearl necklace around Kansa's neck, a gold amulet on his upper arm, diamond and gold bracelets on his wrists and a sword with gold scabbard on his waist. Just then an attendant entered and whispered something into Kansa's ear.

'Friend Vasudeva, something very urgent. I will just go and be back in a moment.'

'But, we will require more than a moment. You are forgetting it is our *Jamai Raja's* first visit after our wedding.' It was a smiling Asti followed by maids carrying huge marble plates and bowls full of choicest dishes and fruits.

Vasudeva stood up with folded hands. 'Sister-in-law, I beg to be excused. Today is not a day for formality. I have come only to meet Kansa for some very urgent discussions.'

'*Jamai Raja*, once you come to your in-laws' place, your urgency does not matter any longer. You no longer have any choice or option, but to comply with the instructions given.

And I have brought you our family deity's *prasad* which no one can refuse.' Asti smilingly turned to Kansa, '*Aryaputra,* you may take your time, *Jamai Raja* is under our custody.'

'Friend Vasudeva, even I cannot extricate you from this position,' Kansa departed, laughing.

The maids placed the plates and bowls on a table in front of Vasudeva. Vasudeva again folded his hands. 'Sister-in-law, please pardon me. It is just not possible.'

Just then a damsel entered the room. 'Sister-in-law, you called me here?'

'Yes, yes, just see, this gentleman is refusing to eat. Maybe you could persuade him.'

The damsel turned towards Vasudeva and both froze. It was Devaki! For a fleeting moment their eyes met and in a flash Devaki drew a veil across her face. Asti laughed aloud. 'Devaki, in less than two months you and *Jamai Raja* are going to be wed. It is time you get to know each other. And don't worry, you can trust me to keep your secrets.'

Vasudeva's ears again assumed a beetroot hue while Devaki stood fixedly gazing at the floor, the veil covering her face. Asti finally came to the rescue of the beleaguered couple. '*Jamai Raja,* you were brought up in this palace. Tell us some interesting incident that you might have experienced here.'

When Kansa returned, Vasudeva was animatedly telling the duo of an incident when he had lost his way in the palace. Asti and Devaki sat with their palms on their chins, intently hearing him.

'My dear Vasudeva, cherish these last few days when you speak and Devaki hears. Thereafter the conversation will be the other way around. See me and Asti….' Kansa laughed aloud.

'This is a totally false accusation,' Asti rolled her eyes. 'When has *Aryaputra* seen me lecture him?'

'Just see her rolling her eyes...the point stands proved,' Kansa laughed again.

Was the meeting with Asti and Devaki stage-managed to soften him up before the unpleasant discussions? Vasudeva now wondered. *Devaki had assured him that she knew nothing of the plans, but what about Asti?*

After some more banter, Kansa took Vasudeva to a separate room. Chanur was already there.

Vasudeva came straight to the point. 'Kumar Kansa, Mathura is a republic. We select our monarch. How can you depose the King and foist yourself upon us? Tell me the circumstances in which you imprisoned the King and how did you do it without the concurrence or even knowledge of any of us?'

'Friend Vasudeva...' Kansa started to speak.

'I am not here as your friend, Kumar Kansa. We may be friends or would be close relatives in our private lives but here I am in my capacity as one of the representatives of the Vrishni community which is a stake holder in the governance of Mathura. We have a right to know why the present monarch has been deposed, the conditions he is in and thereafter we have a right to play a part in deciding who the next monarch should be. We also want to meet King Ugrasen and understand the entire affair.' Vasudeva's tone was acidic.

'Please calm down, Kumar Vasudeva,' Chanur stood up with folded hands. 'Please allow us to explain ourselves and we shall do so event by event. We are sure once we have explained ourselves, you will agree that we have acted solely in the interest of Mathura and its people and will communicate the same not only to members of your community but to all people of Mathura. Please let us explain ourselves, here and now.'

Vasudeva calmed down. 'Alright, explain.'

'Kumar Vasudeva, as you are aware, there are at present two main power centres in Aryavarta—Hastinapur and

Magadh. Kumar Kansa was besotted with one of the Magadh princesses and wanted to marry her. It also made political sense since there was a constant looming threat of Hastinapur attacking us. Not everyone was happy with the match though and one such person was our then King Ugrasen. He felt that if we directly aligned with Magadh, Hastinapur would definitely attack us. The threat would actually come to pass.'

'But, King Ugrasen actually gave his consent to the marriage. He was also personally supervising the marriage arrangements. How can you make accusations against him? I have personally seen him going around the city, enquiring about the preparations,' Vasudeva protested.

'Friend Vasudeva, he gave permission only because I went on a fast. But while giving the permission, he had a much more sinister motive, which we came to know only now,' Kansa spoke up.

'He is right, Kumar Vasudeva,' Chanur joined in. 'If you would have noticed, in the beginning, King Ugrasen kept himself totally aloof from the goings on and it was only for the last two and half months that he suddenly developed interest in the arrangements. Before that, it was I who was going from Mathura to Magadh and overseeing the arrangements. It was during the last two and half to three months that Minister Bindudev came into the picture and thereafter King Ugrasen also joined in. Thereafter, they took over all the arrangements on the pretext that the prestige of Mathura was at stake. Personally it was good for me also since it relieved me of a lot of burden. Moreover, when the King and his Minister want to do something directly, things happen much quicker than it would if only I were involved.'

'You keep quiet, Chanur,' Kansa quipped. 'Just think of it, Vasudeva! It was Chanur who convinced my father to arrange the match, it was he who went all the way to Girivraja and persuaded King Jarasandha to agree to the match, it was he who started all the preparations and yet he was unceremoniously ousted from all the arrangements. In fact this ought to have raised a suspicion at that point itself but obviously who could suspect a father to put his son's life and happiness in jeopardy?'

'Kumar Vasudeva, the plan that King Ugrasen conceived was to invite Hastinapur to suddenly attack Mathura during the festivities and capture King Jarasandha. Since Mathura would be busy in wedding festivities and unprepared for any offensive, it would be a smooth affair and would also not raise any suspicion of Ugrasen's involvement. For this help, King Ugrasen would have been richly rewarded and would have been recognised as the foremost ally of Hastinapur.'

'How did you know of all this?' Vasudeva demanded.

'I will just come to it,' Chanur said. 'A month back when Kumar Kansa was appointed as the Commander-in-chief of the army, I consolidated the intelligence gathering wing. From our spies, I got information that Hastinapur was preparing its armies for assault. Not all soldiers, but one elite division. That got me thinking. At the outset, I advised Kumar Kansa to send our armies to guard the frontiers to protect against any surprise attack during the celebrations. Once that was done, it put paid to the hopes of Hastinapur to mount a surprise attack. It then had to get the entire army in a status of readiness and that delayed its attack.'

'Chanur, tell Vasudeva about the letter,' Kansa interjected.

'Yes, I was coming to that. As I told you, I had developed our intelligence network. On the morning of the wedding, my men caught hold of a person carrying a letter embossed with the royal seal which said that Hastinapur should not delay the attack any longer and that King Jarasandha would remain in Mathura for four more days only. On persistent interrogation, the man confessed that the letter had been written in the presence of King Ugrasen and Bindudev, and the letter was to be given to a person from Hastinapur for onward transmission to Bhishma.'

'Show him the letter, Chanur,' Kansa ordered.

Chanur brought out a palm leaf from a case and handed over to Vasudeva. Vasudeva checked the contents and carefully examined the royal seal imprinted on it before handing it back to Chanur.

'At that point of time there still remained an imminent danger of invasion from Hastinapur,' Chanur continued. 'We had nabbed one messenger but it was possible some other messenger had also been sent and had already delivered the message. Therefore, we had to request the Magadh forces also to be in a state of war preparedness. And for that we were compelled to disclose the reason to King Jarasandha.'

'Can you imagine my embarrassment, Vasudeva?' Kansa was livid. 'That was the day of my wedding and I had to tell my would be father-in-law that my father was plotting against him! And through all this, I had to keep a smiling demeanour so that nobody should have an inkling to what was going on in my mind. My God, it was the most harrowing time of my life! From that day I have not been able to sleep a wink. Till today I am not able to face my wives....' Kansa's voice choked off.

Chanur went up to him and patted his shoulder. 'Calm yourself, Kumar. We all understand your position. This is not the time to vent your personal sorrows.'

'No, let me speak,' Kansa's voice was hysterical. 'I will not remain quiet. Why should I and for whom? Let the world know what game has been played with me and that too by my own father! Can you believe, Vasudeva, my own father using me as a pawn for his political ends? He accepted my marriage with the motive that should

King Jarasandha come here, he would be betrayed to Hastinapur… All for a few pieces of gold, all for a small slice of land… Vasudeva, think, my father… He never scolded me even when I went astray… He always let me live my own life. He did not interfere when I made tribal friends. When others complained that I went on plundering missions, he dismissed it as exuberance of youth… He condoned my follies, allowed me to choose my own path and today I realise how wrong I was in my ways… That father…using me as a bait for his political ends, knowing fully well that my honour would be ruined for all times to come… I just cannot believe, Vasudeva, I just cannot believe… How could he have done this to me?' Kansa broke into wild sobs.

Vasudeva could contain himself no further. He went up to Kansa and embraced him. 'Brother Kansa, don't cry. I wish you had taken me into confidence earlier…don't cry…no, just don't…control yourself.'

Vasudeva's attempt to assuage Kansa had exactly the opposite effect than that intended. Kansa's entire body shivered with spasms of grief. 'Who wants the crown, who wants the throne…? Come on, take it… Just give me back that father who would stand by me regardless of what I did. And, see what a son I am… A son who imprisons his own father! Vasudeva, I stand maligned in history for all times to come. I will be recorded as the first son who imprisoned his father… What a wretch I am, Vasudeva, what a wretch I am….'

'No Kansa, no,' Vasudeva protested. 'If it was as you say, history will record you as the commander who performed his duty to the nation, regardless of familial ties…one who did not even spare his father for the sake of duty….'

'Vasudeva, my heart is broken. If this is politics, where a father trades his son for his self interest, then I have no need for this. I do not want the crown of thorns. You take it, Vasudeva and be happy. I have decided to renounce everything and become a mendicant. Take this....' Kansa tore off his pearl necklace and threw it on the floor. The pearls scattered on the floor. 'And this....' He threw off a gold and diamond bracelet.

'Calm down, Kansa, calm down. Tell me what happened thereafter.'

Chanur spoke up. 'Allow me to narrate the subsequent events. King Jarasandha was so livid that he wanted to kill King Ugrasen and annex Mathura then and there. Finally, I managed to convey to him Kumar Kansa's sincerity and our good intentions. I told him that the deeds of one single person should not lead to Mathura's downfall or subservience. After a lot of persuasion, he saw the point and agreed that the marriage ceremony and the attendant feasts should continue as earlier, provided that after he left for Magadh, King Ugrasen would be dealt with. So, after King Jarasandha left, both King Ugrasen and Bindudev were taken into custody. In fact Bindudev has admitted that he had written and sent the letter at King Ugrasen's behest. It was shocking to say the least.'

'But the question still remains that even if King Ugrasen's imprisonment was justified, how could Kansa declare himself the king? Don't you all know how we choose the king in Mathura?' Vasudeva demanded.

'Friend Vasudeva,' Kansa quipped, 'have I announced my coronation? Can there be a king without coronation? What was said in the declaration was only that I had temporarily assumed the powers of the King of Mathura. This I was entitled to do in the interim, since I was the Commander-in-chief of Magadh and the holder of the highest post in the absence of the King and the Minister. Merely because my staff refers to me as the King, in the absence of an alternative, does not make me the King of Mathura. In fact, let me tell you something that Chanur did not. My father-in-law wanted me to declare myself as the King and also promised support of Magadh in the endeavour. But I refused the offer, telling him that I hold you all in the highest esteem and would not dream of doing anything contrary to the will of the people of Mathura.'

'Then you assure that there will be a selection of king in the traditional manner?' Vasudeva wanted a specific clarification.

'Certainly, my friend but you will have to wait for sometime. The next few days entire Mathura will be busy with your and Devaki's wedding festivities and a month after the wedding, when everything will cool down, we will get to the business of calling a meeting of the *Parishad* to determine the trial of King Ugrasen and selecting a new King for Mathura. That new King may be I, you or any other person.'

Vasudeva was relieved. 'Well, Kansa, you have removed a big burden from my shoulders. I have no ambition to be the King of Mathura. And, if you act honourably as you appear to have done, you can count on my support. But, first tell me, where have you kept King Ugrasen?'

'Vasudeva, I am a son. Whatever my father might have done, I for one could not keep him in imprisonment like an ordinary criminal. He is comfortably lodged in the western wing of my new palace with all facilities and conveniences fit for a King. My mother is there to take care of him. There is a temple where he can pass his days praying. The only restriction is that he is not allowed to meet any outsider. One does not know how he may want to influence any person he gets to see.'

'Can I or representatives of the three communities meet him?' Vasudeva enquired.

'My friend Vasudeva, I have no reservation whatsoever regarding you, but I am apprehensive of the others. I already have information that some of the overlords were also involved in the conspiracy. Now if you go to meet *Pita Maharaj*, others may also demand the same and that may lead to the conspirators getting access to him. I think the best course of action would be to wait for the meeting of the *Parishad* and then let it decide what to do. Let us not do anything at this juncture which may precipitate matters.'

'I take your word, Kansa. Let the *Parishad* decide.'

Vasudeva left. Unknown to him and behind his back, Kansa and Chanur winked at each other.

'A great job, Raja,' Chanur complimented Kansa.

'Thank you, Chanur, it was your plan from beginning to end. But tell me, the question of selection of new king still remains pending.'

'Don't worry, Raja, Vasudeva has already supported you in principle. We just need to ensure that he sticks to his stand. I have also played my part amongst the smaller overlords. My Guru taught me the principle of *bhed niti* or divide and rule. Now you will see what happens.'

Vasudeva was not prepared for the reaction of the other Vrishni overlords towards him. The morning after meeting Kansa, he had called a meeting of the Vrishni overlords at his residence to discuss the next course of action. He gave a full account of his meeting with Kansa and asked them their views. There was absolute silence.

'What happened? Kindly come up with your views.' There was a hint of impatience in Vasudeva's voice.

'Kumar Vasudeva, we do not think it would be possible to have a meaningful discussion with you,' Rantidev, one of the lesser overlords remarked.

'What do you mean?' Vasudeva demanded.

'Come on Kumar, you are shortly going to be a close relative of Kansa. Is it not obvious that your priorities have changed?'

'Listen Rantidev, I represent the Vrishnis. Period. Whether I am going to be a close relative of Kansa in my private life, has no relation whatsoever with my duty towards the Vrishni community whom I represent.' Vasudeva retorted angrily.

'Kumar, it is very easy to say lofty words, but very difficult to implement it in real life. Yesterday morning, did you not go to the palace in Kansa's own chariot?'

'So? The situation was urgent and my chariot and charioteer were not available at that juncture. Merely my using Kansa's chariot does not mean that I am aligned to his cause.'

'Okay, even if we grant that, how could you condone Kansa's usurpation of monarchical powers?' Ballava, another overlord demanded.

'I have not. Kansa has assured that the monarch of Mathura would be selected as per tradition. In fact there has been no coronation which clearly shows that he is not the King.'

'Kumar Vasudeva, as per Mathura's tradition, the new monarch is selected within fifteen days of the death of the old monarch. Here there is no death, but there has been a coup. Kansa ought to have called a meeting of the *Parishad* and left the selection of the new king to it. He has not done so. Instead, he is delaying the selection on one pretext or another.'

'But the reason he has given is also valid. It is due to the marriage celebrations.' Vasudeva's voice betrayed anguish.

'So, is not your private marriage celebration coming in the way of the public discharge of duty?' Rantidev was again vocal.

'And, can you deny that you went to meet Kansa first before convening our meeting and deciding what steps to take? Possibly you went to him to take instructions on what to tell us in this meeting.'

Akrur and some other minor overlords vocally protested but they were shouted down by Ballava and Rantidev.

'How could Kumar Vasudeva give time to Kansa?'

'Does he not know Kansa's character? Kansa is a virtual dacoit. How could Vasudeva trust him?'

'If he had such trust on Kansa, then why could he not meet King Ugrasen?'

'He has betrayed the Vrishnis. He is not fit to represent us.'

Vasudeva was now exasperated. 'Alright, you all decide what you want to do. I will stand by you.'

'That is exactly what we want to tell you,' Ballava retorted. 'We do not want you with us.'

'Yes, Kumar Vasudeva, we do not trust you. Who knows, you may be leaking our plans to Kansa. It is better that you stay away and celebrate your marriage.' Ballava was always foul mouthed, but he exceeded his own standards this time.

It was the worst humiliation that Vasudeva had faced in his entire life. The scion of a King, he was the epitome of noble and honest behaviour. To be addressed to in this manner was next to death. 'Very well, I shall not come in your way. Do what you wish.'

It was a crestfallen Vasudeva who went to bed that night, but he was not alone. Kiritavarman, the leader of the Andhakas and Rudrasen, the leader of the Bhojas fared no better from the other overlords of their communities. Their loyalties were called in question, they were denigrated as Kansa's pimps and were virtually ousted from all community consultations.

'We have succeeded in the first stage. The top overlords of the three communities have been ousted from their communities. They now have no choice but to back you,' a beaming Chanur informed Kansa.

'What is the second stage?'

'In the second stage the remaining overlords will quarrel with each other for predominance. We will reward some of them with favours and they in turn will be eyesores for the remaining. Then we go on to the third stage.'

'What is the third stage?' Kansa was curious.

'In the third stage, all the overlords compete to get favours from you and come over to your side.'

'Great strategy, Chanur,' Kansa appreciated.

'Again it's my Guru, Raja. The policy of "*saam-daam-danda-bhed*". You have to adopt a different strategy for different types of people. Some people can be won over by persuasion, good behaviour, detailed explanation and striking an emotional chord. This is what we tried with Vasudeva. This is the policy of "*saam*". Some people, rather most, are prone to greed. Give them money, power, position, women—whatever it takes and they will follow you and proclaim you as the greatest person on earth. This is the policy of "*daam*" and this policy we will follow with some of the overlords. The only thing to keep in mind is that the greed of these persons may take them to those who offer greater inducements and hence the need to exercise caution and keep a constant watch on the behaviour and movements of these persons. The third policy is that of "*danda*" or punishment. This is for people who would not be moved by greed but can be made to act under threat of punishment or harm. This will also work for the general populace. Fear of the King's wrath will force them to follow you although they may not agree with the orders. The last is the most powerful policy—"*bhed*". This is the policy of dividing your enemies and exploiting their weaknesses. Play one group against the other—the Andhakas against the Vrishnis, Vrishnis against the Bhojas and so on. Even against the Vrishnis, set one overlord against the other. We have done it by setting persons like Ballava and Rantidev against Vasudeva. Similarly, Kiritavarman and Rudrasen have been neutralised by setting the other overlords of their community against them.'

'You and your Guru! Really Chanur… But take one instruction from me, cultivate Vasudeva. He will be the most prized asset in my camp. He is popular amongst people and will lend authenticity to my regime. I have not been to any guru, but this much I know of politics that if you have a good mask, you can do many things behind it. Moreover, you forget, Vasudeva's sister is married in Hastinapur and his association will insulate us from any invasion by Hastinapur.'

'That is true, Raja, but keeping him in will be quite difficult.'

'Try, Chanur, try. Celebrate his wedding with Devaki in a grand style. Devaki is my favourite sister and I am her favourite brother. I am sure once he gets married to Devaki, he will come over to my camp.'

Kansa rose and proceeded to go but stopped at the doorway.

'Chanur, in any case, I want Vasudeva in my camp rather than in the opposite camp.'

VI

The Prophesy and the Arrest

Those in possession of absolute power cannot only prophesy and make their prophecies come true, but they can also lie and make their lies come true

...Eric Hoffer

'Vasudeva...Vasudeva...Vasudeva....' Chanur muttered to himself like a chant.

For the last seven days, each day Kansa had called for Vasudeva and sought his advice regarding affairs of the State. 'I have reformed myself,' Kansa had told Vasudeva. 'I promise you, Vasudeva, never again shall I go on any marauding expedition. I have got over what my *Pita Maharaj* used to describe as "youthful exuberance". I am now married and want to conduct myself responsibly as befits the Commander-in-chief of Mathura and the son-in-law of King Jarasandha. Vasudeva, you are known for your noble mind, kindness, selflessness and honesty. Give me sage advice on how to run Mathura for the betterment of people, help me to transform Mathura. And not only I, but the entire populace of Mathura would be indebted to you.'

Vasudeva will be the most prized asset in my camp. The words continued to echo in Chanur's ears.

Chanur sat up. He had decided. Vasudeva's ascent would inevitably lead to his own downfall. And his downfall would not merely be his own personal downfall, it would also spell the end of the hope of tribal resurgence which he was secretly nurturing in his bosom. Time was silently ticking away. Already Kansa was consulting

Vasudeva for all the important matters concerning the State. Chanur could foresee the time when he would no longer be indispensable to Kansa. His Guru used to say that a minister must always make himself indispensable to the King. For that purpose, if necessary, the minister may create conditions that the King is compelled to rely upon him. It is good for the King when he does not have any worry or fear, but that is not a good situation for the minister. The ideal minister needs to keep the King under a tight leash. The King should always be dependent on him. 'Therefore Chanur,' his Guru used to advise, 'when you are a minister, you should explore the King's mind, find out his fears and play on them so that he thinks he would be doomed without you.' Till now, Kansa had not consolidated his authority and was dependent on Chanur. Advent of Vasudeva on the scene would remove Kansa's fear of challenge to his authority. And if Kansa and Vasudeva teamed up, it would spell the end of Chanur.

No, it had to be either him or Vasudeva. There could not be two swords in one scabbard. It was he who was the architect of Kansa's rise to power. It was he who got Kansa married to Jarasandha's daughters and it was he again who plotted King Ugrasen's overthrow. He had invested a lot of time and effort and could not allow any other person to reap the fruits.

Vasudeva was kind hearted, brave, noble and dignified, but unambitious. He was fit to be a king, but was modest about his abilities. In fact, if his recent conversations with Kansa were to be believed, he was not averse to ceding his space to Kansa. It was surprising, considering Kansa's past and his act in imprisoning his own father. In fact, Vasudeva had interpreted the events in his own way and even praised Kansa for not letting familial ties cloud his duties towards his country. If only Vasudeva had been a bit more assertive, he would not have allied with Kansa. This submissive attitude suited Kansa perfectly and that made the task of creating a rift all the more difficult.

But was it that Vasudeva was acting in the manner only on account of his infatuation for Devaki and in order not to upset the marriage? It is possible that after the marriage, Vasudeva may change his stance and stake his claim to the throne… On the downside, after the marriage Vasudeva and Kansa's bond may grow stronger… Vasudeva was deeply in love with Devaki and she was Kansa's favourite cousin. But whatever it was, Devaki was the one link between Vasudeva and Kansa and if that link could somehow be snapped, the two would drift apart… But how? How to snap that link?

Was Kansa getting any secret advice from Dimvaka? Would Kansa go ahead and woo Vasudeva as he did, on his own, without any input from any seasoned adviser? Would Kansa disregard Chanur's advice in the absence of assistance or prodding from any other quarter?

Chanur thought and thought but made no headway. It was night when he reached home. His wife was telling a fairy tale to their infant son to lull him to sleep. There was once a very cruel king who ruled over a faraway kingdom. He had several queens but no son. Finally, a son was born to one of his queens. The king was ecstatic. He called the royal astrologer and asked him to predict the child's future. The astrologer made long calculations and finally informed the king that the child would one day cause his death. The king immediately called his security guard and told him to go to the forest, kill the child and bury it there. The guard took the baby to the forest but could not kill the cherubic baby. He kept it near the hut of a forest dweller and came back. On his way back he killed a rabbit, gorged out its heart and took it back to the king as proof that he had killed the baby. The baby was brought up by the forest dweller and finally killed the king.

Chanur stood transfixed, listening to the story. Could it be true? Could a king ask his only son to be put to death on the words of an astrologer that the son would one day cause his death? Did an astrologer have such power over the minds of men? Yes, he recalled, Kansa was a big believer in astrology. But, but, was it possible to use astrology to drive a wedge between Kansa on one hand and Devaki and Vasudeva on the other? Could astrology be used to put Kansa under a deep fear of personal harm which would somehow emanate from Devaki or Vasudeva?

He was brought back by his wife's words. 'My lord, you are not eating. What happened?'

Chanur looked at the food which his wife had served before him on a banana plantain. He folded his hands at the food and got up. He needed to think.

That night Chanur did not sleep a wink. Before the first light of dawn, he went to the house of Dhenuka, his confidante.

Mathura was gearing up for the next round of festivities. Kansa had planned massive celebrations for Devaki's wedding. The city was already decked up for Kansa's wedding. Now new festoons and new welcome gates were being set up. The palace was being refurbished, the wedding venue was being decorated. Chanur was supervising the arrangements himself. Kansa and Chanur were personally going to the various oligarchs to invite them for the wedding with costly gifts. The King going personally to the houses of oligarchs was something unthinkable. But this was Chanur's idea, to build up relation with the oligarchs. The gesture succeeded. The oligarchs, suspending their political rivalry, assured of full participation in the wedding.

Preparations were on in full swing at Vasudeva's house also. A new wing had been constructed for Devaki. Weavers came in with the finest fabrics, goldsmiths came in with new designs in gold ornaments, *halwais* produced their new recipes in food and sweets. Relatives were coming in from all over Aryavarta. Except Pritha who was away in the forests with her husband Pandu and therefore unable to come.

The buzz in the city however, was of a sadhu who had just come down from the Himalayas after decades of *tapasya* and established himself below an aging banyan tree on the main road. A tall burly man, dressed only in a tiger skin, with his face and body smeared with ashes, his long hair matted and tied up in a bun over his head, his beard reaching to his chest, a trident in his hand—the sadhu's very appearance evoked respect and awe. It was said that he had divine powers. Often on looking at a person, he would get divine vision of his past and future. Only in respect of those that he got divine vision, did he predict, the rest were turned away. But when he got the vision, he knew even the smallest of things about a person and what he said was cent per cent accurate. In no time, almost the whole populace of Mathura had descended upon that banyan tree, each hoping to evoke a vision. From the oligarchs to commoners, stern-looking matrons to dimpled lasses, all converged at the tree with the common human urge to know the future. They brought with them money, fruits and costly gifts, but the sadhu would have none of those. One fruit in the day and one at night sufficed for him, the rest were either directed to be distributed amongst the poor, or declined.

Unknown to the people of Mathura, the sadhu had been brought in by Chanur and all the persons in respect of whom he had vision, were Chanur's hirelings or persons whose information had been procured.

Kansa may not have matched Jarasandha, yet the grandeur of the marriage organised by him, would have put many larger kingdoms to shame. A thousand Brahmin pundits conducted a massive yagna spanning a fortnight to propitiate the deities and the *navagrahas* for the well-being of the couple. Singers, dancing troupes and acrobats from all over Aryavarta were brought in. Chariot races, bull fights, wrestling, archery and fencing contests were organised throughout the kingdom and the winners were honoured by Kansa himself. Invitations with betel nuts and a gold coin had been sent to every single house in Mathura, with specific request that they participate in the feasts for five days during the wedding. According to Chanur, it was necessary to drum up popular support for Kansa in the aftermath of the coup, to ward off any challenge by the oligarchs. And, as intended, the people of Mathura were enthused about the generous new King and forgot all about King Ugrasen, who was a good King but strict about fiscal discipline.

The celebrations reached a crescendo during the five days of the wedding. Devaki was taken to all the temples in the city and wherever she went, silver coins were showered on the masses on both sides of the road. Grand processions were taken out on the road with caparisoned elephants, horses and decorated chariots. Every night the palace was lit up with a million earthen lamps and blazing torches. For the commoners, huge feasts were organised in the parks with the choicest dishes and sweets.

On the day of wedding, from early dawn, the palace was immersed in the soft tunes of the veena played by the palace musicians. Both Devaki and Vasudeva kept a fast that would last till the wedding rituals were complete. The groom arrived at the wedding *mandap* in a grand procession on horseback with a huge entourage, a thousand conches heralding his arrival. Almost the entire Vrishni fraternity was part of the groom's procession, while the Bhojas considered themselves the bride's party. It was a fascinating sight how the union of two individuals became the personal cause of two different communities, who formed two-thirds of the entire populace of the kingdom. The remaining third were however not left out. They came in as guests from whichever side they chose and played the part.

The groom and his entourage were welcomed with curd and honey, garlands and perfumes. Kansa's wife Asti performed the *aarti* of Vasudeva and thereafter the groom was escorted to the altar. Devaki's mother had passed away during childbirth while her father Devaka had become a mendicant soon after and left for the forests. Kansa had always been the protector and guardian of his virtually orphaned cousin since her childhood and this day, it was he who would give away the bride. He welcomed Vasudeva at the altar with gifts and bade him sit. At the other end, Devaki was brought in a bejewelled golden chariot shaped like a dancing peacock. Kansa smiled as the audience gasped at the magnificence of the chariot. It may not have the mechanical contraption of the swan chariot conceived by Dimvaka, but was a sight to behold in its own right. Embedded with blue and green emeralds and lapis lazuli, with rubies for the eyes, handcrafted to perfection, it dazzled the eyes of all and sundry.

Devaki descended from the peacock chariot with a garland in hand, a thin veil covering her face and advanced towards Vasudeva. Vasudeva stood with a garland in his hand. The time which he had waited for, had finally arrived. And as the onlookers cheered and made salacious comments, Devaki, with a shy smile on her lips, garlanded Vasudeva. Vasudeva took a while to adjust the garland and let the moment sink in and then he too put his garland around Devaki's slim, swan-like neck. The bride and the groom were then ushered in front of the sacred fire, where amidst chanting of vedic mantras, Kansa performed *kanya daan,* the act of giving the bride in marriage. The altar resounded with the chanting of sacred mantras by the priests infusing an air of purity and spirituality.

This was followed by *pani grahan,* the holding of hands. The right hand of Devaki was placed on the left hand of Vasudeva, marking his acceptance of her as the lawfully wedded wife. Devaki shuddered at the first touch of her beloved. She closed her eyes as Vasudeva's hand gripped hers, savouring the moment and praying it last till eternity. The gentle nudge from Kansa brought her back to the ceremony.

Amidst chanting of mantras, together they made an offering of puffed rice to Agni, the Fire God followed by seven rounds or *pradakshina* of the sacred fire.

Finally, Vasudeva applied a streak of vermilion at the parting of Devaki's hair and tied a *mangalsutra* around her neck and the priest proclaimed them husband and wife. Then all the relatives gathered around them for *Annaprashan,* where the bride and the groom were required to feed each other. Feeding her husband in front of so many people...Devaki almost died of shame. Friends joked whether she would remain so even at night. Amidst laughter and after much cajoling from her relatives, she finally picked up a sweet and held it midair, still a cubit away from Vasudeva's mouth. Vasudeva smiled but did not bring his mouth any closer. A further round of laughter finally broke Devaki's patience. Still steadfastly looking to the ground, she shoved the sweet towards Vasudeva's mouth. It did not find his mouth though and spread all over his face. The roof came down with the sound of laughter of those assembled.

Chanur in the meantime was busy overseeing the arrangements for the departure. It would be a huge procession, with drummers leading the way followed by elephants and bullock carts laden with gifts, chariots, richly uniformed guards, servants and maids. The arrangements made, he went to Kansa.

'Raja, remember, you have promised to drive the chariot carrying Vasudeva and Devaki?' he reminded Kansa. Chanur had it all planned. He had convinced Kansa that if he took the initiative and drove the newly married couple to Vasudeva's mansion, it would irretrievably bring Vasudeva into Kansa's camp and that would help him keep the crown.

'But would it not look odd?' Kansa was not so sure. 'What would people say? It is always the groom who takes the bride away. I have never heard of the bride's side escorting her to the groom's place.'

'No, Raja, it will not look odd. Obviously Devaki will be wailing at the time of departure. As she is your favourite cousin, you can always be distressed by her wails and in order to console her, offer to drive her down. It will also create a good impression on the general public who will for long after speak about your empathy and humility.'

Kansa looked convinced. Chanur pressed it further. 'Don't worry, Raja, I shall myself precede your chariot and oversee everything.'

As the hour of departure approached, Devaki turned to Kansa. 'My brother…' she sobbed uncontrollably, 'when will I be able to see you next? I do not want to leave you, brother. Don't drive me away from you….'

Kansa's eyes too moistened. 'O my sweet little sister….' He remembered Chanur's advice. 'Don't worry, I shall myself drive your chariot and escort you to your matrimonial home. Come, my sister… Come with me.'

He held Devaki's hand in one hand and took Vasudeva's in the other and escorted them to the chariot. Then as onlookers gasped, he took the driver's seat and took over the reins.

Chanur readied his chariot at the head of the procession and gave the signal to start. The procession snaked through the main streets of Mathura, showered with flower petals and puffed rice and applauded by hundreds of bystanders. Suddenly, Chanur gave the signal to stop.

'What happened, Chanur?' Kansa was now getting impatient with the slow pace of the procession. Though it was the month of *Aghrayan*, it was still hot. He was already ruing having promised to drive Devaki to her matrimonial home.

'Raja, there is a much respected sadhu sitting below the banyan tree yonder, who has come to Mathura from the Himalayas after years of penance. People say and I have actually confirmed that he has divine vision. He is such a saintly man that he survives on just two fruits a day and the food and gifts showered on him by the devotees are all distributed amongst the poor. The entire city, from oligarchs to the poor have all visited him. Devaki*ji* and Vasudeva*ji* have just been married. We should take them to pay respect to the sadhu.'

Kansa was not so eager. The procession had already been delayed and visiting the sadhu would mean further delay. Could the meeting not be postponed to the following day or any time thereafter? But he was restrained by Devaki's soft voice.

'*Bhai raja*, I want to pay my respects to sadhu maharaj.'

Kansa sighed and descended from the chariot. 'Come with me, sister. Come Vasudeva. Chanur, lead the way.'

They walked across to the banyan tree, at the base of which was the sadhu, sitting in the lotus position on a raised pedestal. His eyes were closed in deep meditation, his flowing beard gently swaying to the light breeze. His face and body were smeared with ash. On his forehead was a smear of sandal paste on which a red *tilak* had been applied. He wore a tiger skin and a *rudraksha* garland and his hand rested on a trident. He looked the very manifestation of Lord Shiva.

Chanur went up to the holy man. 'Sadhu Maharaj, Maharaja Kansa along with his newlywed sister Devaki*ji* and brother-in-law Vasudeva*ji* have come to seek your blessings. Please be kind enough to bless them.'

The sadhu opened his eyes. Devaki and Vasudeva kneeled down before him with folded hands. Kansa stood behind them with folded hands.

The sadhu raised his right hand in blessing and suddenly froze. A murmur went through the devotees—he is having vision, he is having vision....

Moments passed while the sadhu remained entranced. Eyes half closed, his entire body swayed. Suddenly with a shudder he came back to his senses. 'Kansa...' his voice boomed. He raised his right hand and pointed the index finger towards Devaki. 'The eighth progeny of your beloved sister will kill you with his own hands. You are the incarnation of the evil demon Kalnemi, uncle of King Ravana of Lanka. Devaki's eighth progeny will be the incarnation of Vishnu. He will kill you and rid the kingdom of evil. This is the will of the gods...it is predestined Kansa...try as you will, you will not be able to change it....' The area resounded with the sadhu's harsh laughter.

For a moment there was a stunned silence beneath the banyan tree. Vasudeva, Devaki, Kansa, Chanur and all the devotees forgot to draw their breath. Even the leaves of the banyan tree forgot to rustle in the wind. The cawing of a crow brought Chanur back to his senses.

'You filthy wretch, you devious fraudster, how dare you call our Maharaja a demon and predict his death?' In an instant he drew out his sword and flashed it across the sadhu's neck. Blood spattered across Vasudeva and Devaki's face as the dismembered head rolled across and stopped at Kansa's feet. Devaki shrieked and almost swooned. Vasudeva caught her from falling.

Chaos reigned as the devotees shouted and ran helter skelter.

Chanur looked at Kansa, whose face had turned ashen. Suddenly he grabbed Devaki by her hair and dragged her up.

'Your child will kill me? It is pre-destined? Now see how I change destiny,' Kansa flashed out his sword.

The glint of steel caught Devaki's eye as she fainted. In an instant, Vasudeva had grabbed Devaki's falling body while Chanur held Kansa's wrist.

'Leave me, Chanur, let go of me, I will not spare this traitor of a woman,' Kansa shouted, trying to wriggle free of Chanur's grasp.

'No…' shouted Vasudeva, still holding on to Devaki's body, looking around with helpless eyes for something with which to restrain Kansa. He had left his sword in the chariot as a mark of respect for the sadhu. Finding no alternative, he covered Devaki's body with his own, his right hand signalling Kansa to stop.

'No Raja, don't...you can't kill your sister,' Chanur shouted, still holding on to Kansa's wrist.

Kansa resembled a man possessed. With a jerk he pushed Chanur aside, jumped and kicked Vasudeva across and seized Devaki. The blood that had drained out of his face had now collected in his eyes. 'I will not let her give birth to the eighth progeny,' he boomed, his sword ready to cut down Devaki.

Vasudeva did not have time to get up to save Devaki. He just dived and grabbed Kansa's feet. 'Don't, Kansa, don't…I promise to deliver you our eighth child. Don't kill Devaki, let her go.'

In an instant Chanur was back on his feet and had again grabbed Kansa's arm. He was joined by Dhenuka who had come running in from the procession.

'Keep them in prison, Raja, kill the child but don't kill your sister. How can you kill your beloved sister?' Chanur implored.

'She is not my sister anymore. She is going to harbour my killer. She must go. Leave me Chanur, let go of my arm,' Kansa was not willing to relent.

'Raja, if you kill her, that would be your end also. People will revolt. Do as I say. Put them both in prison. Then you can kill the child as soon as he is born.' Chanur continued to hold on to Kansa's arm.

Kansa appeared in two minds. Chanur seized on the moment's indecision. He snatched away the sword from Kansa's arm and signalled to the guards who had by now arrived on the scene. 'Take Devaki*ji* and Vasudeva*ji* into custody immediately and put them in prison. Guard them well or you will be skinned alive. Maharaja will decide their fate in due time.'

Six guards instantly fell on Vasudeva, firmly tying his hands, feet and mouth, while another guard picked up Devaki's senseless body. Noiselessly they exited from a route behind the banyan tree, avoiding the procession and the crowd.

Chanur now proceeded to take control of the situation. 'Dhenuka, I am taking Raja to the palace through this other route. He is mentally very upset and needs my support. Send fifty guards this way. Pralamba and Keshi, you call the remaining guards and disperse the crowd. Be careful, the Vrishnis may turn violent. Agha, you take charge of the gifts. Bring them back to the palace. Bhoumya, you rush to the prison and ensure that it is properly secured. The Vrishnis can attack the prison to free Devaki and Vasudeva. I am leaving with Raja. Ensure that what I have instructed is carried out to the letter. Now just hurry off.'

A chariot was waiting on the other road. Chanur helped Kansa board it and the two left for the palace.

As the chariot winded its way, Chanur barely managed to repress a smile. The situation had unfolded just as he had planned. Vasudeva, his rival, was now securely behind bars while Kansa from this day would be in mortal fear of Devaki's eighth born. And with Vrishnis now baying for his blood, Kansa would be totally dependent on him for survival.

And yet, it could all have gone wrong in an instant. If Kansa had managed to kill Devaki, that would have removed his fear of death. Furthermore, if Devaki was killed, two situations could have arisen. If Vasudeva remained free, he would certainly depose and kill Kansa, which would have reduced Chanur to a non-entity or even led to his death. On the other hand, if Vasudeva were also killed, Kansa would have no further fear to his authority or life and his dependence on Chanur would have gone.

Chanur felt a tinge of remorse for the sadhu. The man was a genuine actor. In fact, Chanur had promised him great rewards once the mission was accomplished, but then his Guru had taught him not to keep witnesses. Chanur's brow wrinkled. He must keep Dhenuka under close watch in the times to come....

The chariot reached the palace. As he escorted Kansa inside, Chanur barked out his orders to the commander:

'Send the Magadhi army on the streets.'

VII

Divide and Rule

Divide and rule, the politician cries
Unite and lead, is watchword of the wise

...Goethe

Ati-taranga or *tsunami*.

Chanur had heard that term from Guru Rudracharya. Sometimes, immediately after an earthquake, the sea would seem to retreat unusually, only to come back with a vengeance with gigantic waves that would destroy anything and everything in their wake.

'This is also how common people react when an earth-shattering event occurs,' Rudracharya had warned.

Chanur remembered his Guru's warning as news came in from the site of the procession.

At first, the crowd that had assembled on both sides of the road and were cheering the procession, were not aware of the developments. Then as the sadhu's devotees ran helter skelter, the crowd sensed something was wrong. In an instant, the news spread through the grapevine of the sadhu's forecast and his death. The people stared at one another in disbelief.

'Sadhu baba killed by Kansa's man?'

'How could someone kill a sadhu?'

'He actually forecast that Devaki's eighth child will kill Kansa?'

'He said Kansa was the incarnation of a demon?'

Like an earthquake that starts at an epicentre and spreads all around within the flash of an eye, the news had spread all over Mathura in moments.

But what happened of Devaki and Vasudeva?

Nobody knew.

Only one thing was certain—they had not been seen thereafter. Some claimed to have seen Kansa strike down Devaki and Vasudeva with his scimitar and gave gory details of the massacre. They were supported by some others who claimed to have seen two bodies carried away by guards along the forest road. Some others said the duo had not been killed but imprisoned. Some said it was only Devaki who had been killed while Vasudeva had been imprisoned. Others disagreed. If someone was to be killed, it must be Vasudeva. How could Kansa kill his favourite sister?

The grapevine acquired layers of colour as it spread. It was not sadhu baba's voice that had made the chilling forecast, it was a voice from the heavens, claimed the people. There was no doubt of Kansa being the incarnation of the evil demon Kalnemi. People pointed to the fact how he had imprisoned his own father and now killed the sadhu and dealt with Devaki and Vasudeva in a manner nobody knew. Surely, none but a demon could do such acts. Some said that immediately as the sadhu baba's head fell to the ground, Kansa's appearance had changed. He had grown in height and girth as the banyan tree, bared huge canine teeth and licked the sadhu's blood before resuming his usual appearance. He was a demon—there was no doubt about it.

Thunderstruck by the developments, the crowd discussed and debated, the more adventurous amongst them surged forward to have a closer view of the site below the banyan tree. And as they did, more than a hundred guards on horseback, carrying sticks and swords, rushed towards the curious crowd.

'Leave this place, leave this place immediately,' they shouted, simultaneously waving their sticks at the crowd. There was a stampede as the crowd tried to run to escape the sticks.

The Vrishnis were still undecided what to do, when the guards closed in upon them. Unprepared for the turn of events and dumbstruck over the developments, with no senior figure to guide them and the evening fast approaching, their first instinct was to herd their families and children to the safety of their homes and thereafter take stock of the situation.

The sea retreats unusually but comes back with a vengeance.

The Vrishnis at least, will return, Chanur was convinced. It may be the next day or a day or two at the most, but return they will, to claim back Vasudeva. And they will be joined by the Andhakas and the Bhojas, angered by the killing of the sadhu and the apparent injustice done to Vasudeva. Merely putting the Magadhi army on the streets would not be sufficient to keep peace if the entire populace took to the streets. And any killings by the army would only create martyrs.

'How do we ride over the ati-taranga?' Chanur had enquired of Rudracharya.

'Chanur,' Rudracharya had said, 'you need to first understand the nature of *ati-taranga. Ati-taranga* sweeps away everything on the coast but has no effect on the mainland. So if you are on the mainland, you will not be affected. Secondly, *ati-taranga* is very transient. If you can wait patiently, it will wear out on its own.'

'But what is the role of the King when there is such an *ati-taranga* upsurge of popular sentiment against him?' Chanur had enquired.

'First you need to find a scapegoat on whom the people can vent their ire. The King must stay passively in the background and not attract undue attention. If you use repressive measures at that stage, the King and his entire set up will be swept away by the popular wave. So, just divert the focus of the public ire. After the people have spent up their emotions, they will return to their homes. Then you can use appropriate measures to ensure that they do not rise again.'

Chanur buried his face in his hands. Something had to be done. Urgently. Moments later, he had taken his decision. He summoned Dhenuka.

'Through your contacts spread word amongst the Vrishnis that the Bhojas did not want to honour the pact with the Vrishnis entered into by King Ugrasen. That is why Ugrasen was deposed and Vasudeva arrested after the marriage drama. Tell them the Vrishnis have been fooled by the Bhojas. In fact the Bhojas are planning to attack the Vrishnis and finish them once and for all. And in this the Andhakas are also with the Bhojas.'

Dhenuka gave a crooked smile and proceeded to leave.

'Wait,' Chanur beckoned him. 'Next, start a whispering campaign amongst the Bhojas that the Vrishnis are angry at the arrest of Vasudeva and are planning to attack the Bhojas. Tell them that the Andhakas are also siding with the Vrishnis. They should sharpen their weapons and be on the guard.'

Dhenuka left.

Chanur called the commander of the Magadhi army. 'Tomorrow your only job will be to guard the palace compound. If there is any fighting on the streets, you must not interfere till I ask you… Is that clear?'

After the commander took his leave, Chanur rose. It was going to be a long night ahead. The moment had come and he must seize the opportunity. He called the chief of his intelligence wing to his bedchamber. 'Tonight there will be various clan meetings amongst the Vrishnis and Bhojas. I want an hourly report on who is meeting whom and what is being discussed. Do it properly and you will be richly rewarded by the King.'

The next two days would forever be etched in black in the history of Mathura. The first day had started as any other, without any inkling of what was to follow. As the day progressed, groups of people were seen huddled together, agitatedly discussing the developments of the previous day. Rumours flew thick. And with the advent of noon, groups of youth armed with sticks, swords, spades, rocks, flaming torches and even ploughshares, moved from the Vrishni and Bhoja localities, and headed towards each other as well as towards the Andhaka localities. They were joined by the private armies of the overlords.

Within moments, street after street witnessed pitched battles fought between the various groups. Vrishnis set several Bhoja houses and shops on fire while the Bhojas returned the compliment. The Andhakas were sandwiched as both the Bhojas and the Vrishnis targeted them. They retaliated indiscriminately, leading to further confusion.

The three communities, which had come together and formed the kingdom of Mathura, had now become sworn enemies of one another. Boundaries of blood and hate were drawn between them. Overnight there were clamours for division of Mathura into three separate kingdoms.

Chanur smiled as messengers brought him news from the streets. He had achieved what he wanted. The Yadavas were now irretrievably divided and Kansa, insulated from the Yadavas, would be more and more dependent on Chanur and the tribals to retain his monarchy. The time was now ripe to start the second phase of his plan—weaken the power of the overlords and establish central power all over Mathura. No other Vasudeva should come between him and the King.

He summoned Dhenuka. 'Pit the overlords one against the other. Let their private armies confront each other.'

At nightfall, the rioters dispersed but under the cover of darkness, another group took over. These were men from Chanur's own tribe, specially trained to accomplish whatever was ordered, even at the cost of their own lives. Swiftly they formed small teams and proceeded towards the mansions of the various overlords. As the palace drums signalled midnight, mansions, haystacks and stables of several overlords went up in flames. Throughout history, it is the common man that suffers any onslaught. The leaders mostly manage to somehow emerge unscathed, whether it be riots or war. For the first time on that fateful night, mansion after mansion of the overlords went up in flames. Throughout the night the private armies of the overlords remained busy trying to douse the flames and by morning, the flames had spread from the mansions to the hearts of the overlords.

On the second day, Mathura resembled a war field as the private armies of the overlords, some of them led from the front by the overlords themselves, took on one another. Wave after wave of fighters from the three communities, seeking revenge, fell on one another, trampling upon the dead and the injured that had already filled the streets of Mathura. The death toll ran into thousands, with thousands more maimed, crippled or injured. It seemed as if the God of Death was indulging in his favourite sport.

A servant came to Chanur bearing urgent summons from Kansa. When Chanur reached, Kansa was pacing to and fro in the hall, shouting invectives at all and sundry. As Chanur entered, Kansa shouted, 'Chanur, you are dismissed. What is happening in my kingdom? It has gone to the dogs and you just watched it go? I was told you ordered our army not to interfere? Why? This is treachery. I am going to feed you to the dogs.'

Chanur stood unperturbed. A smile passed along his face. 'Raja, don't get excited. The overlords are fighting against one another. How does it affect you? These private armies of the overlords are the greatest danger to your authority. They need to be cut down to size. So let them kill one another and reduce their respective strengths—it will all enure to your advantage.'

'But Chanur, I am the King. If I do not act and save the people, then who would obey me? And what do I rule upon? A cluster of burned houses? See what they have done to Mathura!'

'Depend on me, Raja, I have thought of that also. Tomorrow morning the Magadhi army will take over the city and immediately thereafter we will abolish all the private armies of the overlords. And by the way, Raja, formally you are not yet the King. You are the Commander-in-chief who has only temporarily taken over the powers of the King. But in order to save the kingdom from falling apart, tomorrow you shall be declared the irrevocable King of Mathura.'

'Chanur, the overlords are powerful. We hardly have any central forces. We are dependent on the overlords to provide men for wars. King…hah…a King without an army! Do you think the overlords will take it lying down? They will all gang up against me and depose me. Come on Chanur, your solutions are as useless as you are. You won't even be able to take control of the city, let alone abolish the private armies. The only consequence will be my downfall.' The harsh tone was returning to Kansa's voice.

'Raja, I have ensured that the overlords are today irrevocably divided. Each believes that the other set fire to his properties. There is no chance of their ganging up. If anything, they will support our move as they will see it as clipping the wings of their adversaries. Now, your question as to how would we do it. We already have about two thousand Magadhi troops. If we immediately recruit five hundred additional men, it would be sufficient for our immediate requirements. No overlord at this stage would dare to campaign against an army of two and half thousand men. Later, we can expand the force further.'

'Ha...ha...recruit five hundred men tomorrow? Chanur, from whom would you recruit your men and when? From these persons who are fighting in the streets? Or from the dead bodies that line the streets? Or do you want to invite the Hastinapur forces?' Kansa's voice was filled with sarcasm.

'Raja, at the time when you had deposed your father, I had apprehended danger and kept five hundred trained tribal men ready for any emergency. With your permission, I will now incorporate that force into our main army. Raja, it is only after we have a strong central force and abolish the private armies, that we can finally say that we have a kingdom where the King rules as he pleases. Raja, Mathura needs a strong ruler. A King is a King only when he is held in terror by his subjects. We need to destroy these overlords who threaten the very sub-stratum of the kingdom. In fact, it is because of these internal factors only that Mathura has not been able to expand its domain. You will see what happens once these overlords have been brought to their knees. You will achieve greatness like none of your predecessors have.'

Kansa was elated. The allure of greatness was too heady to be ignored. The fact that Chanur had without informing him, raised a tribal army of five hundred men, did not even cross his mind. 'Chanur, that is why I adore you. You are a true genius. Go ahead with your plans.'

Chanur summoned the commander of the Magadhi army.

'The King has ordered you to take control of the city tomorrow morning. No person shall be allowed out of his home. Ask your troops to take up positions in the streets of the eastern sector of Mathura before sunrise tomorrow and publicly hang anybody who violates the orders, *irrespective of whichever community to which he may belong*. My men will take care of the western sector.'

The smouldering city woke up at dawn to the drummers and heralds making announcements.

> 'In view of the riots and distrust between the various communities of Mathura and the resultant threat to Mathura's integration, *Parambhattarak* Maharaja Kansa has proclaimed himself as the King of Mathura irrevocably and has ordered every person of this kingdom to cease violence immediately. People are prohibited from coming out of their houses, whatever be the reason. The army shall patrol the streets to maintain peace. All private armies are banned with immediate effect. Any person found violating the orders or indulging in violence, shall be summarily executed. Maharaja Kansa promises that each of the communities in Mathura shall be dealt with absolute equality and each citizen shall have peace and justice as a matter of right.'

The drummers and heralds were followed by marches by armymen in every quarter of the city. A few prominent bad characters from each of the three communities were publicly hanged and their bodies left hanging at the street square as a grim reminder to the public of the consequences of disobedience as also to emphasise the absolute equality and impartiality with which the communities would be treated. A hundred others were arrested and imprisoned.

Despite the deployment of the army, it took two-three days to get the common men back to their homes. The new King, acting through Chanur, had to give them various assurances coupled with a threat of severe retribution if they did not go back. The simmering Vrishnis were assured that their leader Prince Vasudeva would be dealt with as per law. Assurances were given to all the communities of government help in rebuilding the riot-ravaged structures. Chanur's agents however made sure to keep the fires smouldering in the three communities against each other by circulating appropriate rumours and accusations.

Yet, for more than six months, Mathura remained on the edge of a volcano waiting to erupt. The smaller overlords, who were the main victims of the inter-overlord riots, did not provide much opposition, but the bigger overlords did not take kindly to the prohibition on their private armies. Every other day, the private armies of the overlords clashed amongst themselves as well as with the central forces. And this division ensured that the central forces managed to meet each and every challenge that came their way. The central army took on the overlords of one community at a time. Over the months, sporadic skirmishes went on as one overlord after another raised his head. Finally, with the public execution of two of the recalcitrant overlords—Srinjoy and Anangsen—the central forces emerged as undisputed victors and the matter stood settled once and for all.

Their military powers gone, it was only a matter of time before the overlords were denuded of their power to collect taxes from their respective communities and retain a portion to themselves. Chanur revamped the entire organisation, bringing in his salaried men, who would directly collect taxes from the people and deposit in the treasury.

Slowly but surely, Chanur was progressing towards his ultimate goal—the setting up of a tribal state. For that, the primary requirement was funds. He ensured that a large portion of all tax collected was diverted to him instead of being deposited in the treasury. A significant part of what was deposited in the treasury was also siphoned off through various fictitious expenses. Yet Chanur was not satisfied. Mathura was already in the red on account of Kansa and Vasudeva's marriage extravaganzas and mere debt servicing took away a significant portion of the revenues. He reckoned it would take years, if not a decade to collect sufficient funds at this pace. As a solution, he increased taxes on the common man. New types of taxes and newer variants of the existing taxes were conceived and imposed. His tax collectors unleashed a reign of terror. Those who failed to pay were subjected to imprisonment, whipping and torture. Those who paid were not spared either. They were subjected to higher assessments for the next season.

Kansa, in whose name all this took place, busied himself in the meanwhile in savouring the taste of monarchy. Chanur ensured a steady supply of new varieties of liquor and precocious girls of every region and colour to keep him busy. Nevertheless, once in a while, Kansa would arise from his stupor, flex his rusting muscles and clamour to go to war. This was however, one aspect on which Chanur was adamant. There was no question of going to war. Wars were expensive and Chanur was possessive about money. If the treasury was emptied, how would he draw from it for the mission of his life? But most of all, wars were risky. Most of the kingdoms around were either allied to or under the protection of either Hastinapur or Magadh. Unknown and faceless marauders going and plundering a village in a neighbouring country was one thing but declaring a war was completely different. Chanur did not want to test his fortune to the limits. There was no point in losing his all in a few days of indiscretion.

To satiate Kansa's thirst for blood and provide him a diversion, Chanur introduced him to the sport of feeding live captives to dogs. Very soon, Kansa warmed up to the sport and himself devised newer means of doing it. At times the dogs would be blindfolded and made to sniff out their prey. Some other time, the captive would be armed with a small knife or stick to defend himself, while a dozen hungry hounds would be let loose upon him. Very soon the people of Mathura echoed the words of the sadhu—Kansa is indeed a demon, the incarnation of the evil demon Kalnemi, uncle of King Ravana of Lanka. And they silently waited for their deliverer—the eighth progeny of Devaki.

It was during these times that the news came of Devaki's first pregnancy. The whole of Mathura waited with bated breath as the date of delivery approached. Even Kansa was in two minds what to do. Finally, he turned to Chanur.

'Tell me Chanur, what happens after Devaki gives birth to the first child?'

'Raja, is it not obvious that the child has to be killed?'

'No, it is not so obvious. The sadhu had said that the eighth child of Devaki would kill me. Why should the other children be punished? Even Asti and Prapti have been advising me to kill the child, but when I ask them why, they have no answer. Merely because they are childless while Devaki is delivering a child, is not a reason to kill the child.'

'Raja, tell me, when the child grows up, would he not hate you for putting his parents in prison? Would he not become your natural enemy? Would he not try to kill you or at least facilitate any person who tries to kill you?'

'Chanur, Devaki is my sister. How do you expect me to kill her innocent newborn who is not destined to kill me?'

Chanur paused for a moment to collect his thoughts. Then he turned round to Kansa. 'Raja, can we really say that this child would not be the one destined to kill you?'

'What do you mean? Don't you remember, Chanur that it is the eighth child who is destined to kill me, while this is only the first?' Kansa was growing impatient with Chanur's arguments.

'Raja, just visualise a wheel with eight equidistant points drawn on it. If the wheel is whirled round, would you be able to identify which is the first point and which is the eighth? Here also, for all you know, while you keep waiting for the eighth child, Vishnu may change the sequence and come in as the first, second, fourth or seventh. Do you understand the situation, Raja?'

It took a few moments for the words to sink in. Then Kansa literally jumped up. 'My goodness, Chanur, this thing never occurred to me! I was feeling safe in my belief that it is just one child I will have to destroy. But now it appears that Vishnu may appear anytime… Oh my God….'

The people of Mathura recoiled in helpless horror and revulsion as one after the other newborn was flung to the wall. And, on the day the seventh child was flung to the wall, whispers went round at every nook and corner of Mathura—now the deliverer will come, now the deliverer will come….

In the prison cell, Vasudeva tried to rouse Devaki from her faint. Clanking his foot chains, he went across to the water pot, picked up a few drops of water and sprinkled on her. 'Rise, Devaki, rise, it is not the time to sleep. The deliverer is waiting to come. The eighth child, Devaki. He will…kill Kansa, kill Kansa, kill Kansa, kill Kansa, kill Kansa…Death to Kansa, death to Kansa, death to Kansa death to Kansa, death to Kansa….'

Devaki's lips moved. Vasudeva put his ears close to her. A low whining moan passed through her lips. Vasudeva stroked her head. It had been more than a decade since the hair had been last combed. Unkempt and matted, teeming with lice—she who had been a princess, the most beautiful of all maidens of Mathura… Vasudeva felt his eyes moisten.

When he had first been confined to prison, Vasudeva had hoped that Mathura would rise in revolt and free them. In those initial days he would strain his ears at the slightest of sounds outside—were the people coming to rescue them? Then as the days stretched into months and the months stretched into years, hope dimmed progressively. Had the people of Mathura become so emasculated that they would not protest his arrest? He wondered. Again, when his first born was slaughtered, Vasudeva had hoped that the shock and revulsion would galvanise the people into breaking open the prison walls and killing Kansa. Nothing happened. One by one, the newborns continued to be slaughtered. Vasudeva was at a loss to understand.

Much later, when Rohini came to take care of Devaki, did Vasudeva come to know of the events that followed his arrest, of the riots, of the curbing of overlords and of the unmitigated terror that Kansa was perpetrating on the people of Mathura.

Vasudeva struck his forehead in utter disgust. 'It is all my fault. I made a colossal mistake in judging Kansa. I should have known that a panther does not change his spots. How could I have trusted him after his marauding expeditions, sexcapades and finally going to the extent of deposing his father? How could I believe that he had changed? How could I have thought that he had selflessly detained his own father for the sake of the kingdom?'

'My Lord, to err is human. The problem is that you see in others your own mirror image. You find it impossible to think that any person can act in the manner as Kansa has done. Your innate goodness makes you see only the good qualities in others.' Rohini had tried to pacify him.

'No Rohini, no,' Vasudeva was inconsolable. 'And to think that he had imprisoned me and Devaki in view of the sadhu's prediction! That prediction will no doubt come true, but from what you say, even if there were no such prediction, he would have anyway put me behind the bars in order to usurp the kingdom. I am sure there is Jarasandha's hand behind all this.'

'Take heart, my Lord. Each one of the sadhu's predictions has come true. He had very correctly predicted that Kansa is the incarnation of a demon. He has clearly shown that. My Lord, do not think that the sacrifice of your newborns has gone waste. Each one is adding up to Kansa's sins and now his cup of sins is overflowing. I am sure the Lord will take incarnation as sister Devaki's eighth child, slay this demon Kansa and deliver Mathura and all of us from this scourge.'

Rohini's words still rang in Vasudeva's ears as he tried to rouse Devaki. The Lord will come… The Lord will come… He will come in his incarnation as the eighth child of Devaki. Seven have already gone and now is the time for the eighth to make appearance. Devaki…Devaki… listen to the footsteps of the Almighty as He approaches your womb. Rise Devaki, rise, there is no time to lose…. Death to Kansa…death to Kansa…death to Kansa….

As if in reply to his mutterings, Devaki opened her eyes. Vasudeva helped her sit and patted her shoulder. A drop of tear fell from Devaki's eyes.

'Let me bring you some water.' Vasudeva rose and went to the water pitcher in the corner.

A commotion at the end of the corridor stopped him in his tracks. A commander of Kansa's army came in accompanied by prison officials, armed guards and a whole posse of masons and building materials.

'The King has ordered that a wall be put up between the two of you and in his kindness has ordered that the wall will have a hole through which you may see and communicate with each other.'

Part II

VIII

What will be will be

There's nowhere you can be that isn't where you're meant to be
...John Lennon

'O Chhathi Maiya, protect my newborn son
Guard him against pestilence, fevers and worms,
May he live a thousand years and blessed be his life,
I'll worship you with coconuts, flowers and rice.'

Residents of all the five Gop villages had descended on Gokul in their best attire. All roads led to Nandrai's house, where the *shasthi puja* or sixth-day ceremony of Kanha was in progress. Outside the house, on a levelled field, a huge thatched bamboo structure had been set up to seat the guests. Nandrai stood with a beaming face, personally welcoming the visitors.

Meanwhile, after six days in the lying-in room, Yashoda emerged and took bath. She dressed herself in her bridal attire while her family members helped her wear her jewellery. The *dai* oiled and bathed Kanha. Yashoda took out a new yellow dress for Kanha and put it on him. The little infant, not comprehending the attention bestowed on him and stung by the noise of the crowd outside, clung to his mother, weeping and seeking comfort in her breasts. Yashoda smiled. 'You naughty fellow...alright, wait... wait.' She fed him and lulled him to sleep amidst the din. She took the sleeping child to the outer room and softly placed him on a beautiful wooden cradle that Nandrai had brought home for his son.

As soon as Yashoda placed the little Kanha on the cradle, there was a virtual stampede of ladies seeking first glimpse of the child.

'Oh, my…my…such a cute baby!'

'Oh so sweet. Does he allow you to sleep at night?'

'Have you tied a black thread around his waist? It will ward off evil sights.'

The questions, advices and exclamations poured in along with the gifts. Someone had brought a bracelet for the baby, someone gifted a dress, another gave a coin while a small girl just put a peacock feather in little Kanha's shock of hair.

'See the thatch of hair on his head.'

'Oh the hairs will fall off in a few days. But see his nose. He will grow up to be a very handsome lad.'

'Ha ha, see how many hearts he breaks….'

'Well why not, he will make the Gop girls go gaga over him!'

'But his complexion will be dark. Not like his mother.'

'Leave aside the complexion, that will keep changing over time. But just see his face, does he not resemble Yashoda?' a cousin of Yashoda remarked.

'No, no, see his jawline, he resembles Nandrai,' it was a relative on Nandrai's side.

Heated arguments commenced with neither side willing to back off, till the priest, who was sitting on the side, finally called for order. 'If all of you have completed your discussions, we may commence the puja.'

The priest explained to the gathering the significance of *shasthi puja.* Goddess Shasthi was the goddess of children, reproduction and vegetation. As per mythology, she was the daughter of Brahma (the creator of the universe) and one of the six *matrikas* (mothers) who nursed and nurtured Skanda, the son of Lord Shiva and Goddess Parvati. She was a six-headed goddess with a golden complexion who carried children in her arms and rode a cat. She protected children from perils that afflicted them until the age of sixteen.

'The sixth day after birth is the most important day in the life of every person,' the priest explained. 'It is on the night of the sixth day of birth that *Vidhaata Purush,* the Lord of Destiny would creep in and write the destiny of the child in invisible ink. And since *Vidhaata Purush* is a form of Lord Brahma, the father of Goddess Shasthi, therefore the worship of Goddess Shasthi on the sixth day of the child's birth is all the more necessary so that the child has a bright future.'

Little Kanha slept through in his cradle. The women took turns in tugging at a small rope tied to the cradle. Chanting mantras, the priest invoked the *Vidhaata Purush* to give to the newborn a destiny that would make him rich and famous and make his parents, family and the village proud of him.

Prasad was distributed amongst all present and then it was the turn of the feast. Several dozen cane baskets full of *pooris* had been prepared, to be savoured with *aloo sabzi,* lentils, *halwa,* laddoos *and pedhas.* Leaving the sleeping Kanha in the care of the *dais* and other ladies, Yashoda came out to meet the guests. After spending days together in the confines of the labour room, she was finally soaking in the sun and the fresh air. She flitted from one group of guests to the other. Being the wife of the headman, she knew each one of them by name and conversely, she was the one the ladies of the villages would turn to for advice and help. And in midst of it all she twice visited the hall to feed Kanha and again lull him to sleep.

The men had finished eating and it was the turn of the women to be served. Yashoda, as the hostess, insisted on serving them but they forced Yashoda to sit with them.

'Kanha is sleeping, have your food while he still sleeps, else you would find it difficult to get time to eat,' they told him.

The ladies began eating. They made fun of one another and discussed with unison the worthlessness of their respective husbands. The men, grouped on the other side, wondered if the sound of laughter of their womenfolk would not carry to the King's palace.

'Yashoda *chachi,* Yashoda *chachi,*' a five-year-old girl was calling Yashoda in her singsong voice. 'Yashoda *chachi,* where is Kanha? I want to see him. Is he very little?'

'O my sweet little baby, he is in the hall. You can go and see him. But don't touch him—he is too small and make sure that he does not get up from sleep. And, if by chance he wakes up, just run and inform me.'

The little girl ran inside the house and within minutes, came back. 'Yashoda *chachi,* Kanha is not there. *Dai chachi* told me he is with you.'

'What...?' Yashoda sprang up. The unfinished food stained her dress but she could not have cared less. The ladies around her also stood up.

'Come on Yashoda, how can you rely on the words of a little girl? We are all here, Kanha would be in the room only. Don't panic. You sit down, I will go and find out...' Yashoda's aunt said.

Even before she had completed the sentence, Yashoda had started running.

'What happened? What happened?' The guests shouted as Yashoda ran past them. Her *odhni* fell midway, her bridal lehenga caught a thorny bush and ripped apart, her gold bridle fell on the road. She rushed into the outer room, her hair and dress dishevelled, stopped in front of the empty cradle and shouted at the *dai*—'Where is Kanha? Where *is* my Kanha?'

'But *malkin,* you sent a woman to take Kanha to you so that you could show him to the guests outside.'

'What are you saying? I never sent anybody. Do you know that woman who took Kanha?' Yashoda felt a sinking feeling along her legs.

'No, she was dark complexioned and wearing a yellow lehenga but I don't know her. In fact, there are many women in this gathering I do not know. They are all your guests only. And, why would anyone want to take your baby?' The *dai* was defensive.

'You stupid fool, why didn't you go along with her?' Yashoda shouted as she held the *dai* by her shoulder and shook her up.

The men ran inside the outer hall. Yashoda had left the *dai* and turned towards the door. 'Call...someone call Kanha's *bapu*,' her voice gave way. She gesticulated at the crowd to give way as she proceeded to run towards the main gate. But hardly had she run two paces that the world seemed to swirl before her eyes. 'Kanha...my Kanha,' she muttered as she whirled and fell in the arms of her aunt.

Nandrai rushed in like a whirlwind and froze. For an instant he felt his own head in a spin and his capacity to think deserting him. He wavered. Should he go in and attend to his wife or should he rush out and look for his son? The headman of the Gops, to whom the entire community would turn to for instant decisions in crisis situations, was in a stupor. Never before had he to deal with a situation where his own loved ones were in danger. He felt himself in a dark abyss. He tried to shout but found that his voice had deserted him and merely looked at the gathering with vacant eyes.

The gathering panicked. Women wailed, men shouted but nobody knew what to do.

'What are you all doing?' the booming voice of Soham *kaka* brought them out of their collective stupor. He shouted at a group to get water for Yashoda and then at the men to form groups and go in various directions to search for Kanha. 'Don't worry, everything will be alright,' he assured Nandrai.

The crowd was galvanised into action. Men brought out their sticks and ran out in all directions. They searched the bushes, combed the groves, looked into the fields of mustard and wheat. They scanned the countryside for any glimpse of a woman with a yellow lehenga, all the while straining their ears for any faint sound of a baby's cry.

Meanwhile, the women sprinkled water on Yashoda's face. She awoke with a start. 'Kanha…has Kanha been found? Kanha's *bapu*, where are you?'

Nandrai rushed forward. 'Are you alright?'

Yashoda was aghast. 'You are still standing here? My son is lost and you are standing here?' she shouted hysterically.

'Everyone has already gone to search. I was just waiting for you to recover.'

'Can't you see so many people are there with me? Don't you realise Kanha is in danger? How can you continue to keep standing here? Run and get my Kanha back just now or I will give up my life. Gooooo….' Yashoda was beside herself with anger.

Nandrai ran out like a missile unleashed from a sling.

The festivity at Nandrai's house had given rise to wails. Tears flowed down Yashoda's eyes as milk from her breast. Every few moments she would send one of them outside the house to see if someone was bringing back Kanha in his arms.

'Yashoda, how could you be so irresponsible to leave the infant to the sole care of the *dai*? When we were young, we always kept one eye on our children, whatever be the occasion. Nowadays the womenfolk are more interested in enjoying themselves rather than taking care of their children.' An old lady chided her.

Yashoda didn't reply. Only the sniffs gave way to sobs as more of the old ladies took on the role of mothers-in-law and dissected the event scene by scene.

'Stop these discussions about whose folly it was,' another old woman quipped. 'I am more concerned about the baby. Only six days old, how will he survive even for an hour without his mother? Unless our men are able to find the baby immediately, it will be very difficult for the child to survive the ordeal.'

'You know, many years ago, when I was young, there was a *chhathi* ceremony in the neighbouring village,' one of the old ladies whispered to her neighbours. 'Somehow, while feeding the child, it fell to the ground from its mother's lap. Hardly half a cubit, yet it did not survive. I still remember the mother's cries.'

'You know, sometimes infants are kidnapped by *tantriks* also,' it was another elderly matron. 'They perform various rituals with the children.'

'Hold your tongue, *chachi*,' a shriek emerged from across the room. Yashoda's eyes were the colour of burning hot coals. 'Don't dare to say a word more. Let my life be added to my Kanha's. If I have honestly believed in God, nothing will happen to my child. God will surely protect him from all evils.'

Yashoda rose to her feet in hysterical delirium. 'These men are useless. I will myself go and look for my Kanha. Even if the kidnapper has taken him to the nether lands, I will bring him back. Give way...give way...I must go fast....'

The women caught hold of her arms as she lunged forward.

'Let me go, let me go...I can hear my Kanha calling me out,' shouted Yashoda, behaving like a woman possessed, as a dozen women struggled to keep her in.

Meanwhile, the search was on in full swing. Suddenly someone remembered that the kidnapper could be hiding in the vacant houses in the village. Two teams were immediately dispatched to search each of the houses in the village. Of the others, some proceeded towards the Govardhan hills, some towards Vrindavan, some towards the banks of Yamuna and another party towards Mathura. They combed every inch of the territory. But it seemed that the kidnapper had vanished with the infant.

'Seems to be the handiwork of some witch or demoness,' one of the men observed. 'Surely a mere woman could not have vanished like this.'

The search parties had almost given up when one of the men in the team that had gone towards the Vrindavan forests, saw a glint of pale yellow behind one of the tree groves. As he went behind the trees for a closer look, he found a tribal woman wearing a yellow lehenga sprawled motionless on the ground. One of her breasts hung out of her choli and clinging to her breast and sucking on her nipples was…Kanha!

With a yell he fell on her, snatched Kanha and ran towards the village. His team members surrounded the spot and examined the woman.

She was dead.

Shortly, men and women from the village poured in to see the spectacle.

'Is it not Putna?' one of the men asked.

'Who, Maharaja Kansa's concubine?'

'Yes, yes, seems to be her,' two other men agreed.

Putna was a vivacious and beautiful tribal woman who for some time, was Kansa's concubine. She conceived but suffered a miscarriage and the physician ordained that she would never become a mother again. The travails of the miscarriage drained her of her physical beauty and vitality while the shock of not being able to be a mother again, devastated her mentally. But her sufferings had just begun… There was no space in the King's concubinage for women who had lost their beauty, lesser still for the physically or mentally ill. Expelled from the concubinage, she turned to sorcery and witchcraft. No one knew where she lived. Intermittently she would be sighted, sometimes selling potions at fairs, sometimes begging for alms, sometimes pretending to forecast the future. Everytime she saw an infant, she would cling to it and claim it as her own. There were dark rumours that she devoured small children, but nothing was found and her past association with Kansa ensured that she was not hounded.

'So this was it,' Soham *kaka* adjusted his turban. 'This witch would have devoured our Kanha. Thank God we got him back.'

'Seems that since she did not have a child of her own, she was jealous of others bearing children.'

'But how did she die?'

'Arre *bhaiya,* think of the distance she ran. Must have collapsed out of exhaustion.'

'Yes, exhaustion coupled with fear of being lynched alive if she were caught by any of us…' Bholu quipped.

'I don't think so,' Soham *kaka* intervened. 'Those practicing witchcraft do not die so easily. Her facial expression would have been different if she had died out of exhaustion or fear. Didn't you see Kanha sucking her breast? This child does not seem to be ordinary…after all he is our *Mukhiaji's* son. *I think Kanha sucked the life out of this evil woman.*'

At Nandrai's place, the gloom had now given way to ecstasy. A tear in one eye and smile in the other, Yashoda held Kanha tightly to her breasts. 'Nobody, nobody will now take you away from me.'

The guests started leaving in groups, chatting and discussing the events of the day. Yashoda, with Kanha clasped to her bosom, was seeing them off, when she overheard the conversation in one group and stopped in her tracks.

'What an ill omen. The child became the cause of death of a person on his *chhathi*....'

'That's right, of all days, on his *chhathi* day!'

'*Bhaiya,* this signifies that when he grows up, he will be the cause of death of many many persons....'

The smile froze on Yashoda's lips.

As evening approached, a lamp was lit on the stool containing a *bhurja* leaf, inkpot and quill. The lamp signified *Vidhaata Purush,* the Lord of Destiny, who would write the destiny of the child on the *bhurja* leaf with the quill dipped in ink.

That night, Yashoda did not eat. The whole night she sat in front of the lamp with Kanha on her lap, gazing at the flame. 'Please *Vidhaata Purush,* have pity on my child. Let him not be the cause of death of any person in his entire life. Bless him that he may grow up to be the *mukhiya* of his community like his father. Please grant this earnest wish of a mother, O Lord....'

The Lord of Fate smiled at the mother's prayers.

Can a mother's prayer change destiny? *What will be, will be....*

IX

Convince-Corrupt-Cleanse

There is nothing either good or bad, but thinking makes it so

...Shakespeare

Chanur sat on the mountaintop gazing at the Sun setting in the distant horizon. The setting rays of the Sun had turned the sky into molten amber and gold and the dexterous brush of an unseen painter was using the colours to paint an abstract work of art. It was after more than a decade that Chanur was visiting his Guru Rudracharya's ashram. He had last visited after taking over as Kansa's Minister and never found time thereafter. This time he arrived after receiving summons from his guru.

Nestled in the Vindhya range of mountains amidst lush green forests, Guru Rudracharya's ashram was an abode of serenity. Dense forests, interspersed by gurgling streams and rivulets surrounded it. From the nearby mountaintop, the view extended right till the faraway horizon. Seated on the mountaintop, it dawned on Chanur that this range of mountains was also the original boundary of Aryavarta. The chariots of the all-conquering Aryans trod victoriously all over Northern and Eastern Aryavarta, but their southward march came to an abrupt halt at the Vindhyas. For eons, the kingdoms of Malava and Avanti on the foothills of the Vindhyas remained the last outposts of the Aryans. The steep mountains covered with dense tropical forests rendered the Vindhyas insurmountable, till one day, sage Agasthya discovered a route to cross the mountain range.

A sigh escaped Chanur's lips. Although moving men and materials across the Vindhyas was a daunting task, Aryans had succeeded in establishing a permanent presence south of the Vindhyas, thanks to factional and fratricidal fights amongst the tribals. Haihaya, Vidharbha, Asmaka—the list of Aryan kingdoms in the south of the Vindhyas was growing. Chanur could foresee that a time would come when the entire landmass till Lanka would become part of Aryavarta.

This was his second day at the ashram. The previous day was spent in paying obeisance to his Guru, meeting the Ashramites and resting his travel-weary body. It was this morning that he and Rudracharya sat down in the Guru's hut to discuss the state of affairs. Outside, under the shade of banyan trees, teachers taught the students philosophy, history, politics, yoga and ayurveda. A little distance away from the ashram, wrestling, charioteering, archery and fencing was taught to students. From the *yagyasthal,* strains of hymns wafted in with the breeze which carried the smell of incense.

'Chanur, my son,' Guru Rudracharya had started in his soft lisping voice. 'When you met me more than a decade back after being appointed as Kansa's Minister, I had expressed the hope that very soon we shall see an independent tribal state in Aryavarta. My son, I am now ninety-five years of age. My old eyes are still pining to see that what I dream of. I want to die in peace, Chanur, won't you give me this *gurudakshina* before I die?'

'Guru*ji*, your dream is also mine,' Chanur replied. 'All these years I have been preparing for it. Each day during this last decade I have been stashing away money to fund an army. I have been making contacts, trying to get others converted to my cause. It is just that the circumstances have not been propitious for the last decisive move.'

'Chanur, if I am not mistaken, fourteen long years have passed by since you took over. When you had helped

Kansa depose his father in the palace coup and usurp the throne, we had discussed that it should take about ten years to set up an independent tribal kingdom—a kingdom which would be home to all the displaced tribals of Aryavarta. Today, it still remains a dream.'

Fourteen long years... A lot had changed during this time but even today the equations remained in a state of flux. Time and opportunity were slipping by and Chanur was only too acutely aware of it.

'My son,' Rudracharya continued, 'Fourteen years ago, the conditions were pregnant with promise. Kansa was new to administration and totally dependent on you and the other advisers, almost all of whom were tribals. It was easy for you to divert funds towards the cause. You tell me that you have assiduously done this for all these years. You say that the chest is now sufficient to fund an entire army. Then what is holding you back?'

Chanur closed his eyes and introspected for an answer. Hansa and Dimvaka—the tribal ministers of Jarasandha—Chanur had had very high expectations from the duo. Together, they virtually ran the kingdom of Magadha, while Jarasandha led his armies in one war after another. It was only a matter of time, Chanur had predicted, before the duo would supplant Jarasandha, take over Magadha and establish a tribal kingdom. In fact, tribals and backward classes constituted the bulk of the mighty Magadha army and if the duo had taken initiative, there was no reason why Jarasandha could not have been deposed and a tribal kingdom set up. And once Jarasandha was ousted from Magadha, it would virtually break Kansa's backbone and render him exposed and support-less. The rest, Chanur was confident, he could take care.

But, this expected putsch never happened and this totally upset Chanur's calculations. With Jarasandha at the helm in Magadha, it would have been foolish to depose his son-in-law in Mathura. But why did Hansa and

Dimvaka omit to act? Was it out of fear of Jarasandha's wrath in case they failed? Or did they feel bound by the self-imposed fetters of loyalty? Chanur never could really discern. It was too dangerous a topic to even venture to broach, especially to people of the calibre and maturity of Hansa and Dimvaka. If loyalty to Jarasandha was the reason for the duo's inaction, even a whiff of conspiracy on Chanur's part would prove fatal for him.

Moreover, even if the problem of Magadha was solved, the problem of Hastinapur would have remained. Till Mathura was aligned with Magadha, and in fact ruled by Jarasandha's son-in-law, Hastinapur would keep its hands off, unless it wanted an all out war. But the moment Mathura would come off Magadha's orbit, Hastinapur was sure to invade Mathura and claim it as its own. And the probability of Hastinapur's invasion would magnify manifold if Mathura were to be ruled by tribals. It would then have become a case of Aryan pride to redeem the land from non-Aryans.

But then Hastinapur was itself going through internal turmoil and in no position to set its sights outside. After Pandu's self-exile, his blind elder brother Dhritarashtra was appointed monarch. Bhishma, acting as Regent of the new King, was carrying on administration of the kingdom with his practised ease. However, after Pandu's death in exile and his second wife Madri self-immolating herself on her husband's pyre, his widow Kunti came back to Hastinapur with five children, claiming them to be Pandu's sons and in line to the throne.

Kunti's stay in the Hastinapur palace had become a festering wound for the royal family. Kunti was claiming that her eldest son Yudhisthira was elder to King Dhritarashtra's son and therefore the rightful heir to the throne after Dhritarashtra. She had already enlisted support of Hastinapur's minister Vidura in this regard and was using him to drum up support amongst the influential persons in the kingdom. Sooner or later, Chanur was sure, there was going to be a showdown.

Under these circumstances, Chanur had calculated that if somehow the problem of Magadha was solved and he was able to take over Mathura, Hastinapur would not be in a position to interfere. In an extreme situation, he had calculated, he would accept suzerainty of Hastinapur and drive it against Magadha. But Hansa and Dimvaka's inaction consigned all these plans to the bin.

There was an alternative situation also which did not materialise. Chanur did not contemplate Jarasandha and Bhishma to remain in power after so many years. Yet, fourteen years down the line, the duo were hale and hearty and in fighting fit condition. Jarasandha had turned his eyes on the kingdoms to the north of Magadha and was fighting battles with the mountain tribes. Bhishma had recently quelled revolts in the mutinous west and returned to the capital.

'What do I do in these circumstances, Guru*ji*? Till either Jarasandha or Bhishma go, it will be difficult to depose Kansa and declare independence for tribals—a failure will only jeopardise the interests of the tribals.'

'What you are saying is true, Chanur, but if you could not send feelers to Hansa and Dimvaka directly, did you try to speak to their guru or any other person whom they regard or who has some control over them?'

'I have unverified reports that their guru has died. But now that you say, Guru*ji*, I shall make further efforts in that regard.'

'Step up your efforts, Chanur, step up your efforts. I have passed on to you all my knowledge in politics and you are a master at it. You know what to do. Politics is based on the three C's—convert, corrupt, cleanse. First, try to Convert the person to your cause. If not, try to Corrupt him into following your cause. If everything fails, Cleanse the world from that person's influence. All my hopes for an independent tribal state, are pinned on you. I am proud of you and the position that you have secured by your own efforts. But the time has now come to act.'

'Yes Guru*ji*, with your blessings I shall make further efforts.'

'By the way, Chanur, I am getting reports that all is not well regarding your own position in the kingdom? I am told that Kansa is trying to become more popular amongst the masses and that he is relying on Bhoumya and Agha more than you?'

Chanur momentarily looked up in surprise at his Guru's face and then bowed his head. Nestled in the Vindhayas, his Guru had his finger on the pulse of every place. One year had passed since Kansa had flung Vasudeva and Devaki's new born daughter to her death and much had changed in Mathura since that eventful day. Kansa, the King who revelled in watching his detractors being devoured by dogs, who had no qualms in killing newborn infants of his own cousin sister, seemed to have undergone a complete transformation! Yes, death sentences were still handed out, albeit less liberally than earlier, but more importantly, the executions were carried out in a humane manner. Gone were the times when the King would experiment with new methods of torturing the hapless prisoners. Not only that, one day of every week was earmarked for the King to meet his people. And wonder of wonders, the applicants seemed to be getting relief or at least a promise that their grievances would be looked into.

The people of Mathura attributed the welcome change in conditions to Rishi Aritra. The venerable sage had reportedly spent decades of his life in deep meditation in the Himalayas, and was roused from his prayers by divine voices that commanded him to go and meet King Kansa. He came to Mathura and barged in the Royal Court. Looking straight at Kansa, he thundered, 'O King, have you forgotten that you are the incarnation of Rudra? I have come from the Himalayas to remind you of your original self. O King, your kingdom is not the place for your *tandava*, reserve it for your enemies. Bless your people and show them your true form so that they may worship you.'

The sage came forward to the throne. With the tip of his forefinger he touched Kansa's forehead and uttered mantras. Minutes later, Kansa fell in a swoon. When he was revived, the sage was gone. No one saw him thereafter. But from that moment, Kansa's personality had changed. No wonder, Rishi Aritra was regarded by the Mathuraiites as a Messenger of God.

Only Chanur knew the truth....

The most surprising part was that Kansa was fully cooperating in the new dispensation. His fear of Devaki's eighth son also seemed to have subsided. More than a year had passed since killing of Devaki's daughter and she had not become pregnant again. Agha's strategy of building a wall between Vasudeva and Devaki inside the prison seemed to have worked. Slowly Kansa was getting around to believing that the forecast was entirely a hoax. Coming out of the pall of fear had re-energised him. Further, the sight of people prostrating before him in gratitude when their problems were solved in the Royal Court, made him truly believe in what Bhoumya, Agha and now sage Aritra had told him—that he was himself an incarnation of God. Another year, Bhoumya and Agha had told Kansa, that time would be ripe for the next stage—declaration of his divinity and starting construction of a befitting temple for him as the living deity.

'Chanur, remember, when you were a student, I used to repeatedly teach that there must be some fear due to which the King should feel dependent on his Minister. If there is nothing to fear, there would be no need for the Minister. Chanur, I repeated this lesson to you when you took over as Kansa's Minister. In fact, you had till recently done a good job of it. But I am sorry to say that in the last one year, you seem to have frittered it all away....' Rudracharya shook his head in disgust.

'Guru*ji*, the problem is that the other tribal advisers like Bhoumya and Agha do not share the independent tribal kingdom dream. They are all childhood friends of Kansa and would not dream of harming him. I have tried to indirectly reach out to them on the issue but failed. Now these advisers through their cronyism are trying to advance their prospects. They are trying to project him as the incarnation of God and for that purpose have organised the entire spectacle of redressal of public grievances at the King's Court. This is all a show. Even that Rishi Aritra was an imposter. But the public is lapping it up. Bhoumya and Agha have already assured Kansa that a year hence, the time would be ripe to pronounce his divinity.'

'Chanur, what you say is not unknown to me and that is why I summoned you here. You have to act immediately and decisively. If Kansa gets deified and has popular support, then he will totally come under the influence of Bhoumya, Agha and the like and it would become impossible for you to displace him in future. You must keep Kansa in such a position that people hate him and he just manages to remain in power despite public hatred. This would be an ideal position so that as soon as the other circumstances are ripe, Kansa can be removed easily and an independent tribal state proclaimed. And in respect of those who are likely to hinder achievement of that goal, I repeat my three C's—Convince, Corrupt or finally Cleanse.'

Discussions with Guru Rudracharya went on for another two days before Chanur took his leave.

'I do not know whether I will see you again, Chanur. My life bird is impatiently fluttering its wings to come out of this body's cage. But one individual is too small for the cause. The cause must not die. Chanur, keep the cause alive even after I am no more. I shall watch you from the nether world and my blessings shall always be with you.' The Guru's eyes were moist, so his pupil's.

With a heavy heart but a determination of purpose, Chanur set out for Mathura.

X
The Massacre

Those who can make you believe absurdities
Can make you commit atrocities

...Voltaire

Kanha was now about four years of age and the first realisation that dawned on Yashoda was that there was no correlation between the size of a child and his capacity for mischief. Kanha was slim and appeared small in comparison with the other children of his age. But, hidden behind that almost feminine physique and cherubic innocent face, was a phenomenal capacity for inventing new forms of mischief and boundless energy to carry out those pranks to their ultimate conclusion. No wonder he was the undisputed leader of his gang of ten, many of whose members were even two to three years older than him.

But along with that first, was a second profound realisation for Yashoda that mischief could be simultaneously exasperating and exhilarating. So much so that at times, she, the very image of propriety, would secretly facilitate Kanha and his gang of ten in carrying out their mischievous endeavours.

Kanha's favourite snack was butter and he would go to any length to obtain it. The clay pot where Yashoda stored the family butter, was his first target. Very often, in the midst of cooking, when Yashoda would look for butter, she would find the pot not only emptied of its contents but literally polished off. 'Kanha...Kanha...' she would shout, but gifted with an uncanny instinct, Kanha would have gone out of his mother's reach. An hour later, he would return with *Kadamba* flowers for her and Yashoda, having forgotten the butter episode, would take him on her lap, caress his shock of hair and kiss his dimpled cheeks.

At times Yashoda would deliberately hide the butter at places she knew Kanha would locate. At other times it would be a game of treasure hunt with the butter hidden in the most ingenious of places. Finally, one day Yashoda hung the family butter pot from the ceiling, visible, but totally out of Kanha's reach. The whole morning, Kanha went about with a mournful expression till Yashoda could take it no longer. She brought out some butter and gave to Kanha. Kanha's face lit up and Yashoda was assuaged. From that day she would hang the butter pot near the ceiling and hide some butter separately at a place where Kanha could locate after some search. This went on smoothly, till a week later, when she brought down the butter pot and found it empty.

Had she forgotten to keep butter in the pot? Yashoda was unsure.

The next afternoon, Yashoda pretended to go off to sleep. Several moments later, she heard soft voices coming from the kitchen. She tiptoed into the kitchen to see the gang of ten in the process of looting the butter. They had formed themselves into a pyramid, with four children at the base, three above them, then two and finally Kanha at the top, taking out butter from the pot, eating some and passing the remaining down to his friends.

Yashoda stepped in. 'So this is what is happening?' her stern voice could not however hide the gleam in her eyes.

For a moment, the boys froze and the next moment the pyramid collapsed in a heap, the boys running out through the other door. Yashoda caught Kanha as he was in the process of escaping.

'So you have been stealing and eating butter?'

'No *Maiya,* I did not eat butter,' Kanha's face was the epitome of innocence, even as droplets of butter shone around his mouth. 'We were only playing a game....'

'You tiny little imp...you have now started lying to your mother? Open your mouth.' Yashoda managed to retain the sternness in her voice with supreme difficulty.

Kanha opened his little mouth as two droplets of tears rolled down his cheeks.

As she gazed into Kanha's little butter-stained mouth, Yashoda realised that this was her world, this little liar brat was the reason she had come into this world and motherhood of this little being encapsulated all her happiness, joy, love and affection. It was for him that she lived and she would die a thousand deaths if he momentarily escaped her vision.

Yashoda could control herself no longer. Sobbing with tears of joy, she caught hold of Kanha, cuddled him, brought out the butter and proceeded to feed him with her own hands.

At evening when she narrated the incident to Nandrai, he laughed out loud. 'Do you know, I used to do similar things when I was young? Our *Lalla* has taken after me. I used to have a real appetite for butter and devised some really ingenious plans to get it.'

'Yes, yes, it shows,' Yashoda smilingly pointed at Nandrai's pot belly. 'And next time Kanha does some mischief, I know whom to punish!'

The summer was on its way out and all the Gops were on their way to Vrindavan to worship at the temple of Lord Indra, the King of Gods. Lord Indra was the God of rains and it was necessary to worship him to ensure that there were adequate rains in the season. A train of bullock carts set out from each Gop village, loaded with men, women and children, all dressed in colourful attire, holding plates containing coconuts, sandalwood paste, sweets, flowers and small containers of milk—all offerings for the Lord.

At Vrindavan, the Gops took bath in the Yamuna and then took turns at worshipping at the temple of Lord Indra. It was almost noon when they had finished and the convoy began their return. A few furlongs away from Vrindavan, in a clearing in the forest, they halted for lunch. Mats were spread and plantain leaves taken out for serving lunch. It was like this every year. Children especially looked forward to the trip as it was like a picnic in the woods.

After they finished eating, the children went off to play in the forest.

'Children, don't go too far into the forest,' the women shouted almost in unison.

And the answer also was in unison: 'Of course not. We will be nearby only.' The sound of mirth and laughter that followed the answer however showed that there was no intention to comply.

The men loitered in groups in the edge of the forest while the women gossiped and cuddled their babies. Suddenly from inside the forest there were shouts and screams. Men and women left whatever they were doing and rushed to check. A furlong inside the dense forest, they found the children huddled beside a dead body. The men stepped forward to have a closer look and immediately a scream escaped their lips. 'It's Agha, Kansa's adviser!'

There were marks of strangulation on his neck. The eyes had popped out. A faint mark of blood was visible from the side of the lips.

'My God, who could have killed him?'

'Kanha killed him,' two children of the gang of ten shouted.

'Whaaat?'

'Yes, we saw Kanha was sitting on the body and was pressing that man's neck. He said he had killed the man,' the boys spoke up.

'Oh come on, this body has been lying here for several hours now. Don't utter your silly stories to anyone,' one of the Gops warned.

'Yes, don't forget that the man killed was an adviser to King Kansa. Any loose talk can lead to the executioner.'

'Come, come, let's all go back.'

The Gops collected their children and fled from the spot.

The news shook Mathura like a shattering earthquake. When the news reached Kansa, his first reaction was to draw out his sword and decapitate the hapless news-bearer. Killing his childhood friend and adviser Agha was a direct attack on his authority. Rebellion was brewing, Kansa decided and it was necessary to nip it in the bud. Like a raging lion in a cage, he growled and paced about the palace. Whoever and whatever came in his way was kicked out of sight. Finally, Chanur, Bhoumya and Pralamba, their own eyes redshot, caught hold of Kansa and took him to his room.

Investigation into Agha's death was carried out by Chanur and Bhoumya themselves aided by the *kotwal* of Mathura and his battery of sleuths and police personnel. Apart from strangulation marks on the neck, no other injury was discovered. Since the body was found in a forest thicket, no footmarks or chariot marks could be found. The murder was apparently carried out elsewhere and the body brought and dumped in the thicket. People all around Mathura were questioned if they had seen Agha going to the place with anyone. Agha's staff as well as all the known bad characters of Mathura were all rounded up and tortured to extract confession but it was apparent that they were not aware of the incident. For public consumption, two persons were proclaimed as offenders and were fed to the dogs, and the murder was attributed to the offenders being aggrieved about Agha having ordered sale of their land to recover outstanding taxes. But heart to heart, Kansa and his advisers realised that the investigation had failed to reach its goal. Uneasiness lay heavy on their head. If someone could dare to kill Agha, it could be one of them next....

With every passing day, Kansa was getting more and more irritated and frustrated by the team's inability to nab the real culprit who killed Agha. He started drinking heavily and abusing his advisers as well as his near ones. Finally, Chanur proposed that a *tantrik* be summoned to find out the real culprit. There was a very revered *tantrik* in Kashi, whose utterances were said to be next only to God.

The following week the *tantrik* was brought to Mathura. He was a demon of a man. Dark complexioned with long, flowing grey beard and a shock of grey matted hair on the head, searing eyes and holding in his hands a cup made out of a human skull and a polished human femur bone, his very appearance evoked fear and awe amongst the audience. But the *tantrik* would not enter the palace even to meet the King—he went straight to the cremation ground and made it his home. Kansa was forced to swallow his pride and go to the cremation ground to pay obeisance to the *tantrik*.

The next day the rituals began. A big ceremonial fire was lit in the cremation ground. The *tantrik,* sitting on a corpse in front of fire, uttered his mantras. He put in the fire ladles of *ghee,* sandalwood powder, ground pepper and aromatic spices, while ritually drinking liquor from the human skull held in his hand. The yagna and the chanting of mantras went on for three days. Nine virgin girls, representing the nine forms of Goddess *Shakti* were worshipped. Invocations were made to Lord *Mahakaal*—the destroyer of the Universe, as well as to the spirits of darkness.

Finally after three days, Kansa was summoned to the cremation ground. On his arrival, the *tantrik* stood up.

With eyes blazing, he turned to Kansa and roared with a booming voice. 'You foolish King, you relax here with your cronies, while the eighth son of Devaki is growing up by the day and has begun the process of killing your friends one by one….'

'Whaaa…aaat,' Kansa boomed back, 'the last child of Devaki was a girl and I have with these very hands of mine, consigned her to the heavens. What are you speaking of, *Tantrik*?'

'I speak what I see, O King. The *tantrik* never lies. Devaki delivered a son and not a daughter. That son, the incarnation of Vishnu, was smuggled out of the prison on the night he was born and replaced with a daughter. That son is now about four years of age, but he is blessed with divine powers. It is he, who has with his bare hands, killed your adviser. And your other advisers will also follow suit. If he lives, he will kill your advisors one by one, till one day your turn comes, Kansa.'

Kansa suddenly felt his head swirl. Yes, the *tantrik's* words did make sense. That is why Devaki did not conceive after the wall was put up between her and Vasudeva. That was because she had already given birth to the incarnation of Vishnu.

It was Chanur who remembered one crucial aspect. '*Tantrik,* are you out of your senses? The last child that was killed was the seventh child of Devaki and not the eighth. What are you saying? Is it the influence of liquor that gives you the courage to try to terrorise our King?'

'You ignorant being,' the *tantrik* took on Chanur, 'the last child was not the seventh, but the eighth child of Devaki. How can you forget that Devaki was supposed to have miscarried before the last child was born?'

Chanur remained adamant. 'O *tantrik,* a miscarried child is not to be reckoned as per our *shastras*. How can you count that unborn child?'

The *tantrik* laughed aloud derisively. 'You ignorant fools, that child was not actually miscarried. By the maya of Vishnu, that pregnancy was transferred from Devaki to another woman and that child was also born. That is why I count this child as the eighth and not the seventh.'

'But to whom was that womb transferred?' Chanur enquired of the *Tantrik.*

'Chanur, don't beat about the bush with your useless questions. It is the eighth child that we are concerned with because that child has been forecast to kill me. The seventh child does not matter. But *Tantrik,* if you say that the last delivery of Devaki was her eighth, how could that eighth child be smuggled out? There was so much security, in fact additional security had been put up....' Kansa's voice seemed to break. Then suddenly he turned round and bellowed, 'Chanur!'

Chanur's face turned ashen for a moment.

'Chanur, you were in-charge of security. Tell me, how was the child smuggled out? Guards, take this backstabbing rascal to prison. I shall personally feed him to the dogs!'

Four guards ran forward but before they could lay their hands on Chanur, the *tantrik* roared. 'Leave him alone. That minister is innocent. And so are the guards who guarded the prison on that day.'

Now it was Kansa's turn to be surprised. 'What are you saying, *Tantrik*? On one hand you say that the infant was smuggled out of prison but then you say that neither the guards nor Chanur were responsible? Then how was the baby smuggled out?'

'You forget, Kansa, we are talking about the incarnation of Vishnu. With my *tantrik* powers I have come to know that as soon as the child was born, the room lit up. As if by magic, the prison gates opened and all the guards fell asleep. A Voice commanded Vasudeva to take the child and go out of the prison. As instructed, Vasudeva took his son in a basket and went out of the prison gates as if in sleepwalk and thereafter followed the instructions of the *Voice*.'

'But, where did he go? Where did he get the girl from?' Kansa asked anxiously.

'O King, I am the most powerful *tantrik* in this Aryavarta but I am not God. My *tantrik* powers fade before the might of Vishnu. I can only say what I see. Using my powers I have seen that the night was a night of calamity. The skies opened up almost like the sea itself, and the fury of nature caused our river Yamuna to spill onto its banks and the flood waters had reached till the very gates of your palace. I could see Vasudeva with the basket on his head, trudging through the sheet of water. There was a huge snake, the *Sheshnag* himself, following him and I saw that it had spread its hood wide to shelter the incarnation of Vishnu from the rain. The river parted its way as Vasudeva approached. But then, O King, suddenly everything turned dark before my eyes. After a long time, I saw Vasudeva again at the prison gate. This time there was no *Sheshnag*. The baby was different. And, as he came back into the prison cell, the prison gates shut close and all the guards woke up and resumed their duties as if nothing had happened. Vasudeva and Devaki slept off and they too forgot about the entire event. And you King, killed that girl, thinking she was the seventh child of Devaki.'

'But, where is that eighth child of Devaki growing up? Give us this information and you shall get whatever you want. Riches, virgin girls, land, cows—whatever pleases you,' Chanur asked the *tantrik*.

'A *tantrik* does not hanker after riches, Minister,' the retort came swift and fast. 'We live in the cremation ground and that is our world. Like Lord Shiva, the ashes of the cremation ground are our cosmetic, the human bones our adornment and the human skull our drinking vessel. The riches and land are not for us, so do not try to tempt me.

I have told you that for the period after Vasudeva left the prison gates, everything is shrouded in black. Try as I might, I am unable to pierce that veil. That black veil must be the magic of Vishnu because it sets at naught my years of penance. Take my word, O King, find out this boy and destroy him, for if he lives, you will not.'

'But, how do I find him out?' Kansa asked.

'It is clear that this boy is presently in Mathura since he has killed Agha within your kingdom. And remember, Vishnu's maya will be at work, so it will not be easy to identify the particular child. Kill all the children in your kingdom, if so required, but if you fail to kill this boy, no one can save you.'

Kansa returned to the palace but the *tantrik's* words continued to ring in his ears: 'Take my word O King, find out this boy and destroy him, for if he lives, you will not.'

The mood in the palace was sombre. Kansa paced about the room in deep thought. Chanur, Bhoumya, Dhenuka, Pralamba all sat with their heads bowed, ruminating the words of the *tantrik*.

'That means we will have to collect information about all the four-year-old boys in the kingdom—where they were in the last few days, whether there is any report of any supernatural act on their part and so on....' Chanur said at last.

'Is that even practicable?' Bhoumya asked.

'What other means do you foresee?' Chanur retorted. 'Kill all the children as the *tantrik* said?'

'But, can we be sure about what the *tantrik* said?' It was Pralamba this time. 'What if he is an imposter?'

Kansa finally stopped his steps and turned towards the group. 'Pralamba, I am sure about the *tantrik*. Whenever he spoke to me, he looked into my eyes directly. If he had uttered any falsity, I would have immediately come to know. And, whatever he said perfectly fits in with whatever has happened. Ufff...smuggled out of my prison...can you imagine, Bhoumya, smuggled out of my prison...I just feel like going after Vasudeva and cutting him down to pieces. Now what you all need to find out is how you will identify this boy. I would love to wring his neck personally.'

'May I say something?' Dhenuka asked.

'Yes, yes, go on Dhenuka,' Kansa said, 'Any suggestion is welcome.'

'Raja, as Bhoumya apprehends, it may not be practicable to identify the child who we seek from out of all the four-year-old boys of the kingdom. In fact, we are contending with Vishnu, who is the master of maya. In each of his avatars, he has won through trickery. If you remember, in the Puranas, when the *Asura* brothers Sunda and Upasunda were about to take control of the heavens, Vishnu took the form of Tilottama and made the brothers fight amongst themselves. Then Vishnu took the form of a dwarf *Vaman* and tricked the great King Bali into losing his kingdom. You must remain in no doubt that here also he is trying to deceive us. It would be next to impossible to find the correct boy.'

'What do you want to say, Dhenuka?' Bhoumya was getting bored. 'Say it quickly.'

'I want to say that as the *tantrik* said, if it is not possible to identify one particular four-year-old as Vishnu's incarnation, it may be safer to exterminate all the four-year-old children of Mathura so that our Raja remains safe.'

'What? Kill all the four-year-old boys of Mathura? Are you out of your mind? The *tantrik* said and you accepted it without realising the consequences?' Bhoumya was stunned.

'Our Raja's life is certainly far more important than a hundred four-year-old boys.' Dhenuka was adamant.

'Do you realise that there will be a rebellion if we do so?' Bhoumya asked.

'Any rebellion can be suppressed with an iron hand.'

'But even those whom we will use to suppress the rebellion will have children in Mathura and they would not sit idly if their boys are slaughtered.'

'You forget, Bhoumya, we have Magadhi soldiers who have no roots in Mathura and they would not have any problem in complying with our orders.'

This time Kansa spoke up. 'What Dhenuka says is correct, Bhoumya. My life is far more precious than that of a mere hundred boys. And if there is any whiff of rebellion, it will be dealt with by my Magadhi soldiers.'

'But Raja, if you allow this slaughter, you will be permanently branded in history as an incarnate of devil. Your dream of being worshipped in temples will not be realised,' Bhoumya remonstrated.

'Leave your silly ideas, Bhoumya,' Kansa was furious this time. 'If I don't survive, what will I do with your worship? I am the King and my subjects are bound to offer all sacrifices for my long life and safety, even if such sacrifice involves their own lives or that of their boys. Chanur, what do you say?'

'Raja, it would be sad if children have to be killed but if that cannot be avoided, then the sacrifice will have to be undertaken. It is the duty of the citizens of Mathura to come forward and offer their four-year-old boys in sacrifice for the safety of their King. Those who do not comply with the duty, deserve to be punished.' Chanur was categorical.

'Chanur, you have lifted a weight off my heart. So that's settled, the operation must start from tomorrow itself. Seal the borders and see that not a single four-year-old boy escapes. Make no distinction between the Bhojas, Andhakas or the Vrishnis. Nobody knows who sheltered the child.'

'Raja, what happens if there is any misjudgement of age?' Dhenuka asked. 'You know, sometimes a child of four may appear like two or three or vice versa.'

'Dhenuka, this is my order—whenever there is a doubt, just kill. Whichever child can walk, must face the scimitar. I want the operation to be entirely foolproof. And if you find even a hint of revolt, just crush it.'

'I suggest that Bhoumya and Pralamba should take one division of the Magadhi army each and start the killings, locality by locality,' Chanur proposed. Dhenuka and I will take one-half each of the remaining army and crush whatever rebellion is attempted. I will be in charge of the Northern and Eastern sectors of the city and Dhenuka will patrol the South and West. We shall be in constant communication with Bhoumya and Pralamba and whosoever requires additional help shall be assisted by whichever contingent is the nearest. Is that alright with all of you?'

The others agreed. The meeting dispersed.

Chanur smiled to himself. Everything was going according to his plans. Very deftly, he had transferred the job of slaughtering the small children on Bhoumya and Pralamba. Now, without further delay, the *tantrik* had to be dispatched to his Creator. Guru Rudracharya had taught him never to leave any evidence behind. Halfway through to his residence, as darkness descended, Chanur turned his chariot towards the crematorium.

The crimson dawn that broke over Mathura defined the colour that would rule the city that day.

In the colony adjacent to the famous Indra Temple in Central Mathura, people were roused from their sleep by the sound of horses' hooves, instead of the temple bells. It had been a hot, sultry night and most people of the neighbourhood had taken the cots outside their suffocating houses and slept under the canopy of stars, fanned by the cool night air. As the night sky turned to red, army horses galloped in from all sides and pulled up beside their cots. Even before the people could get up from their beds, the Magadhi soldiers, armed to their teeth, jumped down from their horses and pointed naked daggers at them. Bring all your children outside, they commanded the women, or one by one your men will be slain.

'Why, why, why...why do you want our children?' 'No, you can't take away our children!' Wailing cries rent the air.

The Magadhi soldiers with faces of stone did not bother to reply. Some went inside the houses and dragged out all children who could stand on their legs. Mothers who held on to their children had their arms slashed or in some cases, their throats. Men, who even moved an arm towards their children, were mercilessly hacked down. The children, all of them crying piteously for their mothers, were shoved to the middle of the street and then, in front of their parents' eyes, decapitated with swift flourishes of the sword. A river of blood, gore and tears flowed by what was once a road. Innocent bodies lay about in heaps, many of them with their heads unattached. Many of the men and women fainted at the sight, some petrified out of shock while the others lunged at and clung to their children's bodies, beating their heads on the road, too shocked to cry. A long while later, one loud wail pierced the air, then another, then yet another... It was as if the boiling interiors of the Earth had burst out in a volcano of wails, spewing tears of fiery magma, everything dear turned to ashes.

While Bhoumya led the troops at the Indra Temple area, Pralamba took charge at the locality near the Four Banyans. The four banyan trees of ancient linage, which had stood there from times immemorial, would never have witnessed such a spectacle in their entire lifetime. Mother and child, father and child were together cut down with merciless strokes of the sword. Even lactating babies were not spared. The order to kill four year olds got translated into killing all children, irrespective of their age. The entire locality of the Four Banyans was thoroughly cleansed of children by the troops as if they were getting rid of some epidemic or plague.

The operations at the Indra Temple and the Four Banyans were carried out in the early hours of the morn when people were still asleep. But by the time the two operations ended, the day had broken, people had awakened and the news of the twin massacres spread like wildfire. And at every stage of communication, the news was supplemented with rumours. In every locality of the kingdom, people came out of their houses armed with sticks, rods, swords, ploughshares, stones and even vessels full of dust, ready to take on any army that would come to massacre their children. Children were hidden and men and women patrolled the streets. People felled trees and blocked the roads. The landlords of the Bhoja, Vrishni and the Andhaka clans supplied arms and helped their respective clan members to set up defences.

Having succeeded easily in his mission at the Indra Temple, Bhoumya proceeded with his troops to the settlement near the old temple while Pralamba proceeded towards the houses near King Satvatta's statue. People in both the localities were waiting for the troops and fell on them with everything at their disposal. As blazing torches and hurled rocks fell in their midst, the horses of the troops panicked and turned back. Bhoumya and Pralamba had not expected resistance of this order. Urgent messages were sent to Chanur and Dhenuka to send in reinforcements.

Chanur, who was commanding the forces in the Northern and Eastern quarters of the city, came under attack from the surrounding localities. Same happened with Dhenuka's forces in the Southern and Western sectors. However, instead of using the troops to crush the attackers, both Chanur and Dhenuka took up defending positions.

Meanwhile, the Gop villagers under Nandrai erected defences and took up their positions. The women and men stood on guard, ready to kill or be killed. Sure enough, a small contingent of the Magadhi army was spotted at one of the roadblocks and immediately a barrage of spears was hurled towards them. The contingent counter attacked and several Gops were injured in the scuffle but ultimately the contingent could not hold its ground and soon fled the scene.

However, not all localities were successful in defending themselves. As the day progressed, pitched battles were reported from various quarters of the city. The people won some, the troops won some.

Chanur went to meet Kansa. 'Raja, it is advisable to call off this campaign. It will take us nowhere.'

Kansa was shocked. 'Chanur, you all advised me to take this course of action and now you want me to back out of it? What will my people think? It will be construed as my defeat and this will breed rebellion all over the kingdom. The people will know how to depose me!'

'Raja, my Guru used to say that everyone should know when and how to beat a tactical retreat. When I advised you, I expected Bhoumya and Pralamba to act at a lightning pace. In fact it was on my instruction that they attacked even before dawn. But, instead of just finishing off the children and moving on, they engaged the men of the locality, resulting in a fatal delay. The other localities got time to react and erect their defences. In fact, Dhenuka and my troops crashed through defences of several localities and punished the people appropriately for their defiance.'

'Chanur, get me out of this mess with my head held high,' Kansa's voice was cracking.

'Raja, it can be done, but you will have to pay a price for it.'

'What do you mean?'

'You will have to remove Bhoumya and Pralamba from their posts, although they will continue to remain our friends and will advise you as before, albeit in an informal capacity.'

'How will that help?' Kansa was anxious.

'We will put it that after what the *tantrik* said, Bhoumya and Pralamba, in order to save your life, undertook the slaughter. While they acted in a most patriotic manner, this was not the way to go about it and therefore they are suspended from your advisory board. It will be further put out that the *tantrik* was found to be a hoax, that he had manufactured the story about the eighth son of Devaki and that he has been killed. And that as soon as you came to know of what Bhoumya and Pralamba did, you ordered the operations to stop immediately. In this manner you will be rid of all the blame and the people will also feel assuaged. People whose children have been killed will be compensated from the treasury. Later, when the controversy will have died down, we will reinstate the duo.'

'That is right, but how can we do this to Bhoumya and Pralamba? They are my childhood friends, Chanur. How can I treat them in this way, especially when all our decisions were taken collectively?'

'Raja, do not worry about that. We all live for you and for your sake each one of us can sacrifice our life and honour. Bhoumya and Pralamba will also willingly sacrifice themselves for your sake. I will explain to them the predicament we face today. And I will also clarify that they will continue to be your informal advisers and your closest friends.' Chanur assured Kansa.

'Alright, do as you please, Chanur,' there was resignation in Kansa's voice. 'But what about the eighth son of Devaki?'

'Raja, we will find out through our intelligence sources. Maybe it will take a bit of time, but we will find out for sure. Leave the worry to us, Raja. We are more concerned about you than you are about yourself.'

As Chanur left, a glint of smile passed between his lips. 'Convince...Corrupt...Cleanse.' 'Convince...Corrupt... Cleanse.' Chanur repeatedly muttered the mantra in his mind. 'Now see, Bhoumya, what Chanur can do.'

It took several weeks to douse the fire created by the killing of the children. Two days after the incident, a hundred people gathered outside Bhoumya's residence in the evening and threw stones and lighted torches at the building. Bhoumya was outside when the attack took place, but the building was severely damaged. Pralamba and Chanur lived within the palace compound and therefore their houses were spared. A day later, a mob threw lighted torches inside the palace compound. For several days, anyone in uniform, whether of the army or the police, was stoned by the residents. At several places there were pitched battles between the army and the residents. Finally, the army regrouped itself and conducted marches in the town, swooped down on the protesters, arrested the bad characters of every locality and finally restored order. However, the incident permanently scalded the memory of the people of Mathura.

Six months later, Bhoumya's body was found in a drain on the outskirts of Mathura. There were strangulation marks on his neck.

A year thereafter, Pralamba met the same fate....

Whispers spread like a wildfire throughout the kingdom. *'The eighth son of Devaki is alive and out on his mission... The Deliverer is here... The end of Kansa is nigh... Glory to God... Glory to Lord Vishnu....'*

'Chanur, it's the eighth son of Devaki at work again. Bhoumya and Pralamba have gone...it may be my turn next time. My fate is inching towards me....'

XI

Kanha and Radha

So I love you because I know no other way than this
where I does not exist, nor you
so close that your hand on my chest is my hand
so close that your eyes close as I fall asleep

...Pablo Neruda

That afternoon, like all afternoons, a group of maidens in their mid and late teens, assembled at the banyan grove from their respective Gop villages. Their multicoloured *ghagras* fluttered in the wind. They carried empty earthen pitchers on their head and waist to fill water from the Yamuna. While waiting for the other members of their group to arrive, they gossiped and chatted about their husbands, fiancés and home. The three married girls grouped around the recently wedded bashful Harini, wrenching out from her in hushed conspiratorial tones, facts about her newly acquired conjugal bliss. Two of the unmarried girls tried to peep into the conversation, but were sternly shown the door.

Today there was a new member in the group—a pretty lass named Radha. Her father Vrishbhanu hailed from the Gop village of Barsana but had shifted to Kashi with his family. It was only recently that he had returned to his ancestral house at Barsana and busied himself with tilling the land and looking after the cattle. The other girls milled around her asking questions about Kashi, about her family and herself and introducing one another.

When their entire group had arrived, they proceeded in a single file towards the Yamuna. As they neared the

Yamuna, a soft moist breeze filled the air, the scent of moist earth ecstasised the senses and the sound of flowing water soothed the ears.

After snaking their way for a few furlongs, the caravan reached the Sati Anasuya ghat. Named after Sati Anasuya, it was a women's only ghat. It is said that Anasuya was famed for devotion to her husband. The trinity of Brahma, Vishnu and Shiva wanted to test her. They took the form of sages and reached her ashram, which was situated next to this ghat. Anasuya greeted them and paid obeisance. However, when she wanted to serve them food, the sages said that they would accept food only if Anasuya served them without her clothes. Faced with the dilemma of choosing between her devotion to her husband and serving guests who were akin to gods, Anasuya transformed the trinity, who had disguised themselves as sages, into suckling babies and then, shedding her clothes, fed them from her breasts as a mother. No wonder, she is regarded as a great *sati* and worshipped even by gods.

The girls prayed at the temple of Sati Anasuya and then proceeded to the ghat. Safe in the knowledge that no male would venture in, they shed their clothes and waded into the water. They splashed water over one another in mirth. Their laughter rippled through the water, sending the water birds in flight across the sky. Finally, as the amber in the sky darkened to crimson, the girls finished their play, dressed up and filled their earthen pitchers with water. Then, with one pitcher on their head and another in their waist, they walked back to the villages.

Just half a furlong before the banyan grove, suddenly a stone whizzed past and struck the earthen pitcher Radha carried on her head. A moment later, another stone whizzed past and broke the pitcher she carried on her waist. As the pitchers broke and Radha was drenched in water and tears, sounds of muffled laughter and running footsteps behind the neighbouring trees were heard.

'Ohh, it's that naughty Kanha at his work again,' said Mandavi.

'He must have taken a fancy to you, Radha,' Laxmi could not repress her smile. 'Chandravali, see your Kanha is fooling around with others.'

'You know, day before yesterday Kanha kissed Chandravali. She told me today,' shouted Brinda, even as Chandravali tried to close her mouth with her hands.

'What... What...?' a clamour ensued. 'Tell us about it.'

'Yes, yes,' Brinda continued as Chandravali hid her face. 'Yesterday Chandravali was walking home from the banyan grove when Kanha accosted her and started conversing with her. And when they reached a secluded spot, he kissed her and fled.'

'And Chandravali has not washed her face till now!' Mandavi joked.

'Who is this Kanha who feels free to tease the girls of the village?' The girls had forgotten all about Radha. Her sobbing voice stopped them in their tracks.

'O come on, Radha, don't make a mountain of a molehill of such small incidents. Kanha is the son of our headman Nandrai*ji*. He is a very sweet and handsome guy. It's just that he and his gang of ten regularly plays pranks on us. See, our Chandravali is besotted with him.' Brinda chided her.

'I don't know what you think, but I feel that breaking the water pitchers is a very insensitive prank, if it can be called a prank at all. We girls trudge a long way from home to fill our pitchers and then if they are broken, we have to go back a long way to fill it up. Do we not have any other work but to go up and down filling our pitchers again and again? Let this Kanha go one day to fill the pitchers and he will understand.' Radha's voice was full of indignation.

'You are right, Radha,' Kalyani said. 'The other day when he broke my pitcher, the evening was nigh and I had to again go in the dark to fill it. It was so frightening going alone to the river in the dark....'

Two other girls also supported Radha and Kalyani. 'You both are right. We must take some steps to ensure that these boys do not repeat such acts in future. But what is there to be done?'

'Have you not complained to Kanha's parents about this?' Radha asked.

'Yes, yes, several times. Each time Yashoda*ji* has rebuked Kanha but to no avail.'

'Come with me. I will ensure that after this time Kanha will never break anyone's pitcher.'

Some girls accompanied Radha to Kanha's house, while others went back to their homes.

Kanha was not at home. Yashoda received the girls with great warmth and made them comfortable. Radha narrated the incident. 'You see, *Chachi,* this breaking of pitchers has been going on for a long time. We cook, wash dishes, keep the house clean, bring water, take care of the cows, feed them, milk them, take care of the children, take lunch to the fields for the menfolk... We go a long way to bring water from the river to our house. If someone breaks the water-filled pitchers, we have to go back to our house or to the market, get new pitchers, go back to the river, fill it and then return home. That takes a lot of our time and effort. For what? Just to satisfy Kanha's wish to play pranks? *Chachi,* it is time he was sensitised to our conditions and made to respect us all.'

'You are right, Radha. I have rebuked Kanha on numerous occasions but he does not seem to change. What do you propose I should do?'

'*Chachi,* since Kanha has broken my pitchers, he should get two pitchers, fill them up with water and deliver at my house, unaided by any other. And *Chachi,* my family shall not touch a drop of water till Kanha delivers the pitchers at my doorstep.' Radha got up, touched Yashoda's feet and left. The other girls followed her.

Never had Kanha felt so insulted in his life. In the beginning he had outrightly denied having broken the pitchers. Then he refused to carry pitchers to Radha's house. Finally, after his mother said that he would see her dead face if he did not comply, he took two pitchers and went out. But that was not the end of the matter. The children of the village followed him, singing songs and cracking jokes on him. An aspiring child poet impromptu composed two lines and the entire band of children took it up, shouting in a cacophony of voices:

'With a pitcher on his waist
Kanha walks with a woman's gait,
Another pitcher on his head,
Next he'll wear bangles red.'

The procession went on till the ghat on Yamuna where Kanha filled the pitchers and thereafter went to Radha's house at Barsana.

Kanha's dark face had assumed the colour of red hot coal. That night, despite Yashoda's fervent persuasions, he did not eat. Sleep eluded him. Each time he closed his eyes, the scenes from his carrying pitchers to Radha's place, floated before his eyes.

Radha...Radha...Radha... Radha's face danced before his eyes. She had such a beautiful face and such evocative eyes. In fact he had virtually fallen in love at first sight. Even now he was finding it difficult to hate her. But Radha must pay for the insult she had brought to him, Kanha decided. Something that she would remember for a lifetime. But how?

The next morning Kanha woke up with a fever which continued to haunt him for two further days. And, even as fever scorched his body, the spectre of revenge scorched his mind. It was finally a week before a smile returned to Kanha's face and he put his favourite flute to his lips....

It was a bright day and the Sun had tilted a bit towards the west when the maidens descended at the Sati Anusuya ghat and into the cool waters of the Yamuna. Their bare bodies appeared like a flock of swans gliding on the dark waters of the river. For an hour they played and swam free of all cares and tensions, when suddenly the melodious strains of a flute startled them. This was Sati Anusuya ghat, out of bounds for all men. And yet there was no mistaking Kanha's flute. The girls buried their bodies in water and looked frantically around. And suddenly Vimala shouted: 'Where have our clothes gone?'

'Whaaaat?' the other girls shouted in unison and turned their heads towards the steps of the ghat. The clothes had disappeared. And then they all turned their heads towards the direction from which the strains of music emanated. A multicoloured heap lying beneath a *kadamba* tree grabbed their attention.

'There, there are our clothes,' a cacophony of voices shouted out. Immediately they raised their vision to the top of the tree. There was Kanha, perched on a branch playing his flute apparently in deep concentration, unmindful of the surroundings.

'Kanha, give our clothes back right now.' The voices were in unison.

'I am not holding your clothes,' Kanha shouted back. 'Come and get them yourselves.'

'You scoundrel, give us the clothes and get lost immediately or the curse of Sati Anusuya will be upon you.' Kalyani threatened.

'I am sitting on a tree which is the creation of God. God has not prohibited males from this area. I have as much right to come here as you all.' A smiling Kanha said defiantly.

'See how well he speaks!' Chandravali whispered. 'He has stopped even Kalyani in her tracks.'

'Kanha, give back our clothes,' Mandavi warned.

'Why don't you come and get them yourself?'

'You very well know it is not possible.'

'Ah yes, I forgot. You have put on weight and don't want to show your flab…' Kanha laughed.

'You rascal, am I fat? I will thrash you when I come out.'

'Well, I dare not say untruth in this pious place,' Kanha retorted.

A roar of laughter followed even as Mandavi rolled her eyes and showed her fist.

The girls threatened, implored, shouted, cajoled, reprimanded, prayed and begged in turns. Kanha merely smiled. 'Come and get the clothes yourselves if you want, otherwise stay there as you are.'

The Sun had moved several degrees further west. The girls were progressively getting tired. Mandavi and Dhara burst into tears.

'I think I will go and get my clothes,' Chandravali said, while trying to catch weeds flowing by to cover herself.

'Are you mad?' Brinda and Kalyani castigated her.

'You know, I regard Kanha as my husband. In my heart of hearts, I have given him my body, my mind, my possessions. He is my Lord. Why then should I be ashamed before him?'

Brinda held her back. 'Don't be stupid. Actually all this is because of Radha. Kanha is taking revenge for the humiliation he faced the other day. He is today waiting for Radha to go to him for her clothes.'

'As far as I am concerned, I prefer death to dishonour.'

Everybody turned around. It was Radha. Her face radiated the red of the setting Sun. 'If Kanha is happy with my clothes, so be it. He shall not get my body. That shall go to Yamuna*ji*. I am sorry you all had to suffer because of me. Goodbye my friends....'

As the girls watched in horror, Radha held her nose tight with her fingers and dived into the waters. A collective shout went out—'Radha is drowning herself, Radha is drowning....'

The flute stopped.

'Kanha, are you mad? Can't you see Radha is committing suicide because of your stupid act?' Mandavi shrieked.

Mandavi's shriek struck Kanha like a bolt from the blue. With a start, he jumped down from the tree. In an instant he collected an armful of clothes, threw them at the steps of the ghat. 'Here are your clothes, I am leaving, please... please do not drown yourself. I am leaving. Forgive me for what I have done.' Then he ran out of the ghat as fast as he could.

The girls pulled out Radha. She had ingested a lot of water. Her face was red from lack of breath. Her friends lay her on her back on the ghat and got the water out of her system. By and by she came around. It was almost nearing sunset when the maidens started on their way back. A little beyond the ghat, Kanha stood with folded hands.

'Forgive me all of you. I was just joking and never knew it would turn this way. I will never do it again.'

Radha turned her face and walked away. So did all the other girls. Kanha's face fell. He waited for a few moments and then silently walked away.

The next morning, as Radha plucked flowers for worship, Kanha approached her.

'Forgive me, Radha. What I did yesterday was plain stupidity. I will never attempt any such thing in the future.'

Radha's face contorted in anger and disgust. Just one word came out of her mouth: '*Chhi!*' She overturned her flower-filled basket and rushed inside the safety of her home.

'Chhi!'

A small word, yet it sank in Kanha's heart deeper than a dagger. It seemed Radha had given expression to what the whole world thought of him. His head bowed, his limbs bereft of purpose, Kanha turned back and walked on, leaning heavily on his cowherd's staff as he walked. The flute remained tied to his waist. The tune had somehow broken off. He zombied past the meadows, the groves, the canals and the fields. He did not feel the morning sun, nor heard the chirping of birds. The only sound that resonated in his entire being was that utter of disgust: '*Chhi!*'

He reached the banks of the Yamuna and started walking in the opposite direction to Sati Anusuya ghat. He trudged through purposeless and directionless, still leaning on his staff, still with unseeing eyes. The morning Sun kept company, travelling with him towards the noon. The only other companion being the Yamuna which flowed past. Only if it could wash off the past....

Was it his sixth sense or an almost inaudible growl that stopped Kanha in his tracks, it was difficult to say. His mind came out of the stupor in which it had been since morning and his unseeing eyes started taking stock of the absolutely still and silent surroundings. And in a moment he realised where he was. It was Kaliadah, the territory of a mighty black king cobra, who was called *Kalia Nag* by the people. The serpent was huge, estimated to be about thirteen cubits in length, with a pernicious hood.

It had come ashore around a year back and dug its burrow somewhere in this area. Over the past year, it had decimated all of the marine, land and even avian life in this and the adjoining areas. Every attempt to kill it had failed. It would hide at a place where it would be impossible to trace him and then suddenly strike at the returning hunt party. In fact, during the last attempt about six months back, two people had died and thereafter further attempts to kill it had been abandoned.

Kanha held his staff in an attacking stance and rolled his eyes over the surroundings. He cast a piercing glance at the ground, at the trees and the shrubbery. Then he turned around and repeated the act. Turning back, he took a few tentative steps forward, all the time in readiness for a strike. Again he looked back to ensure he was not taken by surprise. He sharpened his ears, waiting for that elusive growl like hiss that king cobras emanate. And it was then that he heard a soft slithering sound followed by a murmur amongst the dried leaves. Kanha bent down and picked up a fistful of dust. Then, his senses on the edge, he stood still, the stick and dust held in readiness, his eyes on the prowl.

A sudden violent hiss at his back had Kanha turn round like a top. The serpent had silently approached from the back and taken Kanha by surprise. The Messenger of Death was jet black in colour with pale yellow cross bands running along its body. On seeing Kanha, it hissed out loud and started rising on its tail. Its pale yellow belly with smooth scales shone in the sunlight. Within an instant it had risen to a height of almost four cubits. Its black hood started expanding. The crescent white line on the hood became visible as were the two curved fangs that came out from the two sides of its mouth. Its eyes were fixed on Kanha as its forked tongue went in and out.

Whether it was design or a plain instinct for survival, Kanha threw the fistful of dust into the serpent's eyes.

The mighty cobra, which was in the process of springing on Kanha, momentarily got blinded. It nevertheless brought its hood down, but Kanha had by then stepped away and brought his staff down on the serpent with a thud. The staff missed the hood and fell on the neck. Had it been an ordinary vertebrate, the force of the blow would have fractured the vertebra. But it was *'the Kalia Nag'*. It absorbed the blow and swung around. The power of vision is only a lesser used power of serpents and Kanha's movements gave him away. The serpent opened its hood and readied himself to launch the next attack. Like a blazing meteor, the angry serpent blitzed across the ground towards Kanha. But the split second delay in ascertaining the position of Kanha proved costly for Kalia. Kanha immediately jumped and as the snake passed under him, he again brought his staff down upon it with all the force that he had. The blow struck Kalia just below his skull and momentarily paralysed him. And that moment was sufficient for Kanha to pick up a stone from the ground and hurl it at the hood. A loud hiss emanated as the hood was mauled. But Kalia was no ordinary serpent. With astounding speed it stood up on its tail, swung itself on the branch of a nearby tree and then suddenly it let go of its body and like an arrow unleashed from a bow, cut through the air towards Kanha. Kanha had not contemplated such an aerial attack but with an involuntary reflex he bent back and the serpent-arrow whizzed past his surprised eyes and lodged in a big thorny bush three cubits away. Without losing a moment, Kanha thrashed the bush with his stick and as he did so, the serpent was pushed further inside the thorny bush and got entangled therein. The thorns of the bush cut into the serpent's skin. Its tail lashed around outside the bush. Several times it struck Kanha like a whiplash, cutting into his skin and drawing blood with every stroke, but Kanha kept up the assault. Finally the serpent was able to bring half its body out of the bush but the posterior half got entangled. And as it struggled to bring its entire body out, Kanha rained blows on the hood with all his force, crushing parts of it and turning it into a squashy jelly. It was after a very long duration that Kalia was able to wrench itself free from the thorn bush, but its condition had become pitiable. Its hood was crushed and its skin had ripped open in parts. The entire body was drenched in blood. Sapped of energy, Kalia drifted off into unconsciousness, even as Kanha continued to rain blows with his staff finally reducing the mighty serpent to a pulp.

At long last he relented and lay down on the bare ground. Exhausted to his last breath and shocked at such a close brush with death, Kanha drifted between the conscious and the unconscious. After a long time he regained his moorings and went down to the river to wash off and quench his parched throat. Finally, with stumbling steps, Kanha set out for his home. He could not however go very far. With supreme effort he managed to hoist himself on the village road and collapsed in a heap.

It was afternoon and the village maidens were again on their way to the ghat.

It was Dhara who first spotted someone sprawled on the road. The girls rushed and found it was Kanha, with injury marks all over his body and his clothes drenched in blood. Two girls brought a pitcher full of water and poured on him. Slowly, Kanha revived.

'What happened to you?' 'Who did it to you?' 'Who attacked you?' A hundred questions simultaneously followed from the girls.

'Kalia Nag attacked me...I killed him.' Kanha answered and again fell back, exhausted.

The news spread like wildfire all over the village and all the villagers came out. They went to Kaliadah, checked out the remains of the once mighty serpent and consigned it to the river. They took turns to carry Kanha on their shoulder to his home and laid him on the bed.

Kanha remained under medication for two days, but the duration was far from restful. Again and again he relived the events of the two days—the events at the Sati Anusuya ghat and the encounter with the serpent. Finally, he opened his eyes and there was Radha seated on the bedside with some other girls.

'Forgive me, Radha,' he murmured.

The girls giggled. 'You have asked for forgiveness from Radha at least ten times in your sleep. This is the eleventh time.'

Radha lowered her eyes. 'It is alright, Kanha. I know you have truly repented your deed. But you need not have put your life in danger in this manner. We are all very concerned about you.'

Kanha's lips curved into a smile of satisfaction and he finally dozed off into a deep sleep.

Kanha had now become a hero in the community. He had done what the entire village had failed to do in several attempts. And, as pointed out by Soham *kaka,* even when the serpent got entangled in the thorn bush, he did not flee the spot but risked his life to beat the serpent to death. The village elders convened a meeting to honour him and alongwith other gifts, gave him a tourniquet with a peacock feather. 'Like the peacock is the king of birds, may you grow to be a king of men,' they blessed.

For the rest of his life, Kanha donned a peacock feather in remembrance of the men and the honour they conferred.

The recognition brought upon a watershed in the life of Kanha. The prankster was gone and replaced by a more matured young man, who now took direct part in the affairs of the village. Whether it be ensuring the huts were freshly thatched before the monsoon or getting the roads repaired, Kanha took a lot of load off his father. He led the villagers in cleaning the riverbank of all the litter and in desilting of the canals. No wonder the Gops had started referring to him as the *Chhota Mukhiya.* The village maidens no longer had to bear his pranks, rather became his close friends. More so, Radha....

Since the day Radha had come to his bedside, not a single day had passed that they did not meet. They met at the meadow, at the riverside, in the forest, at the Govardhan hills and at times even at Vrindavan.

'Where did you learn to play the flute, Kanha?' Radha asked, her head resting on Kanha's shoulder.

'My father taught me to play the flute. I was very young at that time and since then the flute has been my constant companion.'

'When you play, I lose myself in your music.'

'And I lose myself when I see you, Radha. You are so very beautiful.'

'You are also so very handsome, Kanha.'

'Well, it is nice to hear, but you very well know as I do that it is false. You are like the golden full moon when it first rises from the east, while I am like a dark cloud that eclipses your beauty.'

'This monsoon, each dark cloud will remind me of you,' Radha murmured.

Kanha smiled. 'Then I will pray for an overcast sky every day this monsoon so that I am always in your thoughts.'

'Well, only a few days remain for Lord Indra's *puja.* Let us together go and pray to Lord Indra that day.'

'Radha, I always have my reservations on worshipping Lord Indra. See his character. He is always busy watching the dance of the celestial nymphs and feasting his thousand eyes on other people's wives.'

'Kanha, Indra is the King of Gods. Being a King he is entitled to his privileges. Besides, don't forget he is the slayer of Vrittasura and is also the Lord of Rain. He must be appeased so that there is neither flood nor famine.'

'Whatever you say, Radha, I still do not agree. How can you forget that it was Lord Indra who disguised himself as Rishi Gautam and violated Ahalya in her husband's absence? When you worship such a God, you are setting a very bad example for the society.'

'But what of protection from floods and famine?'

'Radha, we are mainly cowherds, not farmers. Rather we should worship our Mount Govardhan. It is Mount Govardhan which traps the clouds and ensures rains in Mathura. Our cattle graze there, we get all our medicinal herbs from there, it is also a line of defence for us. In fact, this time I have resolved to ask our community to shun the worship of Lord Indra and start worshipping Mount Govardhan.'

'Kanha, I agree fully with what you say. But, will you be able to change a custom that has been in vogue for generations?'

'Generations change, Radha. So why should not custom? There is need to bring in new ideas, take note of the changed situations and modify our customs, so that they reflect our present beliefs and remain relevant to our present age.'

But convincing the others indeed proved a very tough proposition. Nandrai indulged Kanha by convening a general meeting of all the Gops and allowed him to explain his stand to the villagers. And expectedly, the villagers opposed vehemently.

'*Lalla,* don't dare to challenge the might of Lord Indra. He wields the thunder as his weapon and can cause both drought and floods. If we don't appease him, we are all gone.'

'But *Kaka,* can you worship someone whose values you cannot respect? Can you respect a person who is wholly bereft of character?'

'*Lalla,* don't compare mere mortals like us with gods or even kings. Gods and kings can do anything but we can't. Our norms of morality do not apply to them.'

'*Kaka,* do we need to bow merely before power? Should we not make a united move to change the system? Whether it be the gods or the king, none can survive before an united opposition. If everybody unites in resolve not to worship or be ruled by a tyrant, both the God and the king will change their ways and become benevolent.'

'*Lalla,* be careful of what you speak. You are too young to comprehend the cruel world. The words you speak can land you in prison. And as to the point raised by you, if you want to ignore Lord Indra, you do so at your own peril. The entire world worships Lord Indra and it makes no difference to his position whether a few Gops worship him or not. But, if per chance he notices our impertinence and wants to punish, then we are all done for.'

'*Kaka,* you worship Lord Indra because you are afraid of the consequences of not worshipping him. On the other hand, our Mount Govardhan is a benevolent God who showers us with his blessings. Yet, merely because he does not pose any threat of destruction, you refuse to worship him.'

'*Lalla,* I do not agree with you and I am sure the other villagers don't either. *Mukhiyaji,* you decide.'

Nandrai got up from his seat. 'Soham *kaka,* since Kanha is my son, it is not proper for me to speak on this subject. In any case, it is the collective decision of the villagers that will count. What Kanha has said is correct from his perspective and what you all have said is also correct. But, there is a third perspective which seems to have been missed out in this debate and which just came to my mind while listening to you all.'

'Yes, yes, *Mukhiyaji,* please speak out.'

Nandrai cleared his voice before speaking. 'You see, we Gops are different from the Yadavas. We were driven out from our lands by the Yadava King to construct the capital at Mathura and resettled far away. Even today, the Yadavas look down upon us even though, as the rearers of the sacred cow, we stand on a higher pedestal. Yet, instead of creating and nurturing our own unique identity, we have tended to copy them in all things, both material and spiritual. We worship Lord Indra as the Yadavas and other Aryans do, although He has no special connection with us Gops. On the other hand, we live in the shadow of Mount Govardhan. If today we start worship of Mount Govardhan, it will imbue us with a special identity. If we do not develop a special identity today, in the near future, we shall be regarded as a servant class of the Yadavas and consigned to the *Shudra* caste. I am not meaning any disrespect to Lord Indra. What I stated is purely from a political perspective, of the need of the Gops to forge a separate identity.'

An excited buzz went round in the crowd.

'Well said, *Mukhiyaji*. This did not occur to any of us.'

'Let us make Mount Govardhan the symbol of our Gop identity.'

A week later, the Indra temple at Vrindavan was a beehive of activity. But, this year was different from the previous years—there was no representation from the Gops.

And then there was the deluge....

The first ten days of the month of *Aashad* had been oppressively hot. A huge dark cloud had built up in the sky but the villagers kept waiting in vain for the time when the bounty of rain would satiate the parched earth and bring succour from the heat. Performing the daily chores had become oppressive. The Gops would somehow take the cattle to the burning meadows but the cows would hardly graze. The output of milk had registered a sharp decline. Even Kanha's flute had fallen silent.

That night, even as the villagers tossed around in their beds unable to sleep, there was a low growling sound of thunder from the skies.

Moments before the break of dawn, the Gops were jolted out of their sleep by the sudden roar of a thousand lions. It was as if the skies had come crashing down. And as they leapt out of their beds, there was the sound of waterfall outside the huts. Within moments, in many of the huts, parts of the thatched roof had come crashing down and the water poured down inside in torrents.

'It's a cloudburst, it's a cloudburst!' exclaimed Nandrai. Outside, the raindrops had merged with one another to form a continuous stream of water that poured down with the ferocity of a waterfall.

One *prahar* passed by, then another, then another. The fury of the pouring waters continued unabated. Slowly, Nandrai's house, which had till then withstood the relentless onslaught due to double thatching on the roof, filled up with villagers and their families, whose huts had come crashing down. The roads outside resembled gushing rivulets and the water level was slowly rising. Most of the Gop huts were built on a pedestal and therefore the rising waters had not yet entered them. But for how long, Nandrai wondered. Inside the hut, anxious faces looked up to him for deliverance. Nandrai tried to conceal his helplessness and chatted up the gathering, knowing that in times of calamity, the most important thing was to keep up the morale of people.

For one full day, the cloudburst raged over the Gop villages. Mathura and the other surrounding areas had heavy rains but were spared the onslaught of the cloudburst. The next morning, the cloud that burst was spent, but fresh dark clouds wafted in, resulting in heavy rains. The water level which had been momentarily arrested, started rising again, almost reaching waist level.

'Baba...' Kanha called Nandrai aside. 'Baba, there does not seem to be any respite from the rains. If this continues, then the rising water level on the streets will enter our homes. Moreover, Yamuna*ji* will overflow its banks and bring calamity on us.'

'Yes, Kanha, I have also been thinking of the same thing. And now that the course of Yamuna*ji* has been shifting, our villages stand in greater danger than ever before of being inundated.'

'Baba, there is nothing that we can do at this juncture except relocate.'

'But where, *Lalla*? Where would so many people get a roof over their head? Had it been earlier, the palace would have opened its gates. But with King Kansa? He would rather order a massacre. In fact, in hindsight it seems we did a very wrong thing in stopping worship of Lord Indra. It is His anger that has led to all this. You are young, but I ought to have known better....' Nandrai struck his fist on his forehead.

'Baba, please do not despair. We stopped worship of Lord Indra and decided to worship Mount Govardhan instead. And now it is Mount Govardhan who will save us. It is He who will provide shelter to all of us.'

'What are you talking about, *Lalla*? Are you out of your senses? This is not a joke.' Nandrai's voice now had a hint of anger.

'Baba, remember, you had told me about the times of King Andhaka when the displaced Gops had first taken shelter in Mount Govardhan before they were resettled in these villages?'

'Yes, yes but this is not the time for stories, *Lalla*.'

'Baba, while grazing the cattle, I have discovered a huge cave in Mount Govardhan with a secret opening which can accommodate hundreds of people. I think it was the cave which our forefathers had used at that time. We can use it now to house all of us till this problem subsists. It is situated on a higher level and there will be no danger from floods also.'

'Are you sure, *Lalla*? Is it true?' Nandrai's voice quivered.

'Yes Baba. How can I speak any untruth to you?'

Nandrai hugged Kanha. 'You have solved my problem, *Lalla.* God bless you.'

A *prahar* later, a caravan of people and cattle emerged in the pouring rain from the Gop villages. They waded through waist-high water, holding hands to maintain their balance. Their destination—Mount Govardhan. The torrential rains pounded them, the muddy swirling waters attempted to sweep them away and yet they trudged, hand in hand, silent yet determined, in the footsteps of their forefathers. Kanha led the way, Radha beside him, while the others followed.

Slowly the caravan reached the foothills of Mount Govardhan and then began the ascent. Leaving the cattle to graze in the foothills under the canopy of trees, the people began the ascent through slippery rocks and dangerous crevices. A little way up, Kanha turned away from the trodden path and climbed up a few rocks. Then sweeping aside a big thorny bush, he uncovered a hole.

Nandrai had crept behind him. 'This is the opening to the cave?' His voice exuded his disappointment. '*Lalla,* you had said that the cave can house hundreds?'

'Baba, the entrance is small. One has to creep through for a few yards. Then there is a big space. Trust me, Baba, there will be no problem.'

Kanha took the lead and crept inside the hole. One by one the others followed him. A few yards of crawling led them to a wide rocky corridor with a height just enough to stand. The corridor winded through and branched into myriad other passages. Kanha was not wrong. Although low roofed, the corridor and the passages were sufficient to house a few hundred people. Nandrai hugged Kanha. So did the others.

For seven days it rained continuously. It was as if the skies had sucked up and stored in them the entire waters of a sea. The plains below the foothills of Mount Govardhan actually resembled a stormy sea, with trees, houses and dead animals flowing past. Like a mother's womb, Mount Govardhan shielded the Gops from the vagaries of weather outside.

On the eighth day, the Lord of Rains finally gave up and the clouds gave way to a bright sunshine. And as Soham *kaka* brought the news, the cave erupted with jubilation. The villagers hugged each other and Kanha and rushed out to see and soak in the Sun. It was a victory over Lord Indra—a victory made possible by Kanha and Mount Govardhan.

It took three more days before the floodwaters receded and the Gops could descend to the plains. But it was only the beginning. The floodwaters had left behind a trail of muck and devastation. The villages had to be virtually rebuilt from scratch. Yet they were thankful that they and their families were all alive. And as they left the foothills of Mount Govardhan, they turned back and paid obeisance to their new Lord. They would come back to worship Him every year, on the day after *Kartick amavasya*. No longer was the name of Lord Indra uttered in the Gop villages. Lord Govardhan was now the Protector of the Gops. And Kanha was now the unofficial leader of the Gop youth brigade.

Spring had come. The trees, laden with flowers, swayed in the fragrant breeze, welcoming the King of Seasons.

Vasantotsav, the festival of Spring, was a celebration of youth, love and friendship. Every year the festival was celebrated with music, dance and merriment, not only in Mathura but the entire Aryavarta. Young men and women went about with their lovers, seeking solitude in the groves, forests, gardens and riverside, where they professed their love for one another. Friends gathered in groups to sing, dance and celebrate in gay abandon.

Kanha led his friends, Radha and a few other *Gopinis* inside the forest. They passed deep into the forest, by the flowering *kadamba, champa* and *gulmohar* trees, around caressing couples and nestling birds till they came to a small brook. Beside the brook was a grove of trees and bushes in which nestled a beautiful little bower. Inside, the floor was of velvety grass and a canopy of leaves and flowers formed the ceiling. Just outside the bower, from the branch of a tree, hung a swing decorated with flowery creepers.

'I have made it over the months for all of us,' Kanha proudly showed them about.

'It's so…so beautiful…just beyond words…,' Radha mumbled.

As Radha went round the place, two piles of something red and yellow caught her attention.

'What are these piles, Kanha? This yellow one I am sure is turmeric and the red one I think is ochre powder used for painting. Why have you kept these here, Kanha?'

Kanha bent and picked up a little of both the red and yellow powders and brought it close for Radha to inspect. And then suddenly he smeared Radha's cheeks with the colours.

For a moment Radha stood undecided—a cheek painted yellow and the other red. And then in a flash she picked up a handful each of the two powders and ran after Kanha. A roll of laughter ensued and soon all hell broke loose.

Everyone smeared each other with the colours. Very soon, each of their faces and dresses were coloured in red and yellow and even the ground they trod on had assumed those colours. Laughing and panting they collapsed beside the brook, when a spray of water startled them. Kanha had waded in the brook and was splashing water at them with his hands.

'You naughty fellow, we'll teach you a lesson,' a collective roar went up. And soon a dozen boys and girls jumped into the brook and splashed water on one another.

Yadu was the first to get out of water. He took out his drum and started beating it. Soon the others trooped out of the water. Drenched to the skin, their bodies danced in tribal rhythm to the beat of drums. Kanha danced with each of the *Gopinis* and each of them felt as if she was the centre of his attention.

In the midst of the revelry, suddenly Kanha found Radha missing. He came out immediately and started searching for her. After sometime he spotted her sitting beside the brook, behind a bush. He went and sat beside her.

'What happened, my love?'

Radha shook her head.

'Nothing, Kanha. You go, the *Gopinis* must be waiting for you.'

'Oh, so that's the thing. You are jealous, Radha. Are you not?' Kanha smiled.

'Yes, I am. So? What does it matter to you?' Radha voice was both indignant and petulant. 'You profess your love to me and then go and cavort with the *Gopinis*?'

'Radha, you shine like the full moon in my heart while the other *Gopinis* are like mere twinkling stars. There is no comparison between you and the others. It is just that my father taught me that when someone approaches you with love, he or she becomes a part of your being, however miniscule and you cannot turn them away.'

'Your example is flawed, Kanha,' Radha smiled sadly. 'The full moon wanes till there is no moon at all. Then even the full moon is prone to eclipse. Just remember one thing. If at any time in your life, the moon in your heart wanes or is eclipsed either by reason of your work or love for another, you will never find me in your life again.'

'That will never be, Radha. You are my muse and will remain so throughout my life.'

Kanha took Radha's hand in his and turned his fulsome gaze into her deep eyes. And then like the sky descends on land at the horizon, his face descended on hers. Her moist lips were sucked into his parched ones like a drop of rain loses itself in the desert. The two bodies turned into one. Time stood still. Only the sound of two hearts beating in unison, resonated through the universe.

That evening, when they returned home, each of them felt fulfilled as never before. Something had changed in their lives. It was also a day that would not come to them again…a day for which each of them would yearn till the last moment of their lives.

Part III

XII
The Wrestling Bout

The entire world is a wrestling arena where mind wrestles with heart, greed with conscience, hope with despair

...The Author

That day all roads led to Akrur's countryhouse on the outskirts of Mathura. The occasion being the annual *mallayudh* competition that had over the last few years become a celebrated fixture in the city's calendar. Several arenas for *mallayudh* had been set up in the vast compound. In each arena, the soil had been carefully prepared by mixing ghee and other ingredients. The wrestlers called *mallas*, flexed their triceps and exercised with heavy clubs, whirling them around their heads with practised ease. Some others rubbed clay all over their bodies and performed body-warming exercises, all under the watchful eyes of their gurus.

Mallayudh was a no-holds-barred form of wrestling. The *mallas* could punch their opponents, pull them by their hairs, bite them and in extreme cases, even gouge out the opponent's eyes. But these were mostly resorted to in war or in death combats where the issue was settled only by death of one of the combatants. Here, in exhibition tournaments, there were several restrictions on the combatants. Hitting below the belt was strictly forbidden as was inflicting any grievous injury on the face. These led to disqualification.

Akrur himself went round overseeing the arrangements. Short and stout, he had himself been a reputed *malla* in his youth. He had started this tournament, albeit on a much smaller scale, during the reign of King Ugrasen itself.

Akrur looked around. The *mallas* were practicing mock fights with one another, getting into the groove before the actual fight. Akrur's eyes fell on one a slim, dark young *malla* with a handsome face, who was practicing some kicks. How could such a comely lad even dare to take part in a *mallayudh* tournament, Akrur wondered. Yet there was something unusual about that *malla*. Akrur tarried for a few moments and soon the cause dawned upon him. The cherubic face disguised the body of an agile leopard. The muscles continued to ripple on completion of a successful kick even as his face broke into an innocent smile. Akrur's lips curled into a hint of a smile as he walked on, overseeing the arrangements.

It was Kanha's first *mallayudh* competition and a large number of his friends had come to cheer for him. This was the third year in succession that Gops were participating in the tournament. Three other Gop boys, apart from Kanha, were also participating. None of them had any formal training and merely relied on the skills developed during their cowherding periods. The quartet warmed up in unison and practised their kicks and moves on one another. Moments later, the bugle called participants to the arena.

The participants were divided into two categories on basis of their estimated weights. Those weighing two and half *maunds* or above were placed in the first category and those weighing below were placed in the second. The two categories were to have separate tournaments. Kanha naturally came in the second category. In the first category was Balarama, the son of Vasudeva and Rohini. Just a year older to Kanha, he nevertheless had a massive build and bulging biceps and was a trained wrestler.

The competition started in right earnest in both the categories. People crowded around the arenas, cheering and jeering the competitors in equal measure. Many placed bets on the outcome of the various bouts. The first bout that Kanha had was with a *malla* who was both taller and heavier than him. The very start was disastrous for Kanha as his opponent picked him up with ease and threw him on the floor. Undaunted, Kanha swung around, jumped and gave a flying right kick that hit his opponent on the shin and quickly followed it up with a left kick to the opponent's chest. The opponent, not used to flying kicks, was momentarily taken unaware and the next kick floored him. With blazing eyes he jumped up and sprinted towards Kanha, aiming to run him down under his massive body and crush him. At the very last moment however, Kanha swerved out of the way and tripped the opponent with his foot. The crash was severe and was followed by Kanha jumping on top of his floored opponent and punching him to submission.

Elsewhere, the *mallas* were busy grappling, punching and kicking one another. Perspiring bodies clashed with one another like massive trees in a storm. The entire atmosphere was electrified. The audience roared and clapped. Balarama was leading in the first category, pummelling through the opposition. In the second category, Kanha's unconventional pyrotechnics were flooring the opposition. The heavy-built *mallas* who were primarily used to grappling and punching, and using their reach to triumph over their opponents, had no answer to the aerial kicks, which was a new technique for them.

The first category final was expectedly won by Balarama. In the finals of the second category, Kanha was to take on Kodanda, the son of one of the Vrishni clan leaders.

The crowd was rooting for Kodanda and baying for Kanha's blood. The few Gops were like an island in the ocean and despite valiant full throated efforts, were thoroughly outshouted.

At first sight, the contest was a total mismatch. If there was one word to describe Kodanda, it was 'hulk'. He was the heaviest in the category and infamous as a bonecrusher. 'The two contestants are like a tiger and a deer,' someone in the crowd commented. The 'tiger' went around the arena, thumping his chest and flexing his bulging muscles. The crowd roared its approval. Kanha stood in his corner, his eyes momentarily shut in meditation, focusing his energies. When he opened his eyes, they blazed upon his opponent.

The bout started. Kodanda charged menacingly towards Kanha like an elephant, intending to throw his opponent down and trample him. Kanha parried the charge with a deft feint of his body and in the same motion kicked him in the back. And as the roar of the crowd ebbed, the Gops laughed out loud in derision. 'Come on Kanha, kick that fat asshead out of the arena. Yes, that's the way to go....'

The night was never darker than Kodanda's face at that instant. The kick on his back hardly displaced his bulky body, but it rattled his ego. With the speed of a spinning top he turned around, forced Kanha into a corner and pounced upon him. Raining punches all over Kanha's body, he closed in, gripped Kanha in a death embrace and threw him far away on the floor. Kanha landed on the floor with a thud even as Kodanda flexed his triceps and proceeded towards him. The 'Bonecrusher' ran a few steps and suddenly with outstretched hands, threw his two-and-half maund body into the air in Kanha's direction. A roar of approval went up from the crowd. But even before the roar reached its crescendo, Kanha slid forward on the ground on his back and kicked hard upwards. The vicious kick caught Kodanda's falling body on its chest and flung it to the side of the arena. A gasp escaped the crowd but even before they drew their breath, Kanha had flung himself on his opponent, hitting him with his elbows and raining punches on his body. Then he got up and with both hands, picked up his sprawled opponent's legs and held them above his shoulder.

With a swift movement Kodanda brought his legs into a scissor position around Kanha's neck and before the crowd could bat an eyelid, he had flung Kanha to the ground. Egged on by the hollering crowd, the opponents stood up and warily sized up one another. Kodanda moved his hand across his bleeding nose and brought it up. The sight of his own blood maddened him. This time he did not rush for Kanha, but moved with deliberate slow steps, in an effort to push his opponent into a corner and then give him an embrace of death. Kanha looked at Kodanda in the eye and kept backing away towards the north-eastern corner of the arena. The crowd was now on its toes, cheering their local favourite. The Gops, after their initial exult, fell into an apprehensive silence.

Kodanda reached the middle of the arena. Kanha had already backed down to the extreme corner. Kodanda's face contorted into a ghastly smile. He had got his opponent in the position he wanted. He stretched his arms wide, ready to catch Kanha should he attempt to flee. This was the moment he was waiting for. He took another calculated step in Kanha's direction. The crowd held its breath as a hush fell in the arena. 'Come on Kodanda,' someone shouted from the left side. Momentarily, Kodanda's attention wavered and in that instant, Kanha swung around and delivered a stinging kick that hit his opponent on the bridge of his nose and displaced him. What followed thereafter was one swinging kick after another as Kanha did not allow his opponent to regain his balance. Kodanda was clearly unsettled by the aerial onslaught. Kanha took advantage, got closer and started punching the hulk all over. The 'tiger' and the 'deer' had reversed their roles. The Gops regained their volubility while the majority of the audience fell into a sullen silence.

The decisive moment had come. As Kodanda cowered, his hands covering his face to protect against the blows, Kanha went back and with a short run, jumped in the air to deliver his famous aerial kick and finish the game. The kick was aimed at Kodanda's chest. Kodanda saw the kick coming at him with fearstruck eyes and backed down the arena. His backing down caused the kick to land on his groin instead of the chest where it was aimed. Kodanda doubled up in pain and sprawled on the ground clutching his groin.

The referee immediately stopped the fight. Moments later, as Kodanda recovered, the referee announced him as the winner! Kanha had been disqualified for hitting below the belt. Immediately a big cheer went up in the crowd.

The Gops protested vehemently. The hit was not intentional. It was a travesty of justice, they shouted. Clear case of partiality, they growled. Why allow the other communities to participate if none but a *Vrishni* could be declared a winner? Kanha sat in a corner, dejected, holding his head in his hands, his face darker than a pregnant cloud.

The gathering began to disperse. Kanha got up. It was time to leave. Suddenly one of Akrur's men came to him. 'Raja wants to meet you. Please come with me.'

They went inside the mansion into a room decorated with hunting trophies. Akrur, who was reclining on a cushion, looked up as they entered.

'Come, my boy,' Akrur bade Kanha to sit beside him. 'You fought very well today. It was a misfortune that you were disqualified.'

'Well Sir, I thought I should have won. The decision was not fair to me.'

'My boy, tell me, in life do all your acts get the result you deserved? There are good deeds for which you do not get rewarded and bad deeds for which you do not get punished. So, just as you accept God's will, so you should accept the verdict of the referee. Just give your best performance every time and very soon the rewards will follow you instead of the other way round. Remember, my boy, in every contest, the referee is always right.'

'Yes Sir.'

'Who is your father, my boy? Where do you live?'

'My father is Nandrai. He is the leader of the Gops. I live in Gokul.'

'Have you undergone any formal training in *mallayudh?* Who taught you all those aerial kicks?'

'No Sir, there is no formal training. I practise with my friends in the meadows where we graze our cattle. And as far as those kicks are concerned, I have developed them myself.'

Akrur's mouth opened in amazement. 'You developed those kicks yourself? That's amazing!'

'Thank you, Sir.'

'What is your name, my boy? I forgot.'

'Kanha, Sir.'

'Yes, yes, Kanha. Now Kanha, I would like you to come here and take formal training in *mallayudh* from a guru. Your talent must be further developed.'

'But Sir, today I virtually defeated all those who had learnt from gurus.'

'Kanha, my boy, in life, never forsake learning. And always remember, there is no end to learning. Remember the scissor grip by which your opponent floored you? And as for your aerial kicks, the others who have seen your techniques, will develop their answer to it by next year. In any case Kanha, a warrior must always add to his repertoire. I can make out that you are built to be a warrior. *Mallayudh* is not the be all and end all of training. Archery, fencing, chariot riding...these all are skills that you should develop. In life, you never know which knowledge saves you from the jaws of death.'

'Yes, Sir.'

'And of course, all costs shall be borne by me. You just have to come on the days ordained by the Guru and learn all you can.'

'I will, Sir. Thank you.'

Akrur took out a gold ring from his finger. 'Take this, my boy. This is my recognition for your efforts today. See, as I first said, you may not get what you expect but you may get what you don't expect. Now smile, my boy.'

Kanha's face broke into a smile. He bent down and touched Akrur's feet.

'God bless you. Your new Guru will also be here tomorrow morning.'

'Yes, Sir.' Kanha turned around and left.

The next morning onwards, thrice a week at the crack of dawn, Kanha would jump on one of the milk-laden bullock carts and proceed towards Akrur's countryhouse. There he trained with the other boys and learnt the various grips, techniques and styles of *mallayudh.* He was taught how to extricate himself from the various holds, how to block the punches and how to topple the opponents. He learnt to prepare the soil of the arena, the correct techniques of body building and breathing techniques for developing endurance.

That entire week, Akrur's countryhouse was a beehive of activity. Hectic preparations were on to welcome Akrur's guru—Rishi Sandipani. The countryhouse was adorned like a bride, decked up with flowers, garlands and strings of mango leaves.

Akrur called Kanha, Balarama and a few other chosen trainees. 'My boys, it is our good fortune that my guru, the esteemed Rishi Sandipani has graciously consented to set his foot on this land and be my guest. He is a sage of the highest order with profound knowledge and spiritual powers. I want that all of you should attend on him, benefit from his preaching and secure his blessings.'

The venerable Rishi Sandipani, his flowing white beard reaching upto his navel, his matted hair rolled in a massive bun over his head, his forehead smeared with sandal paste, with a vermillion mark at the centre, was addressing the trainees at Akrur's countryhouse. 'My children, there are only three things that can deflect your course and hold you back from achieving your dreams—ego, avarice and fear. Always remember, like the Sun sets and then rises again the next day, we all will die one day and then be reborn. Why should we harbour ego? We do not know what we were in our previous birth, nor do we know what we will be in our next. It all depends on our deeds. No work is low, no person is low, no creature is low. They are all part of our cosmos.

Now avarice. We have come empty handed into this world and shall go back empty-handed. All your material possessions will be left behind. Similarly, all your family and friends will leave you when you die and in a matter of years, even months, totally forget you. There is no point in committing sins to nurture those who after a time will leave you or forget you.

Finally fear. We will all die and we will all be reborn. This life is not the end of the journey, it is only a bridge between two unknowns. So, why get attached to it? If this life goes, another will come. So expend the life for a good cause. Live for your cause and die for your cause and your deeds will ensure that when you are reborn, it will be in positive surroundings. Why fear death? My children, look around you. If you see suffering and injustice, make it your life's cause to remedy it. If you succeed, you make this place itself a heaven. If you fail, your deeds will ensure that you go to heaven and your next life will be an exalted one.'

Two days after the initial sermon, Kanha got an opportunity of serving Rishi Sandipani in his room. The Guru lay sprawled on a mattress. Kanha massaged the Guru's legs as he sought to dispel his doubts. 'Guru*ji*, the other day you said that we will all be reborn. But the body is destroyed at death. How can a person be reborn?'

The Guru opened his eyes. 'My son, when we die, we return to the five elements—air, water, sky, earth and fire. And from these we are recreated by God into a new being. The new being may be a human, bird or even an insect. It all depends upon our deeds.'

'But that will be an entirely new creation. How can we relate it to our earlier life? I mean, how can we say that the new body contains that particular air, water, sky, earth and fire which the previous body had disintegrated into?' Kanha persisted.

'My son, it is our ignorance that prevents us from relating to the past. When absolute knowledge is attained, the darkness will give way to light.'

'But Guru*ji*, then a common man will never know whether he had any past life or what he was in that life?'

'My son, in rare cases, God himself shows the way. I give you a very recent example. My disciple is the *rajpurohit* of King Drupada of the Panchalas. He came to meet me a few days ago and told me that the youngest son of the King on attaining the age of five years, suddenly went into a trance and proclaimed that he was the incarnation of Amba, the erstwhile daughter of the King of Kashi and had been reborn to take vengeance on Bhishma, the regent of Hastinapur.'

'What? Why vengeance?'

'Bhishma had abducted Amba and her two sisters from the site of their *swayamvar* at Kashi because he felt insulted at not being invited to the ceremony. The two younger sisters got married to the Hastinapur King Vichitravirya but Amba was left out. Her lover King Salva refused to accept her since she had been abducted. When she came back to Bhishma, he too refused to marry her. In fact, Amba even got the legendary Rishi Parashuram to duel with Bhishma to avenge her insult, but that too failed. Bhishma was inconquerable. Finally, Amba prayed to Lord Shiva to resurrect her in her next life as a warrior who would take revenge upon Bhishma. This has now happened. Unless there is rebirth, how else will a five-year-old boy know about Amba and Bhishma?'

'But Guru*ji*, when Amba died and her body was destroyed, her entire identity was destroyed with it. It is not possible to recreate that particular air, water, sky, fire or earth that had constituted the earlier body. So, if there is a rebirth of the identity in a new body, it must mean that when the earlier body is destroyed, not all is destroyed. There must be something that survives when the body is destroyed, something that can give identity to the next and succeeding births?'

Guru Sandipani sat bolt upright. 'What is your name, my boy?'

'My name is Kanha, Guru*ji*.'

'Kanha...Kanha...but if I am not mistaken, when you came into the room, somebody was calling you by some other name....'

'Yes Guru*ji*, the other boys derisively call me Krishna because of my dark complexion.'

'My boy, from now on I will also call you Krishna. And, this is not in derision. This is a challenge for you to prove to me that even with a name like Krishna, you will one day make kings and emperors bow to your feet. You have a superlative intelligence, Krishna. You have just now raised an issue which I or the other sages have not thought of yet. We will have to do a lot of *tapasya* to find the answer. Or maybe when you grow up, you will find the answer yourself and spread it to the world. I bless you, my child, that you may attain heights which no one else has achieved. Tell me, who is your father and how much have you studied?'

'Guru*ji*, my father Shri Nandrai is the headman of the Gops. We live in the villages near the Govardhan mountain and supply milk to the city. My father taught me to read and write. I know how to maintain accounts for the milk sold and that is all.'

'How old are you, Krishna?'

'Guru*ji*, I would be around eighteen this *Bhadra*. In fact my father tells me I was born on the same night that King Vasudeva's daughter was killed by King Kansa... What... what happened, Guru*ji*?'

Rishi Sandipani's pupils were dilated, he was sweating profusely and his entire body was shaking.

'I will just go and call help, Guru*ji*,' Kanha proceeded to leave.

Rishi Sandipani motioned him to stop and with a supreme effort, controlled himself. Slowly his breathing turned to normal.

'Guru*ji*, are you alright?'

'Yes, I am well now. Krishna, repeat what you had last said to me about your birth?'

'Guru*ji*, I had said that I will be eighteen this Bhadra and that my father had told me that I was born on the same night that King Kansa had killed King Vasudeva's daughter. In fact, he had told me that it was a night of unprecedented storm and rain and the Yamuna had flooded the ramparts of the palace also.'

'Kanha, listen to me very carefully. You will not disclose to any other person in any circumstance, without my or Akrur*ji*'s permission that you were born on the same night that King Kansa had killed King Vasudeva's daughter. Do you understand?'

'Yes Guru*ji*, but why?'

'Do as you are told, Krishna, else you will be in great danger.'

Kanha nodded in acceptance. The befuddled look on his face however remained.

'Now go and call Akrur. Tell him that I want to meet him immediately.'

Kanha went out on his errand.

Rishi Sandipani sat with his brows furrowed. Was this the beginning of a new destiny for Mathura? Could the son of a Gop change the political history of the Yadavas? Would he be allowed to do so? The vermillion mark on his forehead glowed like a third eye as the venerable sage concentrated his thoughts.

XIII
The Preparation

You were born to win, but to be a winner, you must plan to win, prepare to win and expect to win

...Zig Ziglar

So much had changed and yet nothing had changed. Chanur wiped away a droplet of tear that had spilled over from his eyes and furrowed its way to his cheek. The messenger who had brought the news of Guru Rudracharya's death, had left.

An era had ended. And yet, sunshine poured inside the room, birds chirped happily and the Yamuna flowed by like a youthful damsel. Life continued as if nothing had happened. Individual life is transient but life itself is eternal, the Guru used to say. How true, thought Chanur. It was more than a decade since Chanur had last met his Guru. He did not have the courage to meet him thereafter.

For the most part of the last decade Guru Rudracharya was confined to bed, the messenger had said. Bereft of his faculties on account of old age, a vacant expression on his face, he nevertheless clung on to his breath for as long it was possible, hoping against hope that he would die in his independent tribal homeland. Chanur could almost hear the last murmur of the departing soul: 'Chanur, Chanur... do something, act my son, act now....'

Chanur wrung his hands in despair. The scenario around Mathura was fast changing. New kings were coming to power, succeeding their departed fathers. For the last few years, the kingdom of Panchala had had a new King, Drupada. Same with Kashi, Kunti, Matsya and Kosala. Boundaries were being redrawn. And yet, nothing had changed. The two constants—Hastinapur and Magadha—remained at the two ends of the political spectrum as they had a decade back.

Bhishma and Jarasandha had aged, but apart from the greying of their hairs, they remained at their fighting best. Jarasandha was now more active of the two. He was bent upon fulfilling at the earliest, his dream of becoming a *Rajchakrabarti.* The proper course for that would have been to perform an *Ashwamedh* yagna where a horse would be set free to roam around the various kingdoms as it pleased. It would be accompanied by the royal army. If any kingdom dared to hold the horse hostage, the army would fight and conquer the kingdom. After a year, the horse would be brought back to the kingdom and ritually sacrificed in a huge ceremony attended by all kings through whose territory the horse had passed. It was said that if anyone could perform a hundred *Ashwamedh* yagnas, he would be elevated to become Indra, the King of Gods. But, so long as Bhishma remained the head of Hastinapur, Jarasandha had no hope of performing the *Ashwamedh* yagna. So he took an alternative morbid route to realise his dream. He vowed to detain a hundred kings and once the tally reached a hundred, to ritually sacrifice them before his deity, Lord Shiva. The larger kingdoms around Magadha were already his allies—Kashi, Poundra, Banga, Odra, Kalinga, Utkal and even faraway ones like Chedi and Vidharbha. So, Jarasandha wandered with his army through mountains and valleys, in search of smaller kingdoms, whose kings he could imprison to fulfil his vow.

Bhishma, on the contrary, was bogged down over the last decade by palace politics. Hastinapur was split in the middle on the issue of succession between Duryodhana, the eldest son of the present blind King Dhritarashtra and Yudhisthira, the eldest son of the deceased King Pandu.

Yet, despite the internal haemorrhage, Hastinapur could not be totally ignored, as was brought home the hard way to its immediate neighbour, the Panchalas. Panchala King Drupada was on a hunting expedition very near to the Panchala-Hastinapur border. Secure in his knowledge that the internal fissures in Hastinapur had rendered it toothless, King Drupada did not deem it necessary to take any extra precautions having regard to the proximity of the border. He was ambushed by the sons of Pandu, also known as Pandavas. The third Pandava prince, Arjuna, who was now touted as the best upcoming archer of Aryavarta and and the second prince Bhima, who was euphemistically said to have the strength of a thousand elephants, captured Drupada and forced him to relinquish half of the Panchala kingdom in favour of their Guru Dronacharya, who in turn installed his son Ashwatthama on the throne.

There was however a lesson to be learnt, Chanur contemplated. Hastinapur had got away with dividing Panchala without getting embroiled with Jarasandha. True, Panchala was no ally of Jarasandha and had maintained its independent identity, but it was also true that if in its hour of crisis it had appealed to Jarasandha, he would not have been able to help.

Jarasandha was too busy scouting the hills and forests in search of kings he could capture for his intended sacrifice. His focus was elsewhere. This was the time to strike.

Chanur got up. He had made up his mind to act. He remembered his Guru's words: 'Chanur, my son, change will not come by itself. It must be brought about. What distinguishes great men from mere mortals is the ability to take risks and change the status quo.'

Chanur stood in front of the mirror and passed his hand through his hair. The silver grey strands signified the years he had wasted waiting for change to occur in the natural course. Any further delay and his entire life would stand wasted. He had decided now. He would himself be the harbinger of change. All this while he had waited fearing Jarasandha's attack if he deposed Kansa. No more. After deposing Kansa, he would send emissaries to the tribals in Jarasandha's army urging them to join him in creating their own independent homeland. He would split Jarasandha's army right along the middle and hand him a defeat he would remember for his lifetime. The fear of death could hold him back no longer. 'When the time comes, we shall see. What will be, will be,' Chanur murmured to himself.

The immediate task on hand was deposing Kansa. For that he would have to use the resources he had amassed all these years to create a tribal army that would train deep in the forests and then on the appointed day, assemble at the capital and take over. The simplest of plans were the best made and executed. But for the plan to succeed, there must not be any suspicion in the minds of the King or the people. 'Act like a conjurer,' Guru Rudracharya used to say. 'Deflect the attention of people so that they see what you want them to see and miss out on your sleight of hand.'

A temple for Kansa.

Yes, it was originally the idea of Bhoumya. Chanur's lips twirled into a sarcastic smile as he remembered his late friend, colleague and adversary. *A temple for Kansa.* He would build a grand temple for Kansa. It would be a proof of his devotion to the King and like a magnet, it would attract all the attention of the King and his subjects for the entire period of its construction. This would enable his tribal soldiers to come into the capital in the guise of construction labourers and have a feel of the ground. Then on the day of consecration, there would be a grand function. Under the cover of the grand function, his tribal soldiers would come in and complete the coup.

One and half years. That would be the time taken to construct the temple. And then....

Chanur touched a *rudraksha* garland that his Guru had given him and which he wore around his neck. 'Guru*ji*, I swear by you to depose Kansa and create an independent tribal homeland,' he murmured.

It was a secret room in Akrur's countryhouse—a room built within a room. With extra thick stone walls and lined with absorbent wood, the room was soundproof. Despite the safety measures, it was in hushed tones that Guru Sandipani spoke to Akrur.

'You remember, Akrur, the events just preceding the massacre of the children?' Guru Sandipani spoke in an agitated tone.

'Guru*ji*, are you referring to the *Tantrik* who had come to the cemetery?'

'Yes yes, don't you remember what that *Tantrik* had said?'

'Yes, he had said that the eighth son of Devaki is growing up by the day and has begun the process of killing Kansa's friends one by one....'

'Exactly. He had said that Devaki delivered a son and not a daughter. That son, the incarnation of Vishnu, was smuggled out of the prison on the night he was born and replaced with a daughter. If he lives he will kill Kansa's advisers one by one, till one day Kansa's own turn will come.'

'Yes, Guru*ji*. But we do not know who that child is.'

'I know him, Akrur, I have found him. He will deliver us from Kansa.'

'Whaaaaaat?' Akrur almost jumped on his Guru in excitement. 'Who is he?'

Guru Sandipani took his mouth near Akrur's ear. 'It is Krishna,' he whispered.

Akrur stood back in disbelief. 'That Gop lad?'

'Yes. He was born on the same night as Devaki's daughter.'

Akrur sat back bewildered.

'Sit up, Akrur, now it is time to act. Now that we have found the boy, we must take immediate steps to take him out of the kingdom before Kansa gets wind of the fact. Then we have to organise resistance, spread the word amongst the people that their Deliverer has come and finally throw out this maniacal monarch.'

Akrur looked up as if in a daze. 'Guru*ji*, do you really believe what the *Tantrik* said? Maybe he said it at somebody's instance with some concealed motive?'

'Akrur, the question is not my believing or not believing. It is the question of how people are to be made to believe. If you can arouse belief in people, if you can make them believe that the Deliverer has come, if you can make the people rally behind this one lad, the days of Kansa are numbered. I am prepared to clutch at even a straw to kill this King and free Vasudeva from prison.'

'But Guru*ji*, a Gop lad leading the Yadavas? Who will accept him?'

'Akrur, he is not a mere Gop lad. He is the son of Vasudeva and an incarnation of Vishnu. Who will *not* accept him? You do as I say. Get up, Akrur, there is no time to lose.'

'Guru*ji*, I am prepared to do everything and submit to everyone in order to free Vasudeva. You tell me what to do and it shall be done.'

Guru Sandipani smiled.

'Akrur, the way I see it, there will be several stages to our plan. The first and foremost will obviously be to train

Krishna both mentally and physically for the job. He will have to realise and believe that he is the selected one—the *avatar* of Vishnu with the specific job of eliminating Kansa. But the most difficult part of his training will be to wean him away from his Gop roots and convince him to accept Vasudeva and Devaki as his parents. And that will also include counselling Balarama to accept Krishna as his brother. Alongside the mental training there has to be weapons training. Under your custody Krishna has basically been learning *mallayudh* and what I have seen of him, he is now quite proficient in the sport. And since he is a Gop, he will also know how to wield a *lathi*. But he now needs to learn archery and swordsmanship. Same goes for Balarama. This training cannot be done in Mathura because Kansa has his spies all around and we do not want to raise his suspicion. I also want Krishna and Balarama to also learn certain physical skills that would be required if they have to break into the palace.'

'Guru*ji*, it will be extremely difficult to persuade Krishna's parents to let go of him.'

'I have not forgotten that, Akrur. But it will be an integral part of Krishna's training that a person must give precedence to performance of his duty than to his familial relations. He will himself come out of his parents' control.'

'Well said, Guru*ji*. Now regarding the physical training you were talking about, you want to take them to your *ashram*?'

'Akrur, my *ashram* is in Ujjaini. That will be very far from here and it would be difficult to maintain contact with you over such a long distance. I have instead thought of the forests on the other side of the Govardhan hills. That is beyond the boundaries of Mathura, yet near enough for getting regular information about Mathura and keeping in constant touch with you. And since the area is densely forested, the secrecy of the mission will also be maintained.

So, if you can get a suitable area in the forests cleared and a few huts erected, I can start my *ashram* there.'

'I will do that, Guru*ji*. But will you take only Krishna and Balarama there or more people?'

'I think I will also take most of the students who come here to learn *mallayudh*. We will require as many hands we can get because we will ultimately face the Magadhi army and Kansa himself is a champion fighter. The boys I take with me will constitute the core team of fighters with Krishna as their leader.'

'Thereafter, Guru*ji*?'

'While I train these fighters, you will have to engage irregulars and mercenaries. While they will directly take on the Magadhi army and deflect their attention, Krishna and Balaram with the other boys will launch a direct assault on Kansa and his advisers. The Magadhi army will fight only so long as Kansa lives. As soon as he is killed, the Magadhi soldiers will give up the fight.'

'But, what about the people? What will be the reaction of the Bhojas?'

'I was just coming to that, Akrur. You snatch words from my mouth. Shows your keen political sense. Very good.'

'Your blessings, Guru*ji*.'

'See Akrur, you will have to spread a whisper campaign that Vishnu in his incarnation as Krishna, the eighth son of Devaki, has come to deliver the Mathuraiites from the scourge of Kansa. Vrishnis will obviously support you. So will the Andhakas since Kansa has been a very cruel monarch and they also would not have forgotten the massacre of children which started from their locality. The Bhojas are not enamoured of Kansa either, yet they continue to support him for the sole reason that he is a Bhoja. Unfortunately the class factor blinds us to all reason, Akrur. Their children had also been massacred under Kansa's orders. Yet they would continue to suffer Kansa rather than feel free under a benign Vrishni or Andhaka leader.'

'So what is the solution, Guru*ji*?'

'I have thought over it the whole day, Akrur. You have to spread a rumour that Kansa is not a Bhoja.'

'But how is that possible? Kansa is the son of King Ugrasen who is undoubtedly a Bhoja.'

'Slow, Akrur, slow…' Guru Sandipani smiled. 'If Kansa is the son of King Ugrasen, he is undoubtedly a Bhoja. But what if he is not the son of King Ugrasen?'

'What?'

'You heard me, Akrur. Now tell me, does Kansa have any resemblance to King Ugrasen, physically or by nature?'

'No, that he does not. King Ugrasen is of medium build and pale complexion while Kansa is like an *asura* in appearance with a huge muscular body and darker complexion. And, if we see the nature of the two, it is like light and dark. The bloodthirsty and sadistic nature of Kansa has never been seen in any of his forefathers.'

'So, can it not be said that Kansa was a product of rape of his mother by a non-Aryan? Say, by a demon?'

'By a demon?'

'Yes, why not? If you see, Kansa is demonic in his characteristics—both physical and mental. He has created a history in Aryavarta in barbarity and debauchery. It can be said that Kansa's mother Queen Padmavati had gone to visit her parental home where the incident took place and thereafter it was hushed up and Kansa was born as the product of the rape.'

'What an idea, Guru*ji*! If Kansa is not the son of King Ugrasen, he is not a Bhoja and therefore his support amongst the Bhojas will be cut off.'

'Right, Akrur. We can further explain that it is also the reason why Kansa had no qualms in deposing and imprisoning his own father—simply because Ugrasen was *not* his father! And if you remember, the sadhu who had prophesised about the eighth child of Devaki had said Kansa was the incarnation of Kalnemi.'

'True Guru*ji*, but then the Bhojas will always demand that we agree to the return of King Ugrasen.'

'Akrur, there will be many claimants to the throne. Ugrasen will naturally have a claim, Vasudeva will have a claim on account of his incarceration, whoever kills Kansa will also have a claim. But, I think we are counting the crop even before it is planted. Let Kansa be deposed first. The next step will be Vasudeva's release. The rest will follow in the natural course. If you name a King at this juncture, then the forces opposed to Kansa would never unite. So, the answer to questions about succession is that the oligarchs of Mathura will together decide who shall be the next King of Mathura.'

'Right, Guru*ji*. Very well said. But what will be the time frame?'

'I should think that arranging finances, training Krishna, hiring a mercenary army and so on should take about a year and a half, provided we start immediately. You start work on the land behind the Govardhan Hills from tomorrow itself. God willing, in a year and a half, we will transform Mathura.'

Akrur bowed and touched his Guru's feet.

'God be with you, Akrur.'

'No, the question does not arise. I refuse to let him go. I have not raised him by feeding him the milk of my breasts only to let him go away from me.' Yashoda was emphatic in her stand.

Nandrai tried to reason with her. 'Look Yashoda, opportunities like this do not come calling every day. We are all virtually illiterate cowherds. If Kanha stays with us, he will be nothing more than what we are—an ignorant cowherd whose aim in life would be to supply milk and curds to Mathura. What more will he attain? On the other hand, here is a sage like Rishi Sandipani who spots talent in our Kanha and wants to take him along to his *ashram* to train him so that he rises in life. He said that he has great expectations from Kanha. He has forecast that one day people will worship Kanha. Don't you want to see that day?'

Tears flowed down Yashoda's eyes. 'You fathers will never understand a mother's heart. The only time I had entrusted him to another, he was kidnapped. You remember the incident on his *chhathi* when that Putana had kidnapped him? Never again will I commit that folly. How can I entrust him to your Rishi who does not even know how many times he is to be given milk, which vegetables he likes and what time of the day he feels hungry?'

Nandrai smiled. 'Yashoda, the bird has grown. He is now a young man perfectly able to take care of himself and also of others. Stop sheltering him under your wings. Let him go.'

'You remain quiet, Kanha's *bapu*. How will I sleep here, always under the apprehension that something bad may befall my child while he is away?' The son of a Gop will be a Gop. It is no use teaching him the *shastras*. You know well he cannot become a Brahmin. He will be the headman of the village like you and get the same respect that you command amongst the Gops. And as regards art of war, if a drop of blood flows out of my *Lalla's* body, it shall be the end of my life. You want me dead? Then send Kanha wherever you want. But only over my dead body!'

If it was mother Yashoda at home, it was Radha at the bower.

'Kanha, how can you even think of leaving me and going away? Is this your love for me?'

'Radha, you are the love of my life. How can you think I am leaving you? Whether I am here or there, you will remain in my life breath.'

'Why do you have to go, Kanha? We have everything here—you have your herd of cows and will never be wanting in wealth. Nature has laid out its beauty here to feast your eyes. You have peace of mind. You have your flute. And, you have your love. What more can a person seek in this life, Kanha? And as for work, you will succeed your father as the *mukhiya* of the Gops and then you can do as much work you want to better the conditions of our villages.'

'Radha, the world beckons. Being a Gop is not enough. The Yadavas look down upon us as if they are a superior race. I want to show to the world what a Gop boy can do. Guru*ji* tells me that he foresees that I am born for a particular great deed which no one else in the world can do. He says that I will do something for which the world will worship me. Don't you want your Kanha to gain respect in the eyes of the world?'

'I do not know about the world, Kanha. It frightens me. I only know that there is no end to craving. See our King, Kansa. He was born a prince, but he was not satisfied. He wanted to be King and see what he did to achieve it? He imprisoned his own parents! And after becoming King, he is still not satisfied. I am told that he wants to be God. Take heed, Kanha. Do not become a slave to your craving for more—more knowledge, more wealth, more fame, more adulation, more and more of everything. Then one day you will find that the more of everything has so occupied your heart and mind that there is no place for me and then you would not even care.'

'Is this what you understand of me, Radha? Before that day comes, I shall die. It is for you that I would prove myself. Prove that I am worthy of your love.'

'You don't have to prove anything to me, Kanha. I have already given my heart and mind to you. Don't go, Kanha, don't go. I beseech you, Kanha, don't leave me.'

'Radha, don't weaken my resolve. If you say like this, then I will never be able to seek my destiny.'

Radha took a deep breath and closed her eyes. 'Must you go, Kanha? Well then I will not come between you and your destiny,' she muttered. When she finally opened her eyes, it was with a new resolve. 'Come closer, Kanha,' she beckoned.

Kanha came closer.

Radha took his hand and placed it on her heart. 'Here Kanha, I give you my mind, body and heart. Wherever you go, I shall be there with you. My physical body shall be here performing the routine chores of life, but I shall always be there with you. Go, Kanha, seek your destiny, I have already found mine.'

For an instant her lips found Kanha's. And then she was gone.

Kanha strained his eyes till she disappeared in the dusk and pricked his ears to hear the fading tinkle of her anklets till they could be heard no more. And then all of a sudden warm tears flooded his eyes.

It was still dark when Kanha stood on the road outside the village with his belongings, waiting to be picked up. It had been a sleepless night for the family. A tearful Yashoda had been up all night preparing sweets and savouries for her Kanha to take with him.

'*Maiya,* it is already a sackful. How will I take all this?' Kanha remonstrated.

'On the contrary, it will only suffice for a week. What will you eat after that, Kanha? How will you survive on the *ashram* food?' Yashoda's voice choked.

'Don't worry, *Maiya,* I will take care of myself.'

Yashoda burst into tears. 'What will I do without you, Kanha? How will I ever sleep knowing you are away in a foreign land?'

Kanha gently kissed her forehead and wiped away her tears. 'I shall always be in your heart, *Maiya.* And, in your waiting eyes. And before you know, I shall be back in your arms.'

It was a tearful farewell from home. Yashoda insisted on accompanying him to the pick-up spot, but Kanha declined. It would not do to have his mother wailing in front of others. Nandrai accompanied him, carrying the sackful of sweets and savouries.

Soon the chariots came. Akrur was driving the first chariot himself, with Rishi Sandipani and Balarama in the seat. And as Kanha ascended the chariot with his belongings, Nandrai stood with folded hands before Akrur and Guru Sandipani. 'Please take care of my boy and pardon his mistakes.'

They smiled, nodded in assent and started off. There was not a moment to lose. They must cross the boundaries of Mathura before daybreak.

And, as the convoy of chariots disappeared in a haze of dust, Nandrai stood dazed. Had he done the right thing sending the apple of his eyes to the distant lands? For the first time, he was not so sure.

Akrur had dutifully carried out his task. A large area, deep inside the dense forests, had been cleared, levelled and fenced. There were rows of huts for the Guru and his pupils and a large open space for physical activities. A nearby stream catered to the water requirements. A little distance away were the cowshed and the stable. In the open space there were several devices, structures and poles erected for body building and exercise.

Away from their homes and civilisation, it was a new life for the fifty odd teenaged boys. They studied, played and wrestled together, went on excursions deep inside the forest, jumped on hurdles, climbed ropes and at night lit a bonfire and sang songs. The Guru framed a mantra for the group—all for one and one for all. There were of course initial hesitations, frictions and clashes of ego but they were smoothened in the course of time.

Two weeks into the program, the Guru summoned Krishna and Balarama and took them deep inside the forest. There was a separate clearing with two huts. The Guru sat down in one and bade Krishna and Balarama to sit beside him.

'My children, it is destiny that has brought you here. I am only fulfilling my small part in the work that destiny has in store for you. Listen carefully to the story I am going to narrate to you, for this is going to change your lives forever. I know you will have many questions but wait till I finish.

As you know, the Kingdom of Mathura has three major clans—the Andhakas, Vrishnis and the Bhojas. The leaders of these clans together elect a King who rules over Mathura during his lifetime and after his death, a new King is selected by the clan leaders. There is no dynastic rule in Mathura. This tradition has been ritually followed over generations. This was also the manner in which Ugrasen of the Bhojas became King after the death of Vrishni King Surasena.

Ugrasen had a son Kansa by his wife Padmavati. But unknown to him, Kansa was not his real son. He was the son of a demon who had raped Padmavati when she had gone to visit her parents. Kansa inherited the appearance as well as all the demonic qualities of his real father.

Emperor Jarasandha of Magadha was eyeing Mathura as an ally to counter Hastinapur. He married off his two daughters to Kansa. Immediately after the wedding, Kansa, with the help of Magadhi soldiers loaned to him by his father-in-law, imprisoned his parents Ugrasen and Padmavati.

As you are aware, Kansa's cousin Devaki was married to Vasudeva. After the marriage, a rishi predicted that Vishnu would take avatar as the eighth child of Devaki and kill Kansa.

So Kansa imprisoned Vasudeva and Devaki and every child born to them was immediately done to death. One by one six children were killed. Then Devaki had a miscarriage, which was not actually a miscarriage. Her womb was transferred to Rohini, who gave birth to you, Balarama.'

Balarama's jaw fell wide open. He tried to say something but the Guru stopped him with a movement of his hand.

'The stage was now set for the birth of Vishnu's avatar. Exactly at midnight of the eighth day of the dark phase of moon in the month of *Bhadra*, Devaki gave birth to a son.'

'Son? But we all know Devaki*ji* gave birth to a daughter…' Balarama and Krishna spoke out together.

The Guru smiled. 'Patience, my dear children. Hear the story fully. As the boy was born, by the magic of Vishnu the palace guards fell asleep and the gates of the prison and the palace fell open. A Voice commanded Vasudeva to take the newborn baby boy and leave it with Nandrai, the chieftain of the Gops and to bring back Nandrai's baby girl who was born at the same instant.'

Krishna and Balarama were now sweating profusely. Krishna tried to say something but he could not find his voice. Balarama clasped Krishna's hand.

The Guru continued. 'Vasudeva took the newborn boy in a basket and went outside through the open gates. Outside the rains lashed the ground. The waters of the Yamuna had flooded the entire area till the palace gates. Vasudeva, who was in a trance, stepped into the water which suddenly parted and a path came into existence. The Great Serpent Sheshnag came behind them and with his enormous hood, protected the newborn avatar of Vishnu from the rain and water. Vasudeva went to Nandrai's house, exchanged the babies and came back. By the maya of Vishnu, all the protagonists—Vasudeva, Devaki and even Nandrai and his wife, lost all memory of the incident. What they all believed was that Devaki had delivered a girl child while Nandrai's wife had delivered a boy. When Kansa was informed of the delivery, he came and flung the girl to the wall, killing her. But the eighth son of Devaki lived on at Nandrai's house. You, Krishna, are that avatar of Vishnu, you are the one destined to kill Kansa and rid Mathura of the menace.'

Krishna's eyes were full of tears and his body was shaking. 'No, no, that is not possible.'

Guru Sandipani looked at him with eyes laden with compassion. 'You are really that divine child, my boy. And now the time has come to fulfil the purpose for which you have come to this world.'

'No, no,' Krishna shouted in a fit of frenzy. 'I do not believe anyone. My *Bapu* and my *Maiya* are mine. I was not born to anyone else.'

Guru Sandipani opened his mouth to pacify him but by then Krishna had jumped up and run out of the hut.

He ran and ran and ran through the thickets. The thorns pierced his flesh and bruised his body, blood dripped from his feet and yet his mind was so full of what he had heard that there was no space for even the sensation of pain. His mind rebelled. How could Yashoda, *his Maiya,* who would not let him be away from her even for an instant, not be his mother? How could Nandrai, *his Bapu,* who always stood by him, not be his father? It was all false, he told himself. How could he call any other person his *Bapu* or *Maiya,* even if they be the King or Queen of the world? No, he would not go back to these people who were taking away his very identity, his parentage and maybe would go on to take his life itself. No, no, no, it was all false. He would go back to his *Bapu* and *Maiya*. He would not stay here any longer.

It was difficult to say who ran faster—the body or the mind. Finally, the body bereft of the mind, tumbled hard on the undergrowth. The forehead struck violently against the trunk of a tree and the body collapsed in a heap of unconsciousness.

When his eyes opened, it was dark. Inside the hut, a dim earthen lamp only managed to coagulate the darkness. At the bedside, Guru Sandipani caressed Krishna's brow.

'How are you feeling, my son?'

Krishna tried to sit up but the Guru forbade him. 'Take rest, my boy. Do not exert yourself.'

The events of the day flashed through his mind. 'I am not the son of anyone else,' he muttered between his teeth.

'I think you are harbouring a misconception, my boy,' Guru caressed his hair. 'Yashoda and Nandrai will throughout your life remain your mother and father. Nobody can take them away from your life. The status of adoptive parents is even higher in the scriptures than the real parents since they give you love although you do not bear their blood. And you Krishna, you are the selected one who by the grace of God is getting another set of parents in addition to your own. Cherish your blessings, my son.'

It took one whole week of counselling from the Guru to make Krishna come around. 'Let not relationships come in the way of performing your duty. It does not matter whether Nandrai is your father or Vasudeva. Just look around you and you will realise your duty. See the suffering and destruction that the rule of Kansa has brought about. Can you imagine the plight of people who are fed alive to dogs if they cannot pay their taxes when their crop fails? Think of the mother whose infant is massacred because the King sees a potential assassin in the newborn. Think of Vasudeva and Devaki whose newborn children are dashed to the wall in front of their eyes and every instant of day and night they are forced to see the stains on the wall. Do you bear no responsibility to the people of your kingdom?

Think Krishna, about the people of the kingdom. For decades together they have borne excruciating suffering hoping that one day the Deliverer will come. Whenever they have tried any uprising, they have been smothered, broken, ground to the dust. Ultimately they have lost the will to resist. The only light at the end of the long, dark tunnel is the forecast that the eighth son of Devaki will kill Kansa and deliver them out of Hell. Will you break that only ray of hope that has kept the people of this kingdom alive through all the sufferings?

Krishna, God lives in each one of us. Yet we fail to realise it and search Him outside in the nature or in the temples. According to our scriptures, the highest stage of realisation is "*So aham*"—"I am HE". I am here only to develop in you that realisation that *you* are the manifestation of God. You are a part of God. *YOU ARE GOD*. And once you realise this, then it is your duty to rise up to all injustice and suppression and to bring about justice and equity. Arise my son, awake and proceed towards your goal.'

On the seventh day, Krishna and Balarama hugged each other in a tight brotherly embrace.

'We promise, Guru*ji*, that we shall not rest till we have rid Mathura of the tyranny of Kansa.'

Decades later, on the battleground of the Mahabharata war, Krishna would build upon the teachings of his Guru and develop the concepts of the *aatman* and *karma*. There would be a sense of *déjà vu* as Krishna would exhort Arjuna to perform his duty regardless of worldly ties, regardless of success or failure, regardless of life or death. The exhortation that had fired up Krishna was now invoked by the Guru to exhort the other fighters to action.

'You are the chosen ones to deliver this kingdom from its sufferings. And the very *avatar* of Vishnu is there to lead you to victory. You will be the scourge of the evil and the protector of the good. Whether with arms or without, whether on foot, chariot or horseback, whether on land, water or air, you will develop skills that none have achieved earlier or will achieve hereafter. You will be known, feared and revered as the *Narayani Sena*—the Army of Vishnu. And under the leadership of Krishna and Balarama, you will eliminate even the memory of Kansa.'

Very soon Guru Sandipani sent word to Akrur that the first phase of the plan had been successfully executed.

For Kansa, the countdown had begun....

XIV

The End of Kansa

There have been tyrants and murderers, and for a time, they can seem invincible, but in the end, they always fall

...Mahatma Gandhi

It was Sudama, the cook's assistant, who brought the news from the city. The Great Temple of Kansa was nearing completion. It had been announced that the temple would be inaugurated three months later, on the full moon day of the month of *Ashwin,* amidst grand festivities.

The boys milled around Sudama, enquiring about news from Mathura. After all he was their only gateway to the city. Every weekend, the cook and Sudama would make a furtive trip to Mathura to get provisions. They would come back not only with the supplies but also the latest news.

'Have you seen the temple?'

'How big is it?'

'What is it made of?'

'Have you been inside?'

'Have you seen Kansa's idol inside?'

The questions were never ending. But Sudama was patience personified. Not only did he describe what he saw, but also what he believed a great structure should be. Thus the stone of which the temple was built, acquired myriad hues that would put many a pearl to shame, the cupolas acquired an exterior of gold and the height of the temple would dwarf even the Mount Govardhan.

It was obvious that he was basking in these little moments of glory.

Krishna waited till the last of the boys had finished his query and then he came around and held Sudama's hand.

'Friend, did you pass through the Gop villages? Could you gather some information about my parents? And… and…about Radha? It has been more than a year that I have seen them. I don't know how they all are.' His eyes became moist.

Sudama sadly shook his head. This time they had taken another route to prevent suspicion. Maybe next time… He could not disclose that Guru Sandipani had strictly forbidden him from visiting the homes of any of the students.

It was on the very first day of arrival at the camp that Krishna had made friends with Sudama. The humble assistant cook, of almost the same age as Krishna, had been all at sea while serving lunch to the hungry students. One boy called out for rice at one end, another simultaneously demanded vegetables at the other, while many others riled him with taunts and comments. A moment later, Krishna had got up from his place and with a serving bucket in hand, was doling out food to the students. A visibly embarrassed Sudama had tried to stop him but Krishna assuaged him with kind words. Together, the two of them soon brought order to the proceedings. Sometime later, Sudama sought him out with goodies from the kitchen and soon the two became fast friends. Once, but only once, Sudama had managed to visit Kanha's home for a moment, during one of his forays into the city. That was before the Guru's prohibition. Yashoda had, under pressure of time, and all the while shedding tears and deluging Sudama with a barrage of questions, quickly packed some *khichdi,* wheat puffs and clarified butter for her beloved son. That day, while opening the packet, Krishna had cried copiously. Then, when the tears had dried, he had held Sudama's hand in his own and said—'I shall be in your debt forever in life.'

That debt was repaid decades later, when a pauper Sudama had called on Krishna, who was then the King of Dwarka. A pauper friend calling on the King was reminiscent of the pauper Drona calling on King Drupada of the Panchalas, but the similarities ended there. Sudama was no Drona to demand part of wealth or kingdom of his friend, nor was Krishna the haughty Drupada who deemed friendship could only be amongst equals. On hearing that a pauper calling himself Sudama had come to the palace gates and was requesting an audience, Krishna ran barefoot from his throne to the palace gate and tightly embraced his friend who was clad in dusty rags. He held his hand and brought him to the palace, washed his feet with his own hands and like the days of his youth, snatched away the parboiled rice brought by his friend and gobbled it as if it was the tastiest meal of his life. It was many months later that Sudama could take leave of his friend and when he finally reached home, he found that his friend had converted his hovel into a palace fit for a King and overflowing with wealth.

That night the Guru called Krishna to his cottage.

'Krishna, over the past year that we have been together, I have seen you evolve. I have observed the sarcasm and taunts from the other boys you have had to endure for being a Gop. I deliberately did not interfere since I wanted you to be able to deal with your problems by yourself. And I have seen you eventually emerge a leader amongst the boys. But now the time has come for the real test when you have to justify your existence.

My son, as you may have heard, Kansa is building a huge temple for himself and it will be inaugurated three months hence. He has proclaimed that there would be great celebrations in the city at that time. I think that would also be the ideal time for us to strike. The people would be busy in celebrations and the army would be busy controlling the crowds. The King's personal defences would be the weakest at that time.'

'Yes, Guru*ji*. I will wait for your orders.'

'Krishna, I have extensively trained you and the other boys here in martial arts. You have been taught to climb ropes, scale walls with bare hands and feet. Whether knife throwing or archery or swordsmanship, I have trained you in all forms. In addition, I have trained Balarama in mace fighting in view of his raw strength and I have given you lessons in battle strategy. With Balarama by your side and your dedicated *Narayani Sena* behind you, you are now ready to launch a frontal attack on Kansa. I have spoken to Akrur. He will get a few hundred irregulars ready who will divert the Magadhi army and enable you to take Kansa head on.'

Krishna nodded his head in agreement.

'But, Krishna, mere theory or internal practice is not enough. An actual battle is a very hard place because real lives are at stake there. You have to kill or get killed. So, before you take on Kansa three months hence, you must plan small surprise raids against the Mathura army so that your own army is ready for the actual battle.'

'Guru*ji*, I am ready. But for launching such raids, we will require information. We are situated at a very remote place. From here it will be difficult to get information. Can we relocate to the cave in the Govardhan mountain where I had taken my villagers to safety during the great deluge?'

'You may, Kanha, provided you give me your word of honour.'

'What word of honour, Guru*ji*?'

'That till your work is accomplished, you will not contact your parents or any Gop whatsoever.'

Krishna's face fell. He took a moment to compose himself and look up. 'I give my word of honour, Guru*ji*. Till my work is accomplished, no relation nor any tie of friendship shall bind me. I shall work tirelessly and ceaselessly towards my goal, without concern for my own life or death,' he muttered.

'My son, you are the avatar of Vishnu and are destined to succeed. But, being an avatar does not mean that you are endowed with supernatural powers. God does not endow anyone with supernatural powers since that would be a violation of His own laws of nature. The only difference between you and any other person is that an average person has infinite potential but uses only an infinitesimal part of it while you have developed the capacity to use much more of this potential.'

Krishna nodded his head.

The Guru continued. 'Krishna, I am telling you this because you may be a divine avatar, but you have the body and powers of a human being. So be careful in your endeavour. There is no need to take any unnecessary risks. Keep safe. Your accomplishment of the final task is more important than success in these raids.'

'I will remember, Guru*ji*.'

The Guru got up and hugged his pupil. 'May dharma and victory be with you. Always.'

Chanur smirked at the new landmark of Mathura—a landmark that Kansa had predicted, would become the signature of the city. The exterior of the colossal temple complex was now ready and work was going on in the interiors. Just two days back Kansa had himself visited the complex and was evidently thrilled with what he saw.

The huge central temple would bear a huge figurine of Kansa plated in gold with diamonds and rubies for eyes.

The idol was also ready for installation. Surrounding the central temple would be nine small temples set out in an arc, dedicated to nine prominent gods of the pantheon. One of these small temples, Kansa had decreed, should be dedicated to Vishnu. The intent was to show that Kansa was the chief god and the other gods, including Vishnu, were subservient to him.

'We will go one step ahead,' Chanur had remarked. 'The palms of Vishnu would be folded as if paying obeisance to you.'

Kansa's roaring laughter had brought the house down.

'The temple of Vishnu!' Chanur could not help a smile flit across his face. That temple had a secret labyrinth that led to a secret underground hall. If all went well, five hundred men, who were disguised as labourers working in the temple, would hide themselves inside the secret underground hall the previous night and then on the day of the inauguration, would emerge and create mayhem.

He had himself decided that the temple containing the secret room would be dedicated to Vishnu. 'Well, at least Kansa's death should have some connection with Vishnu,' he chuckled.

The news spread like wildfire. Keshi had been done to death along with ten Magadhi troops while patrolling the eastern border areas. There were no survivors to tell the tale of how it all happened. Had the Panchalas conducted a surprise raid at the borders? But the raiders had left no trace. Even the arrows by which the men were shot, had been wrenched out of the dead bodies. The Panchalas never did that in the past. Who could it be?

A fortnight thereafter, there was another incident but this time on the western side. Fifteen troops lost their lives.

Chanur and Dhenuka went personally to investigate but drew a blank. An infuriated Kansa went to the sites to see for himself. Killing of Magadhi troops was a serious matter. Searches were made, rewards were announced, yet the matter remained unresolved.

In the city the grapevine was hyperactive. 'It's the eighth son of Devaki...it's the eighth son of Devaki...' the whispers went viral. 'The Deliverer has finally come.'

Chanur was perplexed. Who could have done it, he wondered for hours on end. Finally, he made up his mind. Whoever might have done it, Chanur would use it to his advantage. Very soon, the major contingent of the Magadhi army was sent to guard the borders of Mathura.

Only a small force remained to guard the King and the city.

It was festive time in Mathura. The inauguration of the temple was preceded by weeklong celebrations. Never since the marriage of Vasudeva and Devaki had there been celebrations on this scale and the people, after decades of ruthless repression, let their hair down and participated in the revelry with gay abandon.

A band of acrobats entertained the crowd with a superb display of physical skills. The band performed near the temple complex and then at various points along the palace gates and the palace wall and people thronged to see their performance. And, as evening approached and the band packed up after giving the last performance of the day, one of the members took their leader aside.

'Krishna, Akrur*ji* has sent a message for you. You and Balarama are to secretly meet him tonight in his city house.'

Krishna nodded.

It was a long night for Krishna and Balarama. Their rendezvous with Akrur went on well past midnight as Krishna and Akrur discussed threadbare the modus operandi of the operation.

'Leave me out of this, Akrur*ji*,' Balarama had said midway. 'This strategy business goes right over my head. I frankly don't understand what is there to devise such elaborate plans. You just command me to fight and I will ensure that each head is smashed to the smithereens.'

Krishna smiled. '*Dau,* the problem is that we are too few compared to the army. I am sure you can take on fifty or even hundred soldiers at a time but the others are not as powerful as you. That is why we need to plan.'

'Then allow me to go and catch up on my sleep. Just tell me when and where to fight and I shall be game for it.' Balarama left in a huff.

Krishna smiled indulgently at his petulant brother and went back to the drawing board. There were three days left for the inauguration of the temple and both Akrur and Krishna were in agreement that the operation should be conducted on that day.

'Krishna, from the information I have gathered, on that morning Kansa will get up at sunrise. The first *prahar* will be spent in ceremonies at the palace itself. He will be bathed with water from the seven rivers and anointed with sandal paste. There will be a *havan* performed by the *Rajpurohit*. Then at the gong announcing the commencement of the second *prahar* of morning, a massive procession will start from the palace to the temple. At the head of the procession will be the heralds, flag-bearers and standard-bearers. They will be followed by a cavalry contingent of the army. Then dancers, jugglers and performers will follow. Behind them will be Kansa riding on his elephant. He will be followed by his wives Asti and Prapti on palanquins and several maids. Another contingent of the Magadhi army will bring up the rear. This procession will pass through the main thoroughfares of Mathura and reach the temple in a little over one *prahar* time. Once they reach the temple, there will be consecration of Kansa as the living deity. He will then unveil his idol. The idol will then be worshipped. It will be about noon. There will be food offerings to Kansa and his leftovers would be distributed amongst the common men as *prasad.* Kansa would then preside over a "wish fulfilling" ceremony in which he would fulfil the wishes of his subjects. Finally, he would preside over a *mallayudh* competition to be held in the temple premises and then just before sunset, he would return to the palace in a procession.'

Akrur paused for a moment and started again. 'In my opinion, Krishna, you should attack while the procession is on way to the temple. My irregulars can attack the cavalry contingents on both sides and you and your team can attack Kansa directly and fell him.'

Krishna mulled over the suggestion in his mind. 'No Raja, that will not be an appropriate moment. I am sure that when the procession will pass, the King will shower coins from atop the elephant. There is bound to be a mad scramble for the same. It would be difficult to launch a frontal attack in such a melee. Further, I am sure the flanks would be protected by a column of soldiers in order to keep the crowd at bay.

I suggest that we attack at the precise time the procession reaches the temple gate. It will be a bottleneck and there will be confusion amongst the soldiers and others in the procession. That would be the ideal time to strike.'

'Well, we can go by that.'

'Raja, your irregulars are all in city?'

'Yes, they sneaked in during the last one week in the garb of performers just like you and your team came in as acrobats.'

They discussed for hours the various possibilities and strategies. It was decided that Akrur's irregulars as well as Krishna's team shall wear white cloth armbands for easy mutual identification. Finally, Akrur concluded the meeting.

'Krishna, you are the General of the expedition. You shall decide the entire strategy. Guru*ji* has spoken very highly of you and after speaking to you, I realise why. Tomorrow night I shall introduce you as Vishnu's avatar to some Vrishni overlords, who are my confidantes. We need to start a whispering campaign amongst the people that Deliverance is nigh. We meet here again tomorrow.'

As Krishna turned to move, Akrur stopped him. 'Krishna, for the people here, divinity is equated with supernatural powers, not with *karma*. So when we meet the overlords tomorrow, I may have to speak about your life events and link them to supernatural powers.'

'Do we really need to?' Krishna hesitated.

'Krishna, politics is like war—it starts with games of the mind. For the success of your expedition, we require unstinted support of the people. That will come about only if people feel you are on a higher pedestal. If they feel you are just one of them, they will try to pull you down. That is why the need to project supernatural powers. People do not want to believe in success achieved through hard work and dedication because that would set a precedent which they would be expected to follow. So, any outstanding feat is promptly attributed to miracles and the supernatural. If we are to succeed, we must play on what they believe and use their support for our cause.'

Krishna nodded. Guru Sandipani had taught him that in politics, the ends were more important than the means. In the cosmos, there was nothing as a permanent truth. Even the Sun changed directions.

Only a mile away from where Krishna conferred with Akrur, another meeting was in progress. Chanur was speaking to the captains of his tribal army.

'Friends, the day has come for us to fulfil our dream of a tribal homeland. Till the Aryans came, we were the owners of all this land. The Aryans displaced us with their superior weaponry and superior battle strategy. You have all heard how our forests were put on fire and whoever came out was hacked to death. But enough is enough. I had promised to my Guru Rudracharya that I shall set up an independent tribal homeland. The time has now finally come when we shall redeem our freedom. The path of our freedom shall start with Mathura and then will spread all over Aryavarta. This is our chance. Remember friends, if this opportunity goes, another may not be available in centuries.

Friends, you have worked hard at building the temple. And, on the third day hence, you shall decimate the living God therein and install the image of our own God. That day Kansa shall come in a huge procession from the palace to the temple. You all shall remain in hiding inside the secret chamber in the Vishnu temple. Wait till I send my messenger. And then you will come out like a wave and fall upon all those inside. My men will lock the main gate of the temple so that Kansa cannot go out and his men cannot come in. And once Kansa is killed, his Magadhi army will flee. As it is, a large part of the Magadhi army has been stationed by me at the borders and so the number of them in the city is minimal. Do not restrain yourself. Kill as many as you can. And then on these ruins will be built the great tribal homeland. Once Mathura goes the tribal way, Magadha will follow and soon we shall have a vast homeland spanning from Mathura to Magadha.'

Amidst cheers and calls for victory, Chanur bid them adieu. 'We shall next meet at the ceremony to declare creation of our Tribal homeland, nay, Our Homeland.'

'*He* is the boy you spoke of, Akrur*ji*? *He* is going to deliver us from Kansa?' The sarcasm in the voice was palpable.

It was the meeting with the Vrishni overlords that Akrur had promised Kanha the previous night.

'This dark-skinned boy cannot be the son of Devaki*ji* and Vasudeva*ji*. He is not an Aryan and in any case not a *Kshatriya*. You are mistaken, Akrur*ji*.' Another overlord spoke up.

'Sir, you are much elder to me but I feel that you should judge a person by his ability and work rather than by his appearance,' Krishna protested. 'And, as for the colour of skin, please don't forget King Rama of Ayodhya was also dark skinned and yet he is regarded as the doyen of the *Kshatriyas* and a King of Kings.'

'Akrur*ji*, do you listen? Now this fellow is comparing himself with King Rama! King Rama had killed Ravana. This fellow is too young to give battle to any of Kansa's watchmen, leave alone Kansa.'

'Sudershan*ji*, I think I will need to narrate all that this young fellow has already done to convince you that he is indeed the avatar of Vishnu and the eighth son of Devaki and Vasudeva,' Akrur was not one to back out from the argument. He narrated Kanha's conquests from Putana to Kalia and Agha to Bhoumya and Pralamba and described them as his *leelas*. He set out how Kanha saved all the Gops during the mighty cloudburst by taking them to Mount Govardhan and opening up the bosom of the mountain.

'Sudershan*ji*, cast aside your doubts and believe in Krishna. He is the real avatar of Vishnu and it is He who will deliver us from Kansa.' Akrur implored.

'Raja, I beg to differ with you on this aspect,' Krishna intervened. 'I am not here to deliver you all but to show you the path to your deliverance. All these years you have remained in servitude because you waited for someone else to come and deliver you instead of unitedly fighting for the cause. Rather you fought amongst yourselves. You did not deem yourselves as Mathuraiites but as Andhakas, Vrishnis and Bhojas. And Kansa took advantage of your internecine quarrels and incited each group against the others. He divided you and ruled over you.'

'Akrur*ji*, what he says is true.' It was Sushena, one of the overlords. 'When we look back at the events, it is clear that our quarrels have led to our downfall.'

'Yes, yes...very true.' There was a chorus in agreement. Sudershan also nodded his head in agreement.

'Krishna, you have told us the cause of our downfall. Now tell us how to get out of it.' Sudershan had now come around.

'Sudershan*ji*, my *Narayani Sena* and I plan to directly attack the King when he disembarks at the temple day after tomorrow. Simultaneously, Raja's men would attack the Magadhi army contingents on the flanks. I would request you and your men to conceal daggers under your cummerbunds and carry sticks in your hands that day. As soon as the attack starts, you all must immediately fall upon the Magadhi troops and kill whatever number of them that is possible. Please remember, God also helps only those who help themselves. If you and your men do not come forward day after tomorrow, you all will be cursed with a lifetime of slavery and ill fate.'

'We will all do as you say, Krishna.' Sudershan spoke on behalf of the gathering.

They discussed and mulled over the strategies. And by the end of the session, Krishna had won them all over.

And as the overlords left one by one, one of the overlords, Subahu, pulled Sushena aside.

'Suppose this Krishna would rid us of Kansa, would he become the King?'

Sushena smiled. 'It is the *Parishad* which will decide the next King. Let Krishna rid us of Kansa if he can. We will then decide who will be the King. Don't worry.'

Subahu smiled back, reassured.

The next day there were whispers all over the city: 'The Deliverer has finally come… The eighth son of Devaki, the avatar of Vishnu is here to rid us of Kansa… His name is Krishna… Tomorrow we shall be rid of Kansa… Prepare yourself.'

Spies brought the news to Chanur. His brows furrowed on hearing the gossip circulating amongst the people.

'Who is this pretender claiming to be the eighth child of Devaki and Vishnu's avatar?' He wondered aloud. It was he who had created the story. Who could it be that was acting out his story without his knowledge? Who was this Krishna? Nobody seemed to know. What were his origins? Who were his parents? How did he look like? Where was he at the moment? All these answers were eluding his spies and seemed to be steeped in mystery. Time was too short and so were the available personnel. Too many outsiders had thronged the city and the spies were in a tizzy trying to keep a watch.

Chanur did the only thing that could be done in the circumstances. He sent a message to the commander of his tribal army holed in the secret chamber of the Vishnu temple.

'Someone else is also trying to kill the King. Be on your guard.'

It was virtually a sleepless night for Krishna. The next day was the reason for which he was born. *Would it go as Guruji had predicted? Would he be able to discharge the trust and responsibility so many had placed upon him?*

Was he the avatar of Vishnu? What could he do what others cannot? The answers eluded him. Self-doubt crept in. He was up against the merciless Kansa and his experienced Magadhi army. And, what did he have? Only about fifty trained boys and a few hundred irregulars. Were the scales not turned against him? What if he were captured? What if he were killed? What if he failed? How would those, who were singing his paeans today, treat him then?

And as he closed his eyes, images of his father, mother and Radha floated in his mind's eyes. So many months had passed by since he had last seen them. Did they know that tomorrow may be the last day of his life? What would happen to them if he were to die?

No, this would not do. He must not let negative thoughts take control of his mind. He steeled his mind and concentrated on his Guru. And yet, moments later it was Radha who had occupied his mind. How was she? Did she continue to think of him as he thought of her? He thought of their last parting. The manner in which she had placed his hand on her heart and given him her everything—mind, body and heart. And the last parting kiss....

The Sun had already risen when he awoke. Kanha jumped up and came out of his tent on the banks of the Yamuna. After paying obeisance to the Sun and the Yamuna, he got ready and proceeded to the palace to ascertain the state of preparedness of the procession. The security at the gate barred him from entering but from the open gate he could watch the soldiers ready with their horses. The King's elephant was being readied. The mahout was draping the elephant with fine tapestries. The gold *howdah* had been brought for the King to sit on. A little distance away the palanquin bearers were cleaning and draping the palanquins on which the two queens would be carried. From inside the palace, sounds of the conch could be heard. The King was being worshipped. Krishna confirmed from the guards that the procession would start at the gong of the second *prahar* of the morn, as Akrur had stated. Then he turned around and proceeded towards the temple.

The boys of the *Narayani Sena* were already there with their white armbands. He could also see the men of Akrur's irregulars mixed in the crowd. Only Balarama was missing. Krishna looked around for him and then sent one person to fetch him. Krishna found it difficult to conceal his irritation. During the last phase of their stay with Guru Sandipani, Balarama had taken to smoking marijuana which he had found growing in the wild. He did it stealthily so that the Guru would not be able to find out. Now, after coming to the city, he had started to drink as well. Krishna had remonstrated with him only to be told that a little bit of intoxication increased one's strength during battle. But intoxication causing delay on such an important day was a bit too much. He would have to speak to Balarama later, Krishna decided.

Close to the temple was a small secluded area covered with thick elephant grass. Krishna had selected this place to hide their weapons. Swords, spears, bow and arrows and Balarama's mace lay concealed in the grass. A few of his men kept watch, ready to fend off any loitering busybody. Just nearby, one of Akrur's men had camped with a few horses, posing as a horse-seller from the land of the Mlechchhas.

Soon the gong at the palace sounded the second *prahar* of the morning and immediately Krishna and his men tensed up. At the palace, the heralds announced the arrival of His Exalted Holiness, the God of the Gods, Bhagwan Shri Kansa Maharaja, the protector of his devotees and the nemesis of his enemies, to the procession along with Her Exalted Highnesses the Queens of Mathura. Kansa, dressed in a flowing robe made of golden threads, bedecked with gold and diamond jewellery and a big gold and diamond crown specially made for the occasion, arrived. His one hand was raised in the position of granting boon while on the other he carried a mace plated with gold. He was flanked by his wives Asti and Prapti, both looking suitably divine. At their first sight the onlookers prostrated before them and the next instant erupted with cries of victory to the living god. With a beatific smile on his face, Kansa ascended the gold *howdah* on the richly caparisoned royal elephant while his queens ascended their respective palanquins. Chanur and the other advisers, including Akrur, followed them on horseback. The soldiers, resplendent in their new uniforms, took up their respective positions. The cavalry contingents, on white horses and carrying shining open scimitars, took up positions at the head and rear while two lines of foot soldiers carrying golden shields and golden lances guarded the flanks of the procession. Thereafter, the procession took off towards the temple.

It was a magnificent sight to behold. The bright blue sky with a nip in the air provided a perfect backdrop to the grandeur that was unfolding on the street. The sun reflected a thousand times from the golden shields and lances and dazzled the gathering. The entire population of the kingdom was on the streets. The army struggled to maintain a semblance of order and keep the road free for the procession to pass. Intermittent showers of gold coins from top of the King's elephant worsened the situation as it almost caused a stampede. Every few hundred yards the procession would halt and the dancers would perform to the accompaniment of foot-tapping music. The grandeur of the occasion made the people of Mathura forget the decades of oppression and join the armed personnel in shouting victory to the living god.

Krishna baulked at hearing the cries of victory to Kansa. Balarama had finally come and Krishna took him aside. '*Dau,* are you sure we are doing the right thing?

The King appears to be so popular that the crowd is rooting for him.'

'You forget Krishna, this man has imprisoned our parents. My hands are itching to smash him with my mace,' Balarama muttered, his breath mildly reeking of liquor.

Two thirds of the morning's second *prahar* was gone by the time the procession reached near the temple complex. And for the first time Kansa did not betray any irritation at the slow progress of the procession. The elation on his face was palpable as the crowd raised slogans in his praise. Only a few *muhurtas* remained before he would be consecrated as the living god. Which ignorant fool had predicted his demise at the hands of the avatar of Vishnu? Here in the temple Vishnu's idol would remain with folded hands behind his own idol. Kansa threw another fistful of gold coins at the crowd, watching with satisfaction as they fell head over heels in trying to catch them. It was so easy to win over people. This could have been done decades earlier. These advisers were absolute idiots. He would now apply his own mind to State policy, he decided.

The *Narayani Sena* and Akrur's irregulars, who had waited patiently since morning, now took up their positions. They constituted the only crowd in that area, having pushed away the others. There was nothing to distinguish them from the regular crowd, except for the white armbands. Clandestinely, swords were taken out from the place where they had been concealed and passed around. For the last time Krishna looked around and ensured that all was going right. Finally he looked up to the skies and muttered a small prayer.

As the trumpets announced the arrival of the procession, the priests came out of the temple with gold plates containing flowers, sandal paste and offerings to welcome the God and King.

The heralds, the advance cavalry contingent and the performers marched ahead of the temple gate and then waited while the royal elephant carrying Kansa and the two palanquins carrying the queens arrived. The priests started chanting *mantras* in a loud voice. Krishna's heartbeat stopped for a moment. He waited for the elephant to sit before giving signal to his men to attack and the wait seemed an eternity.

'Krishna, what are you thinking? We must start immediately.' Balarama thought Krishna was vacillating. And then without waiting for Krishna's reply and before Krishna could stop him, swung his mace and shouted: 'Attack!'

The next moment all hell broke loose. Akrur's irregulars fell upon the advance and the rear contingent of the cavalry with their swords even as Balarama crashed his mace against the shield of a soldier guarding the flank of the King's elephant.

Krishna struck his forehead at the blunder. The King's elephant was still standing and it was no ordinary animal. It was the mighty Kubalayapir, Kansa's war elephant. Trained for war, it was used during peacetime to crush Kansa's prisoners under his feet. Had Balarama tarried for a moment, the elephant would have sat down and then Kansa would have been an easy target. Instead, they would now have to contend not only with Kansa but that mountain of an elephant.

What followed thereafter was utter confusion. The priests threw down their offerings and ran inside the temple complex. The hundred maidens waiting to shower flowers on Kansa, shrieked and ran helter skelter. And as Krishna and the *Narayani Sena* fell on the soldiers guarding the flank and on the King's elephant, the animal trumpeted and charged on them. It swung its trunk viciously and missed Krishna by a whisker. Another member of the *Narayani Sena* was flung away to death. Krishna brandished his sword causing a deep gash on the trunk of the elephant while Balarama hit it with his mace. Maddened by pain the tusker roared, rose on its hind legs and came crashing down on two others.

Krishna drew out his dagger and threw it at Kansa atop the elephant. But the elephant moved and the dagger missed Kansa by a whisker. The next moment Balarama threw up his mace. The mace crashed into the side of the gold *howdah*, smashing one side. But Kansa again remained unscathed.

'To the palace, to the palace,' Kansa shouted instructions to the mahout.

Just then, a wave of tribals swinging machetes over their heads, rushed in from inside the temple. They were the tribal army of Chanur, who had heard the noise outside from their hiding place inside the Vishnu temple and had come rushing out.

Immediately there was a stampede amongst the crowd who had come to watch the procession. People fell and were crushed under the feet of others. Women shrieked, children cried and there was pandemonium everywhere.

Meanwhile, many of the Vrishnis in the crowd took out their daggers and sticks and fell on the Magadhi foot soldiers who had been guarding the flanks and a massive riot broke out. And as the news spread of the attack, people came in hordes and started pelting the royal soldiers with stones and whatever else that came to their hands.

The mahout brought down the *ankush* on the elephant's head but Kubalayapir did not need any egging. Trained to fight as well as to protect its Lord, the elephant tore into the crowd which parted like butter before a knife. Trumpeting its defiance of the crowd, trampling all that came in its way, the mighty tusker ran towards the palace.

The Magadhi army was now under attack from three quarters. Akrur's irregulars engaged the two units of cavalry at the two ends. Chanur's army fell upon the advance unit which was near the temple while a huge crowd attacked the foot soldiers who had been guarding the flanks. The battle-hardened army was however an equal match for the numerically superior but inexperienced attackers. They retreated into a formation and dourly defended with their shields, occasionally launching incisive counter attacks.

The sudden attack had caught Chanur unaware. But then he saw his men battling the guards and Kansa escaping towards the palace and immediately turned his horse in pursuit. He had finally decided to take the lead in this struggle. He would draw out Kansa alone in the palace and drive his dagger into his back. Once Kansa was killed, the royal army would flee and he would then lead his tribals against that third group. He was still trying to find out who that person by the name of Krishna was, but could not succeed. However, he had seen Balarama in the attacking group as also several Vrishnis. So the third group was that of Vrishnis, who must have made out somebody called Krishna as the eighth child of Devaki.

Akrur was stupefied by the sudden rush of fighters from inside the temple complex, who fell upon the royal army. They were not his irregulars. He could spot his men by their white armbands. So, who could these fighters be? He looked closer and soon the reality dawned on him. The fighters appeared to be of tribal origin. If so, then it must be Chanur who was trying to wage a coup. His mind started calculating. Once Kansa was killed or his army decimated, there would then be a struggle for control between the tribals and the Yadavas, which could go either way. It was therefore necessary to kill Chanur too along with Kansa. Krishna and Balarama must be informed immediately. He turned his horse towards the temple gate where the fight was in progress but then his eyes fell on Asti and Prapti. The two queens were huddled in the palanquins. The palanquin bearers had run away. Fear was writ large over the faces of the queens. Akrur felt pity for them. Having a husband like Kansa must have been punishment enough. He saw Subahu nearby and hailed him. He put him in charge of protecting the queens and escorting them safely to the palace when the situation got better. The task of humanity accomplished, he turned his horse towards the temple gate.

In a fraction of a moment, Krishna had made up his mind. The royal forces were sandwiched between Akrur's irregulars and the other gang, who Krishna could not figure out. Nevertheless, he and the *Narayani Sena* need not detain themselves here. It was necessary to go right after Kansa and decimate him. The only problem would be that the palace gates would be closed shut as soon as Kansa entered and there would be some guards inside as well.

Krishna let go a shrill whistle that was an indication to his *Narayani Sena*. Within a moment they milled around him. He sent one group to the wasteland to get the ropes, weapons and horses and with the remaining forces he seized a few of the panicky horses that were running riderless.

Akrur rushed in. 'Krishna, that other group fighting the soldiers is Chanur's tribal army attempting a coup. Chanur has gone behind Kansa towards the palace. He must also be killed.'

'Yes, we are rushing towards the palace. Please come with us. Balarama, come along.'

Within moments, a cloud of dust arose as the band of riders galloped at the speed of wind towards the palace.

Kansa's elephant rushed through the open gates of the palace. 'Close the gates, close the gates,' Kansa shouted. 'Don't allow anyone to enter.'

He got down from the elephant at the doors of his royal quarters. 'Guard the doors with Kubalayapir,' he ordered the mahout, 'and trample anyone who tries to get inside.'

The massive gates of the palace closed shut with a bang, even as Chanur reached outside.

'Open the gate. Let me in. I am Chanur here.' Chanur shouted.

'Sir, Bhagwan Maharaja has commanded that the gate be closed and no one be allowed to enter.'

'That is for the enemies, not for me. Open the gate immediately and let me in.' Chanur commanded.

'Sir, we are just sending a person to inform Bhagwan Maharaja and take his orders.'

Chanur swore at the guards in frustration even as he saw Krishna, Balarama and the Narayani Sena tear in on their horses.

'Open the gate, open the gate...quick! Let me in...the enemy is upon us.' Chanur pleaded.

'*Dau*, see there is Chanur. You take care of him. We are going inside.' Krishna shouted.

Balarama did not need any direction. He leapt from his horse towards Chanur and pulled him off his horse.

Chanur was no mean warrior. From his childhood, alongside his academic progress, he had assiduously cultivated his physique and the art of *mallayudh*. He had been part of every expedition and adventure that Kansa had undertaken in his youth. It was just that the years as minister had made him indolent and a little rusted. The urge for his life made him shake off the indolence and the decades of rust and when Balarama drew him down from his horse, he managed to turn round, catch hold of Balarama and throw him to the ground.

A fierce fight ensued between the two. Youth and experience battled each other in a fight to the finish.

And as the crowds ran in towards the palace with *lathis* and sickles hearing of the putsch, their mud-splattered bodies crashed like two iron maces, their fingers gripped into a gridlock and their arms muscled against each other.

In the meantime, Krishna and the *Narayani Sena* were throwing the ropes up against the palace wall. The ropes were knotted and had big hooks attached at the end. And, as Balarama and Chanur battled it out, Krishna and his boys managed to get the hooks of the ropes attached to the battlements and soon filed up along the ropes. The people of Mathura had never seen such a sight. The boys steadily climbed the steep walls, balancing their feet on the knots on the ropes and within moments, they were on top of the wall and coming down on the other side.

The few guards who came to resist were soon decimated while the rest fled the scene. The boys rushed to open the palace gates. At the same time, Balarama picked up a weary Chanur by his legs and swung him in circles. Then with a thud he smashed Chanur's body on the ground. There was no scope for any doubt. Chanur's squashed, lifeless body lay prostrated on the ground just outside the palace gate.

'The minister is killed, the minister is killed,' a gasp of excitement spread through the crowd.

'That is Balarama who killed him. Devaki's eighth son Krishna is inside searching for the King himself,' a person in the crowd shouted.

'Come on, come on, let's also go inside. We will help Krishna finish the job,' there was a roar in the crowd.

With scimitars dripping blood, Krishna, Balarama and the *Narayani Sena* fanned out in the palace complex in search of Kansa. They searched the wing built for Kansa's queens room by room. They searched the gardens and even the trees to ensure that Kansa was not hiding there.

And as they crossed the compound into the royal quarters, suddenly Kubalayapir charged at them.

Kubalayapir trampled through the flowers and shrubs of the palace garden and with its trunk broke a big branch of an Arjun tree and hurled it at Krishna. As Krishna stepped aside and avoided the blow, the feared war elephant virtually hurled itself at him. The training in dexterity that Krishna had undergone at Guru Sandipani's ashram saved his life. As he dived aside, Kubalayapir also lost his balance and tripped to the ground with a thud. And within a moment Krishna was up on his feet and had grabbed a spear thrown in by one of the boys of the *Narayani Sena*. As Kubalayapir tried to get up, Krishna jumped up and thrust the spear on the tusker's forehead just between its eyes.

There was a deafening roar like a thousand claps of thunder as the mammoth pachyderm toppled over and doubled in pain. Even a furlong away the surging crowd stopped at the sound. Hidden inside the palace, Kansa shuddered at the death roar of his beloved carrier. For a moment even the *Narayani Sena* was taken aback. And then thirty boys with their spears fell upon the notorious beast and punctured it till it moved no more. An icon of Kansa's rule had fallen.

'Krishna!' 'Krishna!' 'Krishna!' 'Krishna!' The crowd cheered, delirious with joy. 'Our Deliverer is here. Now we will go and finish Kansa. Come on, search for the tyrant… We shall feed him to dogs as he had done to our people….'

The massive wooden doors of the royal quarters were bolted from inside. The crowd brought in logs from the palace garden. Together they held the log and rammed it on the wooden doors. Once, twice, thrice…till the old doors could bear no more and fell apart. A roar of delight went up from the crowd. They fanned out into the halls and rooms, hunting for Kansa. They looked inside the vases, under the beds, inside the almirahs. They kicked aside the mantelpieces, tore down the tapestries and searched out the dark alleyways.

It were Krishna and Balarama who finally spotted him, sitting in a concealed room, holding the crown on his head with both hands. His face was calm but ashen.

'He is here, he is here!' A shout went out and the entire *Narayani Sena* sprang to the place. The crowd too rushed in.

'Catch him and lynch him!'

'No, let's catch him and feed him to the dogs!'

'Fry him in boiling oil like he used to do!'

'No, even that would be too easy. We must devise a more torturous punishment as he used to do to our people.'

Akrur stopped them. 'Destiny has ordained that Krishna will deal with Kansa. Allow him to do so.'

Krishna stepped forward. 'Kansa, I am Krishna, the eighth son of Vasudeva and Devaki, the avatar of Vishnu. I am here to kill you and fulfil my promise to the world. Come, fight me.' Without giving him a moment, Krishna caught him by his heavy gold chain, dragged him out of the room and punched him in the face. 'Fight me, you imbecile. For long you have tortured the people of this kingdom. For decades you have imprisoned my parents and deprived me of my identity. You creature of hell, you did not even hesitate to imprison your own parents! The urn of your sins has long overflown and so I have come to rid the world of you.'

The mention of Vishnu made Kansa rise out of his stupor. With a toss of his head he flung aside his crown and pounced upon Krishna like a wounded tiger. 'Vishnu, my bare hands are sufficient to kill you.' Balarama advanced to help but Krishna stopped him with a show of his hand.

'Always beware of a person who is fighting for his life,' Krishna remembered his Guru's words. 'A deer when pushed to the corner by the tiger, will brandish its antlers and attack back. If the tiger is not careful, the deer can even puncture its stomach.'

The two champion *mallas* fixed their eyes on each other as they moved around in a circle. Each knew it was a fight to the finish. The limiting rules of tournaments would not apply here.

And then there was a clash of their torsos. Kansa was fired with the natural instinct of self-preservation while Krishna was fired with the rage of youth. They grappled, kicked, punched and dragged one another with such animal ferocity as would befit two lions battling for territory. The mention of Vishnu's name had converted into rage the years of dread that Kansa had suffered. Now that the moment of reckoning had come, he sought to prove that he was greater than Vishnu. He did not stop to ponder whether the crowd would let him go if he could kill Krishna. He menacingly moved towards Krishna, wanting to catch him in an embrace of death and shatter his bones to smithereens.

Superior strength clashed against superior skill and came up second best. Krishna deftly parried Kansa's manoeuvres and as age and despondency caught up with the tyrant, he unleashed a deadly barrage of kicks and punches. Kansa doubled up in pain and immediately Krishna caught him by his neck, toppled him and thrashed him to the ground. Then sitting atop Kansa, Krishna delivered a final chop at the throat. The tyrant gurgled and then turned motionless.

For one full moment there was a complete silence of disbelief. The people of Mathura could not believe that they had been rid of their tormentor. Then, as Kansa's body lay on the floor, people went up close and checked if he was still breathing. And in an instant, there was an explosion of spontaneous celebration.

Kansa is dead! Kansa is dead! He is finally dead!

It started as whispers and within a moment reached a crescendo. Inside and outside the palace, the crowd turned delirious. People shouted, laughed, danced, cried and then a wave of people picked up Krishna and Balarama over their heads.

At the temple, the fighting had ceased. The royal army as well as Chanur's fighters fled on coming to know that their masters had been done to death. A section of the crowd chased them and lynched a hapless few, while the rest managed to escape. The others barged inside the temple complex. They yanked out the idol of Kansa from its pedestal and threw it down on the ground. The frustration and anger of decades was let loose on the idol. The diamonds and rubies were wrenched out, the gold leaves covering the statue were chiselled out and then the denuded statue was battered with hammers and broken to pieces which were kicked around by an enthusiastic crowd.

That evening, night did not descend on Mathura. Torches were lit in every nook and corner and people went wild with celebrations.

It was with the greatest difficulty that Krishna and Balarama descended from the backs of the crowd. And immediately they went to Akrur.

'We want to meet our parents. Please take us to them.'

XV
The Ordeal

When you left, my eyes went with you. Now how will I cry?

...Rumi

'Death to Kansa...Death to Kansa...Death to Kansa... Death to Kansa,' Vasudeva continued to mutter under his breath.

Since morning he had been in a disturbed state of mind. Something was happening in the city, but he could not make out what. In the dungeon the thick walls shut out all the sounds and light. Only one small ventilator at the end of the corridor gave a faint indication whether it was day or night. From that small ventilator, time and again wafted in a faint murmuring sound. Vasudeva strained his ears to catch each of those elusive sound waves. Was it the sound of the crowd? Why had they gathered? Was it some celebration? Or was it...was it a revolt against Kansa? He called out to the guards but received no reply. Disconcerted, he paced up and down the cell.

In the adjoining cell Devaki sat motionless, her head crouched between her knees. After the death of her seventh child, she had stopped talking altogether. It seemed she had become oblivious to everything...hunger, thirst and even her husband. Even when Vasudeva would call her through the small hole in the wall between their cells, she remained motionless, lost to the world. Everyday at mealtime two lady guards would come and feed her with the greatest difficulty.

In the afternoon the murmurs increased in their intensity. Vasudeva got up and resumed his pacing and muttering.

And then suddenly, a maddening sound—difficult to describe but more like an earth-shattering wailing trumpet stopped him in the tracks and shook him to the core. For once, even Devaki momentarily looked up. Vasudeva rushed near the iron grills of the gate of his cell and strained his eyes down the corridor. Sadly the ventilator was away from his line of vision. The next moment he could see the prison guards running around.

'What has happened? Will someone tell me what has happened?' He shouted at them. There was no response.

'Death to Kansa…Death to Kansa…Death to Kansa… Death to Kansa,' he shouted till his voice became hoarse. No guard appeared.

Each moment appeared to last an hour. And, after what seemed a decade, sounds resurfaced. Much like the buzzing of a swarm of bees. And they were nearer than the sounds he had heard in the morning and louder. Possibly the sounds originated within the palace compound. Vasudeva strained his ears again, then shook his head and sat down. He had become used to silence during all these decades that he had been incarcerated. And now the sound was maddening. He clapped his hand to his ears. 'Stop it… stop it…stop it…stop it…' he muttered continuously.

When they came, Vasudeva was still in that crouched position, his hand to his ears, muttering to himself. Akrur did not want the boys to meet Vasudeva and Devaki in the prison conditions. He could well imagine the physical and mental state the prisoners would be in. He pleaded that his staff first go and free Vasudeva and Devaki, take them to the palace, clean them and dress them before they met Krishna and Balarama.

'Seeing their present state of being will scar you for your lives,' he repeatedly warned them. But the boys were insistent.

They broke through the dungeon gates and searched through the catacomb of cells. King Ugrasen was found in one of the cells, still sane but drooping with age and almost unrecognisable amidst the grime and the tattered clothes. He was taken up to the palace to be revived. Queen Padmavati had not survived the ordeal. The very thought of having been imprisoned by her own son, had consumed her.

But if Akrur thought that the condition of King Ugrasen had prepared the boys as well as himself for the sights to come, he was wrong. When at the end of the catacomb they finally found Vasudeva and Devaki, Krishna and Balarama were speechless, benumbed with shock and horror.

Akrur gently placed his hand on their shoulder. 'I told you so.' And then the Yamuna flowed out of their eyes. Balarama repeatedly hit his forehead to the prison wall. 'How could I have enjoyed and slept all these years while my parents were in this wretched condition? Why did I not even try to kill Kansa all these years?' Akrur and Krishna tried to calm him. 'It is all destiny. It has a time for everything. Everyone has to go through the travails and sufferings that have been ordained by destiny. Nobody can change it.'

'Raja,' Akrur addressed Vasudeva. 'Raja, see your boys have killed Kansa and have come to free you.'

Akrur's words did not register with Vasudeva. He continued to mutter 'Death to Kansa...Death to Kansa... Death to Kansa...Death to Kansa....'

Akrur went and shook him. 'Raja, I am Akrur. Kansa is dead. Do you hear, Kansa is dead! Your sons have killed Kansa. You are free. Do you hear, Raja, Kansa is dead, you are free.'

Vasudeva started from his stupor and clutched Akrur by his upper garment. 'You are lying. Kansa must have sent you. How can he die? My eighth child is not yet born. It is all a conspiracy. Yes...Yes...You are an agent of Kansa. Go away...go away....' He shoved Akrur across, walked back into the cell and sat down, with his back turned to them.

Devaki still sat motionless in her cell. Krishna and Balarama touched her feet and called her but their calls had no effect on her.

'Don't get disheartened,' Akrur consoled Krishna and Balarama. 'After so many decades of suffering, they will take time to come around. We will take them to the palace and bring on the best physicians. Trust me, all will be well.'

With a heavy heart and tearful eyes, the boys came out of the prison. Attendants carried Vasudeva and Devaki to the palace.

'Raja, my work is done here. Permit me to go to my village to meet my parents. I have not seen them since eons. Don't worry, I will come back.' Krishna could no longer bear even a moment of further separation from Yashoda, Nandrai and...Radha.

'Krishna, I understand your anxiety, but have you forgotten your Guru's teaching that you must properly complete the work you have started?' Akrur asked. 'It is just today that you have killed Kansa. Your physical presence in town is imperative or else a fight for power would immediately ensue between the Vrishni, Andhaka and Bhoja overlords. There would be complete anarchy in the kingdom. Guru Sandipani will arrive here tomorrow. He will guide you. Then the day after I am calling over all the overlords of Mathura to decide the next course of action. Your presence is essential at the meeting. Have patience, my child. One false move can undo all the good work you have done.'

Krishna's face turned pale. Yet, he nodded. He could not endanger innocent lives for his personal needs. 'Alright Raja, I shall wait for the situation to stabilise and leave immediately thereafter.'

It was a long secret meeting between Akrur and Guru Sandipani. 'Akrur, Krishna is the only hope today for both the Vrishnis and Mathura,' the Guru explained. 'Vasudeva has been rendered incapable of assuming the reins of the kingdom. Balarama has the brawn but not the mental faculties to rule. He is also incendiary and therefore dangerous to have as a monarch. And you, Akrur, have the greatest mental faculties but not the leadership qualities of a King. You can be a kingmaker and guide the kingdom but not become the King yourself.'

Akrur nodded. 'But Guru*ji,* will the Andhakas and Bhojas accept Krishna? And the same also goes for our Vrishni community. Will he not still be regarded as a Gop?'

'All those problems will of course arise, Akrur, and we need to face them squarely. Krishna is the son of Vasudeva, the slayer of Kansa and an avatar of Vishnu. Nobody but an incarnation of God could have delivered Mathura from a demon like Kansa. He is the perfect combination of physical prowess, intelligence, modesty and human values. He is the perfect candidate for the King. And you will guide him as minister.'

'But Krishna insists on going to his village. He says that he has completed the task for which he had taken birth. And now he wants to go to meet his parents and his love. He says that he will come back but....'

'Have you enquired into the situation in his village?'

'No Guru*ji,* I was busy preparing for the uprising and could not keep track of the developments in Krishna's village.'

'Akrur, this has been a failing on your part. You must always have all information related to all key people who are either associated with you or opposed to you. Now as regards Krishna's wish to go to his village, my answer is: no. He has to be stopped. No question about it. Once he goes to his village and meets his parents and his ladylove, he may as well decide to settle there for the rest of his life. His presence in Mathura is crucial to stability of the kingdom. If he goes, the kingdom will divide in three. And one thing you are forgetting, Akrur. Kansa was Jarasandha's son-in-law. As and when the news carries to him, he will attack Mathura with all his force to avenge Kansa's death. Our soldiers will blow away like straws in the wind unless they are assured that they are fighting under the avatar of Vishnu and so victory will be theirs. Krishna is crucial to Mathura's existence.'

'But what do we do?'

'Anything. Ethical, unethical...anything that will sow division between him and the Gops. Tear him away from the Gops because these relations are only maya which will impede his karma. He is the future of Mathura. And the future of Mathura is more important than his personal emotions. Besides, he cannot escape his destiny. He is born to rule, not to herd cows. Send your agents, Akrur. I shall hold Krishna back for three-four days till you make the necessary arrangements.'

For the next few days it was celebration time in Mathura. But the problem arose from those whose family members had been tortured or killed under Kansa's regime. They got together and tried to seize and defile Kansa's corpse. They demanded the corpse be hung on a pole at the gate of the palace and that his wives be thrown in the dungeon. It was with the greatest difficulty that Akrur and Krishna managed to pacify them and hurriedly cremate Kansa's body. Asti and Prapti were sent back to Magadh with a small retinue of guards. The guards were specifically instructed to take their own time before reaching Magadh.

Jarasandha would obviously know but the later he knew, the better for Mathura.

It was after decades that the overlords of Mathura, representing all the three clans, were meeting together.

The *Parishad* had to be reconstituted. Many of the original members had died and were represented by their successors. Akrur, who had convened the meeting, addressed the gathering. The *Parishad* would now have to elect a King for Mathura. The next meeting would be held a fortnight hereafter, he declared, wherein the new King would be selected.

Some of the Bhoja overlords objected. Where is the need to select a new King, they asked. King Ugrasen had been wrongfully deposed by Kansa. Now that Kansa was dead, King Ugrasen should revert as monarch for the rest of his lifetime. The Andhaka and Vrishni overlords were up on their legs refuting the theory. Arguments and counter arguments ensued which in a matter of moments almost degenerated into a virtual brawl. Finally, Akrur got up. 'We have a fortnight to sort out the issues amongst ourselves. Today was just a preliminary meeting. We shall all ruminate upon the issues in the interregnum and at the next meeting all the views will be considered and appropriate decision taken.'

As the Govardhan hills came into view, Krishna's heart leapt with joy. He egged on the horses. A little while more and he would be with his parents...and Radha.

'Kanha has come...Kanha has come....' The children shouted as Krishna's chariot negotiated the last turn before Nandrai's house. Even as the chariot approached the gate, Yashoda ran out of her house, the ladle still in her hand, her hair dishevelled, her garment stained with turmeric. And even before the chariot came to a dead stop, Krishna had jumped out of it and into his mother's bosom. Their lips smiled and eyes cried even as their arms hugged each other in the tightest embrace. 'My Kanha, my *Lalla*...' she muttered, her voice choked with emotion.

'My *Maiya,* my *Maiya...*' Krishna purred back. Nandrai had come out of the gate and stood smiling, soaking in the scene. Moments stretched to eons before they finally eased out of the embrace and Yashoda took a full good look at her son. 'O my *Lalla,* you have become so thin. But don't worry. Now that you are back, I will pile you with fresh milk and butter and in no time you will get back your health.'

'Yashoda, will you keep *Lalla* waiting outside the gate? Won't you bring him inside?' Nandrai quipped.

'Baba...' Krishna rushed to Nandrai and touched his feet. Nandrai pulled him up and embraced him tightly. 'You have grown taller than me,' he laughed. 'They say when the son grows taller than father, they become friends,'

The entire neighbourhood poured in at Nandrai's residence to greet their Kanha.

'Did you go to Mathura?'

'Do you know Kansa has died?'

'Do you know, the eighth son of Devaki and Vasudeva killed Kansa?'

'Yes, you know, somebody by the name of Krishna. He is said to be the avatar of Vishnu. Have you seen him?'

'Are the celebrations still going on in Mathura?'

'Who gave you this chariot?'

The questions came thick and fast from all directions and in a torrent, without giving any opportunity to reply. Yashoda went inside with other women to prepare *chhach* for the guests and sweets for her beloved son.

Krishna smiled and turned to his father.

'Baba, I killed Kansa.'

If ever there was a state of soundlessness in the universe, it was there at that moment in Nandrai's living room.

Even time held its breath for an instant, finally releasing it with a collective shout of '*Whaaaaaaat?*'

Krishna merely nodded his head in affirmation.

'But you are Kanha. And we all heard it was somebody named Krishna who killed Kansa.'

'Yes and that Krishna is the eighth son of Vasudeva and Devaki.'

'And we all know you are son of Nandrai*ji* and Yashoda*ji.*'

'Kanha, don't joke!'

'Come on, the slayer of Kansa is the avatar of Vishnu. You are a mere cowherd.'

Krishna smiled. 'Can Vishnu not take a cowherd's avatar?' Then he turned to Nandrai. 'Baba, I am your Kanha but I am Krishna as well. And, it is I who killed Kansa with my own hands.'

'What are you saying, Kanha?' Somak *kaka* was aghast. 'You are Nandrai and Yashoda's son. How do Vasudeva*ji* and Devaki*ji* come into the picture?'

Kanha was going to say something but Nandrai gestured him with his eyes, to stop. 'Somak *kaka,* don't you understand, it was to hide Kanha's identity and protect us and our villages from Kansa's wrath that he was given an assumed name and described as Vasudeva*ji* and Devaki*ji's* son.' He turned to Krishna. 'Kanha, your mother is yearning to speak to you. Go and spend some time with her. And take some rest. You must be tired.'

Nandrai had buried the issue so far as the villagers were concerned, but between him and Kanha the issue would remain alive and raw. His heartbeat suddenly increased in anticipation of the approaching showdown.

When the last of the visitors had left, Nandrai called Kanha to him. 'Kanha, are you ashamed of being my son that you claim to be son of some other?'

Krishna sat down and held Nandrai's feet in his arms. 'Baba, please don't take it otherwise, but I need to tell you something that my Guru told me. As you are well aware, at the time of Vasudeva*ji*'s marriage with Devaki*ji*, it was predicted that their eighth child will be the avatar of Vishnu and will kill Kansa. Kansa killed six of their children. The seventh child was transferred from Devaki*ji*'s womb to Rohini*ji*'s womb and everyone thought that Devaki*ji* had undergone a miscarriage. That child was born to Rohini*ji* as Balarama. Then came the time for birth of the eighth child, which everybody assumed to be the seventh. On that apocalyptic night, Devaki*ji* gave birth to a boy, that was me, while *Maiya* gave birth to a girl. By the maya of Vishnu, the guards fell asleep and the prison gates opened. Vasudeva*ji* carried me in a basket in the rain, the water parted before him and he reached here. He placed me beside *Maiya,* took the girl and went back to prison. That moment the gates shut and the guards woke up. They heard the wails of the girl and informed Kansa. Kansa came the next day and killed her.'

'That is wrong, Kanha,' Nandrai shouted. 'I vividly remember that night. I had gone out for some time to attend to the villagers whose huts had collapsed. When I came back, I opened the door and called out to the *dai.* At that instant you cried out. The *dai* came and said that a boy was born. I washed myself, went inside and saw you. Your mother was also conscious and it was she who gave you the name Kanha then and there. There is no question of us being asleep with a girl child and Vasudeva*ji* changing the babies. You are my boy Kanha, get all that crap out of your mind.'

'Baba, Guru*ji* told me that due to the maya of Vishnu, Vasudeva*ji* and Devaki*ji* thought they had given birth to a girl and you and *Maiya* thought you had given birth to a boy.'

'No *Lalla,* you have been misled, I do not know for what purpose and what end.'

'Baba, if you remember, Kansa had called a *tantrik* after the killing of Agha. He had also said the same thing what my Guru said. In fact, it was after that *tantrik's* prediction that Kansa ordered the general massacre of all children in the kingdom. My Guru*ji* is a Rishi, Baba. He will not speak untruth.'

Nandrai sat crestfallen.

Krishna caressed his father's feet. 'Baba, when I first heard this fact, I was so disconcerted that I could not eat or sleep for a week. Then Guru*ji* explained that the position of foster parents is even higher than that of real parents. And that I was lucky to have two sets of loving parents. Baba, I have known only you and *Maiya* all my life and the fact that I have another set of parents does not make a difference to our relationship.'

'But it makes a difference to me, Kanha. Yashoda and I have remained awake the whole night whenever you had fever. We almost died of shock on your *chhathi* ceremony when we discovered you had been kidnapped. You do not realise what we went through during your absence for the last one year. Now when you say that our blood does not flow in you, my world is devastated. I do not know what your mother will make out of it. Maybe she will die of broken heart if she comes to know.'

'Baba, what do I do? Where is my fault? How can I choose between you and my Guru? I love and respect you both....' Krishna broke down in tears.

Nandrai also broke down. A moment later he lifted Kanha and hugged him. 'Don't cry, my son. You will always remain my *Lalla*. No one can take that away from me. Just one thing...don't tell your *maiya*. She may not be able to bear it.'

It was not until the sun had reached its midday peak and Yashoda had piled him with the choicest dishes, that Krishna could come out of his house. At long last he would be going to meet Radha. He checked the ring tied securely in his dhoti. He untied the horse from the tree and secured it to the chariot, when he saw his friend Pundarika come by.

'Where are you going, Kanha?'

Kanha blushed. 'I am going to meet Radha.'

'What? Haven't you heard about Radha?'

'No. What happened to her?' Krishna's feet seemed to be heavy as lead.

'Radha was forcibly married off by her father to Ayan Ghosh.'

'Whaaat? When?' The world seemed to collapse before his eyes.

'A few months back. But that is not all. Her in-laws constantly berated Radha for her love for you and now she is just a mute, lifeless body that just goes through the motions of life. You won't recognise her if you see her.'

A volcano of rage surged up from his insides. He left the horse and rushed inside the house, where the volcano erupted.

'Baba, how could you allow Radha to be married off to Ayan Ghosh? You knew that we were in love.' For the first time Krishna had shouted at his Baba. 'How could you, Baba, how could you?'

'*Lalla,* her father fixed her marriage. You had gone to your Guru and there was no indication when you would return. It could have been a decade. How could I have compelled her father to await your arrival?'

'But...but, could you not send across a word to me? I would have rushed back.'

'I had gone to Akrur*ji* but he did not know of your location. So we could not inform you.'

Tears flowed freely from Krishna's eyes. 'O my Lord, what has happened...what has happened!'

He turned again to his father. 'Baba, you are the *mukhiya* here. Could you not see that Radha was being forced into marriage? How could you allow that? Have you seen what has happened to her?'

Nandrai hugged Krishna. 'My son, as *mukhiya* I cannot depart from the rules or social norms. The father is the guardian of the unmarried daughter. His decision is final. This was not a case of a drunk father selling off his daughter, where I could have intervened. I know you loved each other. Had you been present here, I would have proposed your hand in marriage. But since there was total uncertainty surrounding your return, there was nothing I could have done.'

Krishna took his hands to his head and held his hair in a tight grip. Suddenly he straightened up. 'I will not allow Radha to suffer in this manner. I will get her out from there just now.'

'Kanha, Kanha…come back.' Nandrai shouted after him but Krishna had already jumped upon his chariot and picked up the reins. A pall of dust rose in the air as the chariot hurtled like mad on the dusty road.

'Pundarika, call everybody. We must follow Kanha immediately. God only knows what is going to happen.' Nandrai shouted.

Like an arrow released from the bow, the chariot whizzed through the lanes. Within a matter of moments Ayan Ghosh's cottage came into view. Krishna leapt out from the chariot and shouted: 'Radha, Radha, come out. I have come.'

It was not Radha but Ayan with a dozen others who came out of the cottage, armed with sticks.

'We were told you would be coming here today so we were waiting for you.' Ayan Ghosh could not suppress his grin.

Krishna's dark complexion had turned to purple. 'Ayan, you have forcibly married my Radha and made her suffer intolerably. I have come to take her with me. Give her to me voluntarily or you shall pay for each suffering you have heaped on her.'

In reply, Ayan and his men fell upon him with their weapons. Krishna parried the first blow and then snatched a stick from one of the men. Like the funnel of a hurricane he moved about whirling his stick, leaving his opponents dazed. The fury of his blows flattened heads and broke limbs till the dozen injured bodies lay strewn about the entrance to the cottage. Krishna jumped over them and entered the cottage. 'Radha...Radha...Radha...' he called out repeatedly. 'Radha, where are you, your Kanha has come to take you.'

He found her sitting on the floor, as if carved in stone. Her lotus eyes stared vacantly at the wall ahead. The only thing that moved was a wisp of hair straddling her cheek.

'Radha, I have come to take you, you don't need to stay here, come with me.'

The sound did not register. The sculpture in stone remained as it was, oblivious to the sights and sounds of this world. The unseeing eyes looked through Krishna into the wall ahead.

'Radha, my Radha...' Krishna clutched her arm, 'come with me, I will take you away from here, I will take you with me....'

The faraway look in the eyes did not register a movement. The lips remained silent, colour did not return to the face.

'Radha, Radha...' Krishna persisted.

Outside there was a great hue and cry. Ayan Ghosh's mother raised a ruckus. 'That characterless whore's lover has almost killed my son...Oh, where will I go?

Oh, what am I being made to see in this old age...I will go to the King for justice...O my poor son...' Her daughter pitched in, hurling the choicest of invectives at Radha and Kanha.

Neighbours gathered, undecided what to do.

The wails and the debate had reached a crescendo, when Nandrai accompanied by a large contingent of villagers arrived on the scene.

Seeing him, the wails of Ayan's mother and sister doubled in intensity. 'See *Mukhiyaji,* your son has robbed our honour. He has almost killed my son and a dozen others and molested my daughter-in-law.'

'He is still inside molesting my sister-in-law,' Ayan's sister wailed.

'We want justice, we want justice,' the crowd shouted.

In a glance Nandrai took in the situation and went inside the house, accompanied by the crowd. He saw Krishna clutching Radha's arm, pleading with her to go away with him.

'Kanha, come outside immediately.' It was the voice not of the father but of the *mukhiya* of the Gops.

Krishna looked up as if in a daze, unsure what to do.

'Kanha, it is my command. Come out immediately.'

His head bowed, Krishna came out of the cottage.

'*Mukhiyaji,* you decide what to do.'

Nandrai looked around. 'Since Kanha is my son, would it not be better to refer the matter to five elders?'

'No, no, *Mukhiyaji,* we have full trust in you,' the crowd did not want to delay the justice delivery.

A dark cloud had formed over Nandrai's face. 'Kanha, you have forcibly entered a married woman's home, injured her husband and manhandled her. Do you have anything to say?'

Kanha stood erect. 'Father, Radha was married off in violation of her wishes. A daughter is not a chattel of her father. And all of you knew that we loved each other, yet did not protest when her father forced her into marriage. You did not also protest when she was mentally tortured by her in-laws. And see the consequence of your inaction. See her condition. She has been turned into stone. You all have destroyed three lives. I am not ashamed of what I did because that is the only correct course of action. What more can Ayan get from someone who has turned to stone? And have you not seen how his mother and sister were abusing her? Allow me to take Radha away and all will be well.'

'Kanha, every society has certain norms. If what you say is acted upon, it will result in the disintegration of society. What you have done is punishable. As *mukhiya* of the Gops, I banish you from our community. You will no longer be entitled to live in the Gop villages or to maintain relation with anybody. Go, Kanha, you are expelled from the community.' Nandrai's voice trembled as he uttered the last words.

Krishna's face turned ashen. He bent forward, touched Nandrai's feet and without a word boarded his chariot and set off. He did not look back.

Finally, Nandrai broke down. Tears streamed from his eyes. 'How do I face Yashoda, how do I face Yashoda?' he muttered repeatedly. Inside the cottage, the sculpture in stone remained in the same position. Only, inside her *chunni*, her clutch tightened around a small silver flute.

Behind the grove of trees one person smiled. He had achieved the task assigned to him.

XVI

The Parting

So I wait for you like a lonely house
Till you will see me again and live in me
Till then my windows ache

...Pablo Neruda

Ever since his return from home, Krishna had gone into depression. The image of Radha, frozen in grief, appeared again and again in his mind's eye.

'*You are expelled from the community.*' His father's last words kept ringing in his ears. Krishna cupped his hands to his ears but the sound persisted. Would he never again be able to go back to his Baba or to his *Maiya* or to Radha? How would his *Maiya* survive after hearing the news of his expulsion? Is she still alive? What of Radha? There was a possibility that Ayan and his family would have turned her away from the house. Where would she go? It was maddening.

His room in the palace complex seemed insufferable. He rushed out into the compound. The balmy weather failed to put a balm on his grieving heart. Tormented by his thoughts he walked on, he knew not where. He came out of the palace gates, across the meadow, on the meandering path and onto the banks of the Yamuna. The dark waters of the mighty river invited him. Step by step he walked into the cool waters. The first touch of the cold water on his ankle soothed him. He took a few steps more till the water reached his knees. The torment of his mind was slowly giving way to a state of bliss. The water had now reached till his hips. He felt as if he was entering his *Maiya's* lap. His mind was now at peace. *Maiya* had taken him in her lap and was caressing his hair, kissing his cheek, putting him to sleep. And, as the waters reached his shoulders, his eyes closed. He was entering into a heaven of infinite peace…infinite peace….

'Krishna, Krishna, what are you doing?' screams from the shore roused him. For a moment he felt dazed. His mother's lap was suddenly replaced by swirling waters. Akrur, Guru*ji* and a dozen other people were there on the riverfront shouting at him. A couple of men dived into the water and caught him. *'Maiya, my Maiya, where are you?'* Tears flowing from his eyes mingled into the waters as the men dragged him to the shore.

'Krishna, what on earth…' Akrur was cut short by a glance from the Guru. The Guru hugged Krishna. 'Come with me, my son, come with me.' Leaning on his Guru's shoulder, Kanha slowly walked towards the palace.

Two days later, in a closed-door *havan* ceremony conducted by Guru Sandipani, Vasudeva and Devaki acknowledged Krishna as their son.

Hectic negotiations were underway between the members of the *Parishad* for electing the new King.

The Bhojas were insistent that Ugrasen had been elected King and he was still living, hence the question of succession did not arise. The Andhakas and Vrishnis vehemently opposed. Ugrasen had been deposed by Kansa who became King and ruled for decades. Hence Ugrasen's claim no longer existed.

'But Kansa's rule was illegitimate. He had usurped the throne without reference to the *Parishad*. His reign cannot be considered,' the Bhojas responded.

The Andhakas put forth their claim to the throne. King Sudershan had been a Vrishni, followed by Ugrasen and

Kansa of the Bhojas. The Andhakas had been deprived for a very long time and there would be great unrest if they were denied this time.

But the maximum push came from the Vrishnis. 'For decades we all suffered under Kansa. It is a Vrishni boy who killed Kansa and delivered us. Hence, it is a Vrishni who must ascend the throne this time. Vasudeva has suffered long incarceration in prison. He should be made the King.'

The Andhakas and Bhojas objected. 'Vasudeva may have made the most sacrifices but today he is neither mentally nor physically fit to ascend the throne.'

'And, we have heard he himself does not want to get into politics again.'

'In that circumstance, Krishna should be made the King,' the Vrishnis shot back. 'He is the one who killed Kansa and delivered us from tyranny. It is he who can save us from Jarasandha who is sure to attack us to take revenge.'

'Krishna is too young to be King. And he is also not educated enough. He has been a Gop since his childhood. He does not know of our customs and it would take a long time to assimilate him amongst us Yadavas.' The Bhojas were strident in their opposition.

'We are also not convinced that he is the real son of Vasudeva. Haven't you seen his dark complexion? He does not resemble either Vasudeva or Devaki. Don't thrust a Gop child on us as King, we all will live to regret the decision.' The Andhakas voiced their opposition to Krishna.

'He is the real son of Vasudeva. Have you forgotten the oracles?' The Vrishnis retorted.

'Whatever may be, he has been brought up as a Gop and not as a Yadava. We also heard he was involved with some married Gop woman and was expelled from that community. We can't have someone like that as King.'

'Moreover, this Krishna is so young that if he becomes King for life, both our as well our next generation will stand excluded from claim to the throne.'

The parleys and discussions went on and on, interminably. Guru Sandipani tried to intervene but none of the three clans was willing to back off. The situation was slowly meandering towards a deadlock. No solution seemed in sight.

Finally, after a lot of negotiations and persuasions, a compromise was worked out. Since nothing else could be agreed upon, it was decided as a last resort to continue with Ugrasen as the King. However, the Vrishnis were placated with Akrur becoming the Minister and Krishna being made the Commander-in-chief of the army.

It was a meeting to hear the spy who had come from Magadh. King Ugrasen was unwell and could not attend. Akrur, the other advisers, Guru Sandipani, Krishna and Balarama attended the meeting.

'Jarasandha was mad with rage when he saw his daughters Asti and Prapti in widows' dress and heard of Kansa's death. He has sworn vengeance upon Mathura,' the spy informed. 'And also upon Krishna,' he hesitatingly added.

'When is he likely to attack?' Akrur asked.

'Sir, in fact Jarasandha in his rage immediately gave orders to his army to get ready. But then after he cooled down, he spoke to Hansa and Dimvaka. They advised him to regroup his forces, make further recruitments and then attack. They also advised him to ensure that Hastinapur would not get into the picture. Possibly one of them would personally go to Hastinapur to request that since it was a case of personal revenge, Hastinapur should not interfere when Magadh would attack Mathura. All said and done, it might take about four-five months for the attack to materialise.'

'That would make it sometime in pre-summer to summer,' Krishna calculated.

The spy was sent out and the others continued with the discussions.

'So our doors to Hastinapur may also be closed,' Akrur remarked. 'I had hoped that Hastinapur would help us if Jarasandha attacked.'

'Akrur, Hastinapur is going through its own problems. Even without a formal request from Magadh, they would not have got involved.' Guru Sandipani opined.

'Why Guru*ji*?'

'You see, Akrur, Bhishma has now virtually been sidelined and the blind King Dhritarashtra has taken over the reins of administration. He is guided by his crafty brother-in-law Shakuni whose tactics have sidelined Bhishma. Bhishma today is merely the Commander-in-chief of the army and nothing more. And neither Dhritarashtra nor Shakuni want war because that would again bring Bhishma into prominence. So do not expect Hastinapur to come to your rescue.'

'Then what do we do, Guru*ji*?'

'Raja, it is our battle and we have to deal with it ourselves,' Krishna interjected.

'Krishna, what you say is very true. But do you realise that we would be outnumbered and out-weaponed before Jarasandha's army?'

'Yes, I realise it. And since we would be outnumbered, the only way to win against Jarasandha is by outsmarting him in war strategy.'

'Well said, Krishna,' Guru Sandipani applauded. 'That is like my disciple. What have you thought?'

'Guru*ji*, it is too early to spill the beans. If Jarasandha attacks in summertime and if there is no rain, we have a good chance to win the war. Meanwhile, we must mobilise and train our army. We have four-five months. The most important part of the entire exercise would be to keep the morale of the people intact, that we can defeat Jarasandha. We must start the exercise from tomorrow itself.'

The news spread like wildfire that in a few months Jarasandha would be attacking Mathura. And with the news, panic developed amongst people.

'What chance do we have before him? Our Commander-in-chief is only a boy. Ambushing Kansa is one thing and fighting a war with Jarasandha is another thing altogether.'

'This Krishna was born with the sole purpose of killing Kansa. His work in this world has been accomplished. He is now bereft of his powers. He is now just an ordinary man like you and me.'

It was an emergency situation. Guru Sandipani, Akrur and Krishna went from street to street, addressing the inhabitants.

'Friends, did you ever believe that somebody would kill Kansa? That was done. If Jarasandha dares to attack, that will also be met squarely. Krishna is the avatar of Vishnu. He will protect Mathura from Kansa. We just need to believe in him and in ourselves and do as Krishna says. There is no need to panic whatsoever. Just join the army and be a part of the win against Jarasandha.'

All able-bodied men were conscripted into the army. The blacksmiths worked day and night to manufacture more and more weapons. Swords, lances, bows and arrows, horses and armour were imported from other kingdoms. Balarama practised with his mace, intending to take on Jarasandha in a one-to-one combat while Guru

Sandipani worked day and night imparting training to the recruits.

And while Mathura and Magadh readied for war, thousands of cartloads of straw were gathered by Krishna at various locations in the dense forest beyond the Govardhan hills.

Summer had set in early that year. With the *Flame of Forest* trees blooming with red and orange flowers, the forests literally seemed to be on fire. The bliss of the forest was suddenly broken by shrieks of monkeys. Soon all other sounds were drowned under the sound of creaking wheels, trumpeting elephants, neighing horses and thousands of men. A cloud of dust rose through the trees, blotting out those few darts of sunshine that managed to scrape through the leaves. Jarasandha was proceeding towards Mathura with a *chaturanga* army, an army comprising of four divisions—chariots, horses, elephants and foot soldiers. From Magadh, the army had proceeded through Kashi and Vatsa, along the south bank of the Yamuna, before entering the dense forests of Madhuvan. A hundred miles of dense forests would lead them to Govardhan hills, the gateway to Mathura. This path south of the river involved negotiating more forested area but it would avoid passing through Panchala territory and also avoid crossing the river.

A team of woodcutters slashed through the forest, widening the narrow road used by travellers so that the army could pass through. They were aided by a team of elephants who helped to pull down trees and carried the cut and fallen trees out of the way. In the middle of the convoy Jarasandha sat resplendent upon a golden chariot, his famed mace by his side, a golden umbrella over his head. Five thousand men armed to the teeth with swords, spears, bows and arrows, surrounded him. Behind them were thousands more for manning the provisions and serving the King and his army.

Another twenty miles to Mathura, the guide informed.

'We will reach the gates of Mathura today evening and camp for the night,' Jarasandha told his commanders.

It was too late when they saw the blaze. The burning haystacks set fire to the *sal* forest. From leaf to leaf, tree to tree, grove to grove, the flames leapt all around. The hot breeze, the sun-dried leaves and yet more haystacks suitably placed, facilitated the leaping flames in rapidly spreading from one corner to the other. The elephants who had been transporting the logs, first noticed the flames in front of them. With a hollering roar they turned around and started running on their own men, trampling all that came in their way. Simultaneously a wall of fire suddenly came up on the forest towards the left. It was no longer a blaze but an inferno. Hemmed in by a rapidly advancing fire on two sides and with the Yamuna on the third, a circle of death had enveloped Jarasandha's forces. Elephants, horses and men started running helter skelter. Shrieks and cries rent the air. A general stampede ensued. Bodies piled over bodies and bodies trampled over bodies in the narrow forest path. But that was not all. A barrage of arrows pierced the wall of fire and found their destination on the fleeing men.

Panic.

It was a word that Jarasandha experienced for the first time on that fateful day. His expeditions till this day had centred around two words—'treachery' and 'bravery'. Half his battles had been won through treachery and the remaining half through bravery. Yes, there had been battles which he could not win, an occasional battle that he even lost. But in no battle had he actually panicked. Yet, today, he felt like a helpless prey before the monstrous blaze that looked down on him and his army in joyous anticipation, licking a million tongues of fire.

The horses of his chariot reared up on their hind legs, neighing madly, ignoring even the whip of the charioteer. Several chariots around him lay in broken heaps, flattened by his fleeing pachyderms.

'To the river, to the river!' He shouted.

His voice was drowned in the din. Even his own chariot found it impossible to negotiate the path ordered by him.

The fire was now all over the army. Men ran here and there like flaming torches with their clothes and bodies on fire. Charred bodies lay sprawled on the ground. Hundreds swooned from the smoke and heat and hundreds of others lay dead or injured from the hail of arrows. The stench of burning flesh pervaded the air.

'To the river, to the river...' Jarasandha tore down his armour, jumped down from his chariot and shouted again, furiously pointing out the direction with his golden lance that bore his pennant. With the other hand he wielded his shield to protect himself against the raining arrows. The surviving soldiers followed him and ran through the strip of forest that lay between the path and the river. Almost immediately thereafter the blaze spread over and ignited that strip of the forest. Jarasandha and the surviving soldiers jumped for their lives into the black waters of the Yamuna.

The river was wide and deep, despite the summer. Jarasandha swam across with some effort. But the flying embers caused a stampede amongst the soldiers by the riverfront. Hundreds of soldiers fell headlong into the river with their armour on and drowned immediately.

It was a battle that Jarasandha would not forget for the rest of his life. Of the five thousand troops, only about a thousand survived the ordeal. Amongst the staff, only a couple of thousand survived. The straggling band of survivors finally reached Magadh after a long ordeal, in bare rags.

The world rubbed its eyes in disbelief even as Mathura erupted in joy at the decisive victory. Krishna had become the new household name in Aryavarta. He had done what even Hastinapur with its famed band of *maharathis* did not dare to attempt in all these years. The overlords of the Vrishnis, Andhakas and Bhojas, after a long time, were united in their praise for Krishna and swore their allegiance to him. The same overlords who had earlier resisted his candidature for the throne, now wanted him to replace King Ugrasen, but Krishna declined.

'The avatar of Vishnu is amongst us!' the crowd chanted. Krishna was now more than a King to Mathura. He was their God, their saviour.

But if anyone felt ill at ease at the adulation, it was Krishna himself.

'Jarasandha is not going to rest for a single night,' he expressed his unease to his Guru and Akrur. 'He is not going to digest this insult. He regards himself as an Emperor and this defeat is going to tear his prestige to shreds before the whole world. We have hurt his ego, that too before the whole of Aryavarta. He will strike back and this time he will come with a much larger army and with full reconnaissance.'

'Krishna, we will defeat them again like we did this time,' Akrur said.

'No Raja, in warfare the same tactics do not work. This time when Jarasandha comes, he will send advance parties to ensure that the path which his army takes is properly sanitised.'

'Krishna, we have just dealt him a crushing blow. Let us savour our victory over the next few days. We shall then worry about the future.'

'Raja, when Jarasandha comes this time, he will look to burn Mathura to ashes as we did to his army. We do not have a single day to waste. But even more than that, I am preoccupied with another thought.'

'What is it?' Guru Sandipani enquired.

'Guru*ji*, this victory we have achieved without loss of lives or resources. The next time however, will be different. Jarasandha has an empire, we do not. He can recoup his losses, we cannot. If he wins, he destroys us. If he loses, he regroups his resources and attacks us again. Will we spend the rest of our lives defending ourselves against Jarasandha's attacks? And remember, we cannot sustain war for long. We do not have allies, or any strategic depth. Jarasandha has both. He is not going to rest till he reduces Mathura to dust. So, I want to explore another land far away, where we can relocate our kingdom and be out of Jarasandha's reach. Since finding out such suitable land and building a capital there would take time, we do not have a day to lose.'

'Whaaaaat? Run away from Mathura? What are you saying, Krishna? Are you out of your senses?' Akrur virtually shrieked.

Guru Sandipani remained deep in thought.

'Guru*ji*, have you heard what Krishna is saying?' Akrur now turned to Guru Sandipani to justify his stand.

Slowly the Guru raised his head. 'Akrur, I think what Krishna says makes a lot of sense. We need to think deeper on this aspect.'

They met again the next day and the next day and the next....

They discussed, argued and debated the issue. Then the chief overlords of the Andhakas, Vrishnis and Bhojas were initiated into the discussions.

At first they were aghast. 'Leave the kingdom *en masse* for some distant unknown land? Would we not be a laughing stock for the world?'

Krishna addressed them. He set out his concerns regarding the future, his analysis of Jarasandha's character and his political necessity to destroy Mathura by any means whatsoever. Guru Sandipani supported him. Akrur too, after an initial hesitation, came round to supporting the proposal.

'But if we flee Mathura, would Jarasandha not come after us? Suppose he attacks us at our new kingdom?'

'No, his vanity would be satiated once we leave Mathura. He can tell the world that the avatar of Vishnu has fled before his wrath.' Krishna was emphatic.

'But if we flee Mathura, the world will brand us as cowards. We shall be known as *rann chhod*—one who flees from battle. Why should we bear the ignominy? You all go, I won't quit.' Balarama declared in his sonorous voice.

'*Dau,* do you realise how many lives you will be sacrificing because of your ego? How many women would be widowed, how many children would be orphaned? The entire Yadava clan would be wiped out from the face of Aryavarta. War is never an option. Just let go of your false ego, *Dau.*' Krishna came forward and held Balaram's hands in his own. '*Dau,* if there is stigma, I agree to bear it personally for all the Yadavas. Let the world call me a coward. It does not make a difference to me. But for heaven's sake, do not oppose the proposal.'

'But what if we are able to kill Jarasandha?' Balarama was insistent.

'*Dau,* if it happens, there would be nothing like it. We must hope for the best but prepare for the worst.'

Ultimately after a lot of convincing, Balarama agreed to the proposal. Agents were despatched to all corners of Aryavarta to scout and find out secure land where the kingdom could be relocated. A few months later, the scouts began to come in with their finds. Guru Sandipani weighed each option having regard to the natural defences the place possessed, the availability of adequate land and water, fertility of the land, the kingdoms around it and threats posed by them and so on. He even went to a couple of places to form his own opinion. Finally, he zeroed in on a place in the Sorath region in western Aryavarta, situated beside the sea.

So far as security was concerned, the place was ideal. Not only was the place very far from Magadh, but to reach there one would have to pass through dense forests, high mountains and voluminous rivers. There was also an island on the sea, which could be reached from the mainland by boats. It could provide absolutely safe refuge in times of enemy attacks.

The soil there was black loamy, which was suitable for cultivation of grains. The nearest kingdom was that of the Mlechchhas and that too was separated by a wide branch of the sea and located more than a hundred miles away if one went by the land route. Availability of water was also sufficient. All in all, it was a suitable region in all aspects.

Guru Sandipani did not lose any further time. He gathered men and material and got work started right away. The new city would be known as 'Dwarka', he decreed. *Dwar* meant door. The new city would open the door to a new beginning and new prosperity.

And as constructions began in Dwarka, drums of war sounded in the far east. Spies brought news that Jarasandha was raising a huge army to launch a fresh attack on Mathura and this time he was not rushing headlong into the attack. He was roping in his allies and friends as well so as to launch a concerted attack on Mathura. The armies of Banga, Odra, Kashi, Vatsa and Chedi would march with the armies of Magadh with the sole purpose of setting Mathura ablaze and reducing it to ashes.

'What is to be done now?' Krishna did not have a ready answer this time. There was only one thing of which he was sure. Jarasandha would not take the same route again. He would in all probability pass through Panchala territory on the northern bank of the Yamuna and then use boats to cross the river north of Mathura and march down. If that be so, then the wide arid fields north of Mathura would be the site of the new battlefield.

Messengers were sent to Hastinapur seeking support against Jarasandha. They returned empty handed.

'My Lord, Hastinapur is in mourning. The five sons of Pandu with their mother Queen Kunti had gone on a vacation to Varnavarta. However, the palace where they were residing, which had been specially constructed for them, caught fire and was reduced to ashes and the five sons of Pandu and Queen Kunti were burnt to death. Hence King Dhritarashtra has expressed his inability to assist us.' The chief messenger hung his head.

'What are you saying? Queen Kunti, that is Pritha, the sister of Raja Vasudeva is dead? Her children are dead?' Akrur could not believe what he heard.

'Raja, there are rumours in the public that the fire was not accidental. People are saying that at the instance of King Dhritarashtra's son Duryodhana, the palace was built using inflammable materials like lac and animal fats. And it was set on fire deliberately to kill them.'

'Oh my god! So our family connection with Hastinapur comes to an end.' Akrur sighed. 'No wonder Hastinapur is not helping us.'

'Raja, there is another reason also why Hastinapur is not helping us.' The chief messenger looked up at Akrur. 'After we defeated Jarasandha in the last war, Hastinapur is wary of Shri Krishna. It feels that if we defeat Jarasandha again, Mathura and especially Shri Krishna will become too powerful for them. It wants that Mathura and Magadh should fight out a long-drawn battle so that both are weakened and Hastinapur regains its primacy.'

The messenger went away. Akrur shook his head, dejected. Mathura would have to fight Magadh single-handedly. And it would also not be feasible to go away to Dwarka before Jarasandha came. It would take a long time to make Dwarka inhabitable.

If there was an example of being omnipresent, it was Krishna. One moment he was with the soldiers undergoing rigorous physical and arms training, another moment he was inspecting the city walls and moat and enquiring about the food and water reserves. But the maximum time he spent at the forge, where weapons were being produced. That day he had brought with him an ordinary bamboo handcart and was explaining to the master blacksmith.

'At the lower end of the handcart, a very sharp blade will have to be attached to the box. The width of the blade will be that of the cart's box and in length it should be two cubits. The quality of the blade will be such that if the handcart is pushed through the enemy, it can slice through the bodies. Further, on the upper end of the handcart, just where the box ends and the handrails begin, an iron sheet with slits will have to be vertically installed so that it would shield the persons pushing the handcart from the enemy's arrows.' With a quill Krishna drew the design of the killer handcart and explained it minutely to the master blacksmith. 'Five hundred handcarts will have to be fitted in this manner,' he ordered. Next, he examined the swords and lances. 'Make these a little longer in size. It will take the enemy unawares.'

He next went to Akrur. 'Raja, entry of all outsiders into Mathura, for whatever purpose, will have to be banned for the next few months. We do not want Jarasandha's agents to come to know of our battle plans.'

'But what of traders who bring supplies to Mathura?' Akrur enquired.

'We will form a council of traders who shall negotiate at the gates of Mathura itself. No one shall come in and or go out of the city for these few intervening months.'

'Can such a system work?' Akrur was doubtful.

'Raja, we will have to make it possible if we are to face Jarasandha. He and his advisers Hansa and Dimvaka are adept at treachery.'

Akrur reluctantly agreed and issued instructions to that effect.

It was noon when Jarasandha set up camp near the arid fields to the north of Mathura. There were no elephants this time in his army, only chariots, cavalry and foot soldiers. The army was double in size than the last time and so was the entourage. Yet there was no fanfare as was usual during the march of Jarasandha's army. The clash of cymbals, the trumpet of elephants and the beating of drums were all missing. Yet the neighing of horses and the movement of thousands of men broke the silence of the wilderness. Jarasandha's face resembled a thunderous monsoon cloud, his mind steeled for merciless decimation. He barked instructions to his advisers and himself went round the camp to ensure that everything was in order. The next morning, he would dance the *tandava* over Mathura and deluge the city in its own blood.

That night Mathura did not sleep. The women, children, old and infirm were sent away to the Govardhan hills even as the men tied saffron bands around their heads, ready to make the supreme sacrifice. Krishna, Balarama and Akrur went around motivating the men and giving last-minute instructions.

The armies had taken up positions on the two sides of the field. Jarasandha, intending to launch a cavalry assault, had lined up his chariots and horses upfront. They were followed by his foot soldiers who would pounce upon whatever was left of the opposite army after the first charge. Krishna arranged his army in a half-moon formation, keeping his foot soldiers in the middle, cavalry in the flanks and archers mounted on stands, at the ends. Concealed behind a few lines of foot soldiers were the handcarts, with two soldiers assigned to push every cart.

'*Rajadhiraj*, have you seen the opposite line up?' The King of Banga laughingly remarked to Jarasandha. 'Clearly shows that their Commander is a novice. He has pitted foot soldiers against cavalry. We will tear them to pieces in no time.'

Jarasandha was lost deep in thought. 'Raja, don't underestimate that Krishna. There must be something about his formation, but I just can't get what it is. Anyway, this is an open field. We are superior in both numbers and weaponry. There should be no doubt of our grand success.'

Jarasandha took out his huge conch from his chariot and blew into it. A deep sound resonated through the battlefield. Immediately, the other Kings in his contingent followed suit. Within moments the sound of conches resonated from the Mathura side. Drummers beat up a battle tune.

The battle had begun.

Jarasandha's cavalry and chariots gave the charge. A thousand horses and ten chariots raced down the open field towards the Mathura formations. Behind them the foot soldiers ran, their naked swords and tips of lances glistening in the morning Sun. From the Mathura side the archers shot a hail of arrows towards the advancing brigade but the arrows failed to halt the lightning charge. Jarasandha watched from his post with satisfaction as his stallions galloped at the speed of wind towards the Mathura army. Another fifteen cubits and the cavalry would be all over the Mathura foot soldiers, when all of a sudden, the entire front line of horses tripped and fell with their riders and the second and third line of cavalry who were racing at full speed, could not rein in and fell headlong upon them. The Mathura army had fixed small wooden pegs to the ground and tied ropes between the pegs. The Magadh cavalry could not spot them and tripped over the ropes. 'Go for them, go for them,' Krishna shouted. Immediately with a roar of victory, the foot soldiers of Mathura fell upon the fallen cavalry with their swords and machetes and sliced off their heads.

The Magadh foot soldiers who had been running after their cavalry, stopped for a moment, undecided. Immediately, from behind, Jarasandha raised the red flag of attack. The commanders egged on the foot soldiers and they, with a war cry, rushed towards the Mathura ranks.

The Mathura foot soldiers by this time had despatched the fallen Magadh cavalry to its doom. They did not wait to meet the Magadh foot soldiers, but ran back towards their formations, filtered through the line of handcarts and slipped inside. The next moment, the line of handcarts, with their sharp blades reflecting the blazing Sun, swung in unified action. It was as if a single, half-a-mile long blade was rushing towards the Magadh foot soldiers. And, even before the Magadh foot soldiers could stop their onrushing feet and turn back, the line of handcarts sliced through their ranks. Bodies were sliced in half, right through the abdomen and fell in a heap on the ground, even as the bladed handcarts were pushed over the fallen body parts to slice through the next rank. Simultaneously, the Mathura cavalry raced in from the two flanks and cut off the escape route of the Magadh foot soldiers.

Even before an hour had passed, half the Magadh army stood decimated. The armies of the allies took fright and started fleeing. The allied Kings, fearing Jarasandha's wrath, tried their best to get their armies together and stop the fleeing men, but with only partial success. It was then that Jarasandha swung in action. *'Har har Mahadev,'* he thundered, swinging his mace like a man possessed. The fleeing soldiers stopped and turned. The remnant of his forces, enthused by their emperor in action, echoed the war cry *'Har Har Mahadev'*.

'We still have more soldiers than them. Follow me, I will lead you to victory.' The Emperor boomed, swinging his mace. In a moment his resplendent golden chariot galloped towards the enemy. 'Victory…victory…Kill the enemy,' his army responded as they rushed towards Mathura with renewed vigour.

Like a clash of cymbals the two armies crashed against each other. Sparks flew as steel collided with steel, sword with sword, mace with mace. Jarasandha fought like he had run amok. With every blow of his mace he broke skulls till his mace dripped with squashed brains and gore. The soldiers of Mathura, unable to stand his might, started fleeing before him.

'*Dau,* you are the only one who can take on Jarasandha today. Go and contain him before our soldiers start fleeing the battlefield.' Krishna egged on Balarama. 'I will take on the other Kings in the meantime.'

Balarama did not need any further egging. Wildly swinging his mace, he crashed through the enemy ranks and made his way to Jarasandha. Like two elephants fighting for leadership of the herd, they fought each other. One seething with a desire to avenge the widowing of his daughters, the other seeking revenge for his parents' prolonged incarceration. It was a fight of equals—a fight of richness of experience versus exuberance of youth, a fight of pinnacle of skill versus a high degree of skill blended with raw power and boundless energy. Their maces clashed with sounds like thunder and sparks like lightening. Never since the duel between Rama and Ravana had Aryavarta witnessed a clash of such ferocity.

At the other end of the battlefield, Krishna was proving to be the nemesis for the enemy soldiers. He would rain arrows and the next moment would rush down scimitar in hand, cutting down enemies like ripened crop. Seeing the bravery of their Commander, the soldiers of Mathura got enthused and fought with such venom that the numerically superior Magadh forces were put on the defensive. Akrur and the other overlords of Mathura also fought as if there was no tomorrow and contained the Kings who were part of Jarasandha's camp.

The sun had moved well past its prime when suddenly its blaze was replaced by another, behind the Magadh lines. The supply tents of the Magadh army were up in flames, set afire by flaming arrows shot by a group of Mathura soldiers who had gone behind the enemy lines through the river. The sentries guarding the supply tents were cut down by a volley of sharp arrows. By the time the attackers were repulsed and the sentries able to draw pitchers of water from the river, more than half the supply tents stood gutted.

As the sun dipped below the horizon, blowing of conch shells signalled the end of fighting for the day. Jarasandha and Balarama, perspiring profusely, let down their maces. The soldiers disengaged and prepared to go back to their lines. The charioteers turned the direction of their horses towards their respective camps.

'Who is your Guru?' Jarasandha asked Balarama.

'Guru Sandipani.' Balarama touched his hands to his ears as he spelled his Guru's name.

'Give my regards to your Guru. Nobody, nobody has been able to last before me this long. With a bit more polishing and experience, you would be the greatest warrior of Aryavarta. It was a pleasure fighting you, my boy.' Jarasandha ascended his chariot and turned back.

It was a long night at Jarasandha's camp. He and his subject Kings sat in meeting contemplating the next course of action. In a single day, the army had been reduced by half and half the supplies had been destroyed.

'*Maharajadhiraj*, we may not be able to win Mathura with the remaining army,' the King of Vatsya opined. He was seconded by the Kings of Banga and Odra. Jarasandha sat in deep contemplation. Even if he sent for reinforcements from Magadh, it would take at least several weeks for men and materials to arrive. But retreat at this juncture would mean a loss of face. On the other hand, if he were to persist, there was a fair chance that his army would be handed down a defeat on a scale similar to last time. This fellow Krishna did not play by the book. His strategies and tactics were playing havoc with his planning.

Jarasandha got up. He had decided. 'We retreat now to come back later with a larger force and crush Mathura. Unlike the last time, at least on this occasion we forced the enemy to face us in the battlefield. Next time we shall hold this meeting on the ruins of Mathura.' He paused for a moment, letting the declaration sink in the gathering, before continuing, 'But till the time we come back, Mathura shall not rest in peace. They have played with fire and shall get fire in return. I shall bleed Mathura through a thousand cuts so that when we come back, Mathura shall beg to be taken.' He paced around the room. 'The fate of Mathura shall be worse than death,' he thundered.

The next morning, as Jarasandha's troops retreated, Mathura resembled a lunatic asylum. Liquor flowed freely as people came out into the streets, beating drums and dancing and singing with gay abandon. Thousands converged at the palace, seeking a glimpse of their saviours—Krishna and Balarama. And, as the world around them celebrated, the two of them were engaged in discussions with Akrur on arrangements to be made for disposal of the corpses, medical help to the injured and help to be extended to the families of the dead and wounded.

But that night when the city slept after the day long revelry, flaming arrows fired from beyond the city wall blazed parts of the palace and several quarters in the city. The people, sloshed from day-long inebriation, realised too late and many of them perished in the blaze. Hundreds of homes were gutted. And it was not just that night. Every few days, the flaming arrows, caused havoc in the city. Jarasandha was already acting on his promise to make Mathura pay with fire for playing with fire. As the attacks continued unabated month after month, the residents of Mathura finally made up their minds to abandon the land of their forefathers and escape Jarasandha's wrath.

Guru Sandipani came to Mathura with the message that Dwarka was ready for settlement and further delay should be avoided. Thousands of living quarters had been created for the general populace with the attendant infrastructure and security apparatus. After detailed discussions with all concerned, it was decided that on the auspicious full moon day in the month of *Ashwin*, the journey to Dwarka would start.

Convincing all people was an onerous task and Krishna, Balarama and Akrur were practically at their wit's end. The older persons in particular were extremely reluctant to abandon the homes and hearths of their ancestors and travel to an unknown land. Some cited health problems and some others cited old age for refusing to undertake a journey which would take weeks on end. Some others remained adamant that they would rather die but not be seen running away from battle. It took days of persuasion to convince such persons to join the mainstream.

'Guru*ji*, what about the Gops? Will they move with us to Dwarka?' Akrur asked Guru Sandipani. 'Krishna wants to know…in fact he wants to go there himself to ask.'

'Akrur, obviously Krishna cannot go there since he has been expelled from the community. So you must go there and speak to Nandrai. And when you are there, try to collect as much information as you can.'

'Just one more thing, Akrur,' Guru Sandipani called Akrur as he turned back, 'If the Gops are not willing to shift to Dwarka, there is no need to persuade them further.'

Akrur smiled and nodded his assent.

'And when you come back, report to me before you meet Krishna.'

The next evening, Akrur came to meet the Guru furtively. 'Krishna has not seen me coming. I just returned from the Gop villages and came directly to see you. The news is that the Gops are not willing to relocate to Dwarka. Nandrai himself is willing but a majority of the Gops are unwilling. They feel that the area where we live rightfully belongs to their forefathers who were evicted while constructing the Mathura city. Possibly they are thinking of taking possession of Mathura after we abandon the city.'

'Good for us if they do not come along. Krishna would otherwise get distracted. How are his parents?'

'Nandrai seems to have aged a lot during this period. I had met him once earlier when Krishna was with you. But he has visibly changed. His hair has turned all grey and he has thinned considerably. His wife Yashoda is almost blind from constant crying. But Guru*ji*, there is another important news.'

'What?'

'Guru*ji*, Radha is now living with Nandrai and Yashoda. It appears that after Krishna was expelled, Nandrai pointed out to the villagers the condition which Radha's in-laws had brought her to and offered to take her under his care. The villagers supported him and Radha's in-laws, despite their verbal resistance, were only too happy to be rid of her. From then Radha is living at Nandrai's residence. Nandrai and Yashoda treat her like a daughter. She seems to have improved a lot, though not recovered completely. She and Yashoda are supporting each other in grief.'

'Akrur, don't say anything of this to Krishna. Just tell him that the Gops have decided to stay back and as far as his parents are concerned, they are sad, have aged a bit but are going ahead with life. And, as far as Radha is concerned, you do not know anything. Just remember, Akrur, the entire future of the Yadavas as well as of Krishna is at stake. So whatever you say, pick your words carefully.'

It was the full moon day in the month of *Ashwin* and the first batch of travellers were ready to depart Mathura for Dwarka. In order to prevent chaos, Guru Sandipani had ordered that the emigration to Dwarka would be in batches of about one thousand people and each batch would start a day after the previous one. It had been a monumental effort in organising the departure.

Krishna touched the feet of Guru Sandipani and Akrur and ascended his chariot. He would lead the first batch of people to Dwarka. And, as his chariot moved forward, a hundred bullock carts laden with people and provisions, followed in a line. Tears flowed freely as people tore themselves away from their homes and hearths and slowly proceeded towards the unknown.

The caravan meandered through the streets of Mathura, came out of the city gates and proceeded along the banks of the Yamuna. Krishna wiped away a tear from his eye as he passed by his childhood memories. His heart ached and vision clouded as he thought of those he was leaving behind and would never meet—his Baba, his *Maiya* and Radha. Would he never ever meet them in his entire life? He was passing so close to his village. Could he not for a last time run and meet them for a fleeting moment? Never in his life did he feel so helpless. He recollected the time when he and his friends would form a pyramid and steal butter from pots hung from the ceiling. His lips curled into a smile as he envisioned the little Kanha, his mouth pasted with butter, remonstrating before *Maiya* Yashoda that he had not eaten butter. An arrow of sorrow pierced his heart as he remembered the fiery Radha who complained against him to *Maiya* for breaking her pot and the Radha who would prefer to drown rather than be dishonoured when he had stolen her clothes. And what had she been reduced to...Tears rolled down his eyes as he remembered his bower by the brook where he and Radha passed so many exhilarating days of youth. His heart longed for that first touch and that first kiss.

Krishna broke down. 'Oh God...Oh God...where have you led me to?' He struck his forehead with his fist repeatedly. What would he not give to become Kanha again, even if for a single day....

As the caravan moved away, a figure in white came out from behind a tree grove. Kanha, her Kanha, had just passed her by, weeping. For a moment she wanted to madly rush forward, take him in her bosom and kiss away his tears. But...but...her body was soiled. Can one offer soiled offering to one's god? Then how could she offer her soiled body to her beloved, her god? Maybe in the next life....

She looked longingly at the caravan till the last bullock cart had passed out of her view and the last speck of dust had settled down. And then the tears of parting that had welled up in her bosom for long, finally broke through the barriers and cascaded forth through her eyes. She sat down at the edge of the river and covered her face with her hands while her body shook with spasms of grief. The cool water caressed her feet, attempting to soothe her, but in vain.

The morning turned to noon and yet she sat motionless by the water, an occasional drop of tear rolling down her cheeks, unfelt.

Slowly the water began to turn restless under the influence of tide. The waters that had so long caressed her toes, slowly rose to the ankles and then to her knees, but immersed in the thoughts of her beloved, she remained oblivious to the inundating waters. And, even as the waters reached her chin, she continued to sit in the same position, reliving each moment spent with Kanha. Was it the water or was it Kanha who kissed her lips, her nose, her eyes? And, as her mind and soul became one with Kanha, Mother Yamuna took her in a loving embrace and washed away her tears.

Glossary

Aarti	Ritual worship
Aashad	Month from mid-June to mid-July
Agrahayan	Month from mid-November to mid-December
Akhara	Wrestling arena
Annaprashan	Ceremony of feeding
Apsara	Dancer of heaven, nymph
Arre	A figure of speech
Aryavarta	(literally) Land of the Aryans; old name of India
Ashram	The abode of a Rishi or a Guru
Ashwamedh yagna	The horse ceremony
Ashwin	Month between mid-August to mid-September
Asura	Demon
Baba	Father
Bapu	Father
Bhadra	Month from mid-September to mid-October
Bhaiya	Brother
Bhed niti	Policy of divide and rule
Bhurja	Leaf of a tree used to write ancient texts
Brahmin	Priestly class
Chachi	Aunt
Chhach	Buttermilk
Chhathi	Sixth day after birth
Chhi	Fie
Chhota	Small, Lesser
Dai	Midwife, nurse

Dasiputra	Son conceived through maid
Dau	Elder brother
Dharma	A term incorporating religion and duty
Diya	Earthen lamp
Dwapara yug	The third eon
Gamchha	Towel carried on the shoulder
Gandharvas	A tribe
Ghagra	Skirt
Gops	Community of cowherds
Gopini	Females of the cowherd community
Gurudakshina	Payment/offering made by pupil to his Guru after completion of his education/training
Gurukul	House of the Guru (Teacher) where students lived, studied and served the Guru
Halwai	Confectioner
Havan	Ritual before the sacred fire
Howdah	Seat on the elephant
Kaalchakra	Wheel of time
Kaka	Uncle
Karma	Deeds
Kartick amavasya	No moon night in November
Khichdi	A preparation of boiled rice and pulses
Kotwal	Head of the police force
Kshatriya	Warrior caste
Lalla	Small boy
Chhach	Buttermilk
Lathi	Stick
Leela	Deeds of incarnates of God
Lord Indra	King of Gods and Lord of rain and thunder
Maiya	Mother
Malkin	Mistress

Mallas	Wrestlers
Mallayudh	A form of wrestling popular in ancient India
Mangalsutra	Traditional necklace worn by a married lady
Maund	A measure of weight, approximately 40 kg
Muhurta	Moment
Mukhiya	Headman
Nag	Snake
Narayani Sena	Vishnu's army
Navagrahas	Nine planets
Niyoga	Conception through a third person
Nrisingha	An incarnation of Lord Vishnu with a lion's head and man's body
Odhni	A stole
Parambhattarak	The greatest of the great
Parishad	Committee
Pedha	Type of sweet
Pita Maharaj	Father who is the King
Pradakshina	Taking rounds of
Prahar	Measure of time—roughly three hours
Prasad	Food which has been previously offered to the deity
Purushottam	The greatest amongst men; God; a name of Lord Vishnu
Rajchakravarti	Emperor
Rajpurohit	The royal priest
Rakshasas	Demons
Rathi	Charioteer
Rudraksha	Sacred beads
Saam-daam-danda-bhed	Explain, allure, threaten, divide
Sabha	Meeting
Sabzi	Vegetable preparation

Sadhu	Mendicant
Shastras	Sacred religious texts
Shasthi puja	Ceremony performed on sixth day of birth of a child
Sheshnag	The mythological serpent who bears the earth
Shikha	Tuft of hair at the back of head
Shudras	Caste of persons performing menial and lowly jobs; a derogatory term
Swayamvar	Function where the bride chooses her husband from amongst many suitors who are present
Tandava	The dance of destruction generally danced by Lord Shiva
Tantrik	An occultist
Tapasya	Deep meditation
Tolis	Groups
Treta yug	The second eon
Vaid	Physician
Vaikuntha lok	The heavenly abode of Lord Vishnu
Vaishyas	Merchants class
Vaman	Dwarf; the dwarf incarnation of Vishnu
Vasantotsav	Spring festival
Vidhaata Purush	The Lord of Destiny
Yagyasthal	Place where offerings are made to the sacred fire
Yamaraj	God of death
Yugdharma	Practices of people in the particular age/eon

About the Author

Pranab Kumar Mullick was born on 5th November, 1966 in Kolkata. His family shifted to Delhi in 1971 where he completed his education.

A topper all through school, he received Junior Science Talent and NTSE scholarships. In 1984 he got the national second rank in the CBSE Class XII exams in Commerce stream. The same year he enrolled in B. Com (Hons) in Shri Ram College of Commerce, University of Delhi and passed out in 1987 as First Class First Gold Medallist. Thereafter he did LL.B from Campus Law Centre, University of Delhi and stood First Class First Gold Medallist in the University in 1990.

From 1990 he has been practising as Advocate in the Supreme Court of India and High Court of Delhi. In 1996 he became an Advocate on record in Supreme Court. As an advocate, he has been involved in several historic litigations.

His love for writing was imbibed from his grandfather Dr Raghunath Mullick who was a freedom fighter, a batchmate of Netaji Subhas Chandra Bose and also a scholar in Sanskrit and an authority on Kalidasa. His books *Stories from Kalidasa, Kalidaser Galpo* (with preface written by Rabindranath Tagore) and *Kalidasa Pratibha* are critically acclaimed. His father Late Kali Sankar Mullick also authored several compelling short stories and a book of poems on mythological themes entitled *Pouranik*.

Pranab has written short stories in both English and Bengali. His Bengali short stories have been published in reputed magazines like *Nabakallol* and *Katha Sahitya* amongst others. *Kanha to Krishna—The Journey to Divinity* is his debut novel.